Dental Care and Oral Health during the COVID-19 Pandemic

Dental Care and Oral Health during the COVID-19 Pandemic

Editors

Cesare D'Amico
Pier Paolo Poli

MDPI

Basel • Beijing • Wuhan • Barcelona • Belgrade • Novi Sad • Cluj • Manchester

Editors
Cesare D'Amico
University of Messina
Messina, Italy

Pier Paolo Poli
University of Messina
Messina, Italy

Editorial Office
MDPI
St. Alban-Anlage 66
4052 Basel, Switzerland

This is a reprint of articles from the Special Issue published online in the open access journal *Medicina* (ISSN 1648-9144) (available at: https://www.mdpi.com/journal/medicina/special_issues/Dental_COVID-19).

For citation purposes, cite each article independently as indicated on the article page online and as indicated below:

Lastname, A.A.; Lastname, B.B. Article Title. *Journal Name* **Year**, *Volume Number*, Page Range.

ISBN 978-3-0365-9614-3 (Hbk)
ISBN 978-3-0365-9615-0 (PDF)
doi.org/10.3390/books978-3-0365-9615-0

Contents

Georgia Catton and Alexander Gardner
COVID-19 Induced Taste Dysfunction and Recovery: Association with Smell Dysfunction and Oral Health Behaviour
Reprinted from: *Medicina* **2022**, *58*, 715, doi:10.3390/medicina58060715 1

Ewa Rusyan, Agnieszka Mielczarek, Agnieszka Bogusławska-Kapała, Kamil Adamczyk, Robert Piec and Barbara Szykuła-Piec
Level of Anxiety Caused by the Coronavirus (COVID-19) Pandemic among Dentists in Poland
Reprinted from: *Medicina* **2022**, *58*, 415, doi:10.3390/medicina58030415 15

Catalina Iulia Saveanu, Cosmin Constantin Cretu, Irina Bamboi, Alexandra Ecaterina Săveanu and Daniela Anistoroaei
Title Cross-Sectional Study to Evaluate Knowledge and Attitudes on Oral Hygiene of Romanian Students
Reprinted from: *Medicina* **2022**, *58*, 406, doi:10.3390/medicina58030406 27

Jessica Olivia Cherecheș, Luminița Ligia Vaida, Abel Emanuel Moca, Raluca Dima, Gabriela Ciavoi and Marius Bembea
Orthodontic Adolescent Patients' Attitudes toward Protective Face Mask Wearing during the COVID-19 Pandemic
Reprinted from: *Medicina* **2022**, *58*, 393, doi:10.3390/medicina58030393 43

Georgia Catton and Alexander Gardner
Relationship between Recovery from COVID-19-Induced Smell Loss and General and Oral Health Factors
Reprinted from: *Medicina* **2022**, *58*, 283, doi:10.3390/medicina58020283 59

Yelda Koç, Serap Akyüz and Damla Akşit-Bıçak
Clinical Experience, Knowledge, Attitudes and Practice of Turkish Pediatric Dentists during the COVID-19 Pandemic
Reprinted from: *Medicina* **2021**, *57*, 1140, doi:10.3390/medicina57111140 69

Sarkis Sozkes and Iwona Olszewska-Czyż
Effects of COVID-19 Pandemic on Working Conditions of Dentists in Poland and Turkey
Reprinted from: *Medicina* **2021**, *57*, 1082, doi:10.3390/medicina57101082 93

Laura-Cristina Rusu, Lavinia Cosmina Ardelean, Codruta Victoria Tigmeanu, Anamaria Matichescu, Iulia Sauciur and Emanuel Adrian Bratu
COVID-19 and Its Repercussions on Oral Health: A Review
Reprinted from: *Medicina* **2021**, *57*, 1189, doi:10.3390/medicina57111189 103

Galvin Sim Siang Lin, Sze Hui Koh, Karyn Zuhuan Ter, Chia Wei Lim, Sharmin Sultana and Wen Wu Tan
Awareness, Knowledge, Attitude, and Practice of Teledentistry among Dental Practitioners during COVID-19: A Systematic Review and Meta-Analysis
Reprinted from: *Medicina* **2022**, *58*, 130, doi:10.3390/medicina58010130 125

Javier Santabárbara, Naiara Ozamiz-Etxebarria, Nahia Idoiaga, Beatriz Olaya and Juan Bueno-Novitol
Meta-Analysis of Prevalence of Depression in Dental Students during COVID-19 Pandemic
Reprinted from: *Medicina* **2021**, *57*, 1278, doi:10.3390/medicina57111278 137

medicina

MDPI

Article

COVID-19 Induced Taste Dysfunction and Recovery: Association with Smell Dysfunction and Oral Health Behaviour

Georgia Catton and Alexander Gardner *

Department of Restorative Dentistry, Dundee Dental Hospital and School, University of Dundee, Dundee DD1 4HR, UK; g.s.catton@dundee.ac.uk
* Correspondence: agardner001@dundee.ac.uk

Abstract: *Background and Objectives*: Disruption to taste and smell are common symptoms of COVID-19 infection. The current literature overlooks taste symptoms and tends to focus on the sense of smell. Persisting cases (>28 days) of taste dysfunction are increasingly recognised as a major future healthcare challenge. This study focuses on the severity and recovery of COVID-19 induced taste loss and association with olfactory symptoms, lifestyle and oral health factors. *Materials and Methods*: This study was a cross-sectional survey comparing 182 rapid taste recovery participants (≤28 days) with 47 participants with prolonged taste recovery >28 days. Analyses of taste loss in association with smell loss, age, sex, illness severity, diet, BMI, vitamin-D supplementation, antidepressants, alcohol use, smoking, brushing frequency, flossing, missing teeth, appliances and number of dental restorations were conducted. Differences in the severity of the loss of sour, sweet, salt, bitter and umami tastes were explored. *Results*: Both the severity and the duration of taste and smell loss were closely correlated ($p < 0.001$). Salt taste was significantly less affected than all other taste qualities ($p < 0.001$). Persisting taste loss was associated with older age (mean ± 95% CI = 31.73 ± 1.23 years vs. 36.66 ± 3.59 years, $p < 0.001$) and reduced likelihood of using floss (odds ratio ± 95% CI = 2.22 (1.15–4.25), $p = 0.047$). *Conclusions*: Smell and taste loss in COVID-19 are closely related, although a minority of individuals can experience taste or smell dysfunction in the absence of the other. The taste of salt may be less severely affected than other taste qualities and future work exploring this finding objectively is indicated. The association of flossing with rapid taste recovery adds to the growing evidence of a link between good periodontal health and favourable COVID-19 outcomes.

Keywords: COVID-19; taste dysfunction; oral health; dental care

Citation: Catton, G.; Gardner, A. COVID-19 Induced Taste Dysfunction and Recovery: Association with Smell Dysfunction and Oral Health Behaviour. *Medicina* **2022**, *58*, 715. https://doi.org/10.3390/medicina58060715

Academic Editors: Cesare D'Amico and Pier Paolo Poli

Received: 19 April 2022
Accepted: 23 May 2022
Published: 26 May 2022

1. Introduction

Alteration or loss of sense of smell (olfaction) and taste (gustation) were noted as critical symptoms early in the SARS-CoV-2 pandemic and were the most definitive symptoms of infection [1,2]. It has been shown that sensory symptoms can perform comparably with a polymerase chain reaction (PCR) test of nasopharyngeal swabs. Smell loss has been shown to demonstrate a sensitivity of 65% and specificity of 97%, whereas the corresponding values for a PCR swab are 87% and 97% [3,4]. The high specificity in particular means sensory symptoms are strongly indicative of the disease and public health guidance quickly reflected this, encouraging isolation in the advent of rapid onset smell or taste disturbance [5]. Machine learning models have demonstrated that sensory symptoms in conjunction with machine learning can yield sensitivity of 82%, with smell loss being more characteristic of a true positive than taste loss [6]. Estimates of the prevalence of sensory symptoms vary and range from 87% for smell loss and 56% for taste loss, down to under 15% for either symptom [7,8]. It has been noted that the more recent Omicron strain of the virus, which emerged in Winter 2021, appears to result in less instances of sensory disturbance compared with the predominant strains earlier in the pandemic. Data supports a decrease in the prevalence of olfactory symptoms from 63% to 25% and a decrease in the prevalence of gustatory symptoms from 57% to 27% [9]. Despite a significant decrease in prevalence, sensory symptoms are still seen to affect considerable proportions of infected individuals.

In health, the sense of taste is perceived when taste molecules or ions bind to G-protein coupled receptors (GPCR) expressed within taste receptor cells, which are housed in clusters known as taste buds. Taste buds are primarily located within specialised papillae on the tongue. These include fungiform papillae anteriorly and foliate and circumvallate papillae posteriorly [10]. Upon binding to a GPCR, a signalling cascade mediated by cyclic adenosine monophosphate (cAMP) or inositol triphosphate results in neurotransmitter release at a basal synapse, ultimately triggering an action potential. The nerves that carry taste to the brain in humans are facial, glossopharyngeal and vagus nerves (7th, 9th and 10th cranial nerves, respectively) [11,12]. Smell is detected by an analogous receptor–molecule binding mechanism. Specialised polarised olfactory receptor cells are housed within the olfactory epithelium at the top of the nasopharynx. Odorant molecules are present within inhaled air and bind to GPCRs, initiating a cAMP mediated action potential. This is relayed via the olfactory bulb to the brain by the olfactory nerve, the first cranial nerve [13].

A key difference between taste and smell in humans is the number of tastes compared with the number of smells that can be detected. Taste is currently understood to comprise five primaries, or basic, tastes. These include sweet, bitter, umami, salt and sour. Salt and sour tastes are thought to be ionic, caused by sodium or hydrogen ions, respectively. Sweet taste is caused by molecules such as sucrose or artificial sweeteners such as aspartame. Bitter tastes are caused by a wide range of molecules including many plant alkaloids. Umami taste is a savoury taste caused primarily by monosodium glutamate (MSG) or nucleotides such as inosine or guanosine monophosphate [14]. Humans have up to 400 different odour receptors, which when activated in different combinations allows potential for recognising up to one trillion different smells [15,16]. Due to this vast array of odours, attempts to cluster different smell molecules based on similar odour qualities have been made using ten different categories [17].

It remains unclear how COVID-19 damages the senses of smell and taste. A leading theory is that the virus can bind to, enter and destroy chemosensory receptor cells or neurones via angiotensin converting enzyme 2 (ACE-2) that is expressed by these cells [18]. An alternative mechanism may be via indirect damage to olfactory and gustatory tissue by increased inflammatory molecules such as interleukin-6 (IL-6), tumour necrosis factor alpha (TNF-α) and gamma interferon (γ-INF). These inflammatory markers may impede cell function, including interfering with their natural turnover [19]. Other mechanisms include hypoxic damage interfering with the central perception of taste and smell and changes in oral environment via salivary gland damage affecting function of taste receptor cells [20].

A general overview of the literature on taste and smell loss following COVID-19 infection reveals that studies of smell loss seem to be more than twice as prevalent as studies of taste loss. This is evidenced in Figure 1, which illustrates the number of publications identified by literature searches for the respective symptoms associated with COVID-19 since the start of the pandemic. At the time of searching (April 2022), 410 articles on smell loss and COVID-19 and 178 on taste loss and COVID-19 were returned. The reason for the discrepancy between smell and taste loss may be rooted in several reasons. Firstly, true loss or change in taste was rare before COVID-19, and in many cases is secondary to the disruption of olfaction as much of what is experienced during eating and drinking is attributable to the sense of smell. Recent meta-analysis has added weight to the argument of a genuine disruption to the sense of taste in COVID-19 infection [21]. Another reason may be that due to the lower prevalence of taste disturbance in COVID-19, and thus the lower predictive value of taste symptoms, there has been a tendency in researchers to focus on olfactory symptoms and overlook gustatory symptoms. Another overlooked factor in the study of COVID-19 taste loss is the effect on individual taste qualities which include sweet, bitter, sour, salty and umami. Efforts to capture this information have been recommended in future studies [22].

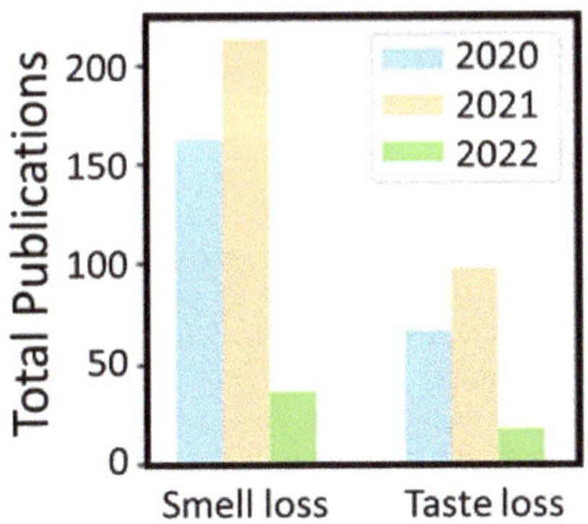

Figure 1. Comparison of total publications on either smell or taste loss and COVID-19 infection since the pandemic began. Data generated by searching the Web of Science using the terms "COVID taste OR COVID gustatory NOT smell NOT olfactory" and "COVID smell OR COVID olfactory NOT taste NOT gustatory" in the title field.

Thanks to global public health efforts, including vaccination and population level screening, SARS-CoV-2 is moving from a pandemic to an endemic status in many countries. The challenges posed by the virus are not yet over, however, with a major concern being the management of morbidity in survivors of the infection. Many studies find that the majority of individuals recover chemosensory function rapidly, with upwards of 80% returning to normal within two months [23–25], and in some studies recovery is even faster [8,26]. Worryingly, there are increasing reports of delayed sensory recovery with chemosensory effects being reported to persist for over a year in up to 30% of cases [27]. Furthermore, there are reports of taste disruption persisting in around one third of cases at six months, whereas smell disruption persisted in only 15% of cases at the same time point [28]. Other work reports that olfactory symptoms show a slower recovery than taste disturbance [29]. Persistent symptoms of COVID-19 have been reported from the early stages of the pandemic, sometimes referred to as "long COVID", although there is a lack of clarity over definitions [30]. A four-week cut off for the persistence of symptoms has been adopted within the definitions of the Centers for Disease Control (CDC) in the United States and the National Health Service (NHS) in the United Kingdom. It is recognised that persisting sensory disruption following COVID-19 has a significant quality of life impact on patients, with a lack of data about the management of the conditions of concern to both patients and clinicians [31,32].

The aim of the present study was to evaluate the loss and recovery of taste function in COVID-19. This included a granular analysis of the intensity and duration of taste loss in relation to smell loss, a comparison of intra-individual evaluation of the intensity of loss of individual taste qualities and an analysis of lifestyle, behavioural and oral health related factors that may be associated with prolonged (>28 day) taste loss.

2. Materials and Methods

2.1. Ethical Approval

This study was approved by the University of Dundee School of Health Sciences and Dentistry ethics committee (ref: UOD\SDEN\STAFF\2020\017, 25 June 2020).

2.2. Survey Design and Dissemination, Data Gathering and Processing

A full description of methodology has been previously published [25]. In brief, a survey was designed using JISC Online Surveys (JISC, Bristol, UK). Following written approval from website administration, the survey was hosted from March to August 2020 at https://www.reddit.com/r/COVID19positive (accessed on 10 March 2021). The survey was open to individuals >18 years old who had suffered COVID-19 infection diagnosed by PCR test, a physician or self-diagnosis, where symptoms included acute changes to smell and/or taste. The full survey can be found in Supplementary Figure S1 (information for participants and questionnaire).

Target variables were maximum severity of smell loss and taste loss and duration of smell and taste recovery to baseline levels. The severity of individual taste modalities (sweet, sour, bitter, salty and umami) were also asked. Umami taste was described as that of savoury food or food containing monosodium glutamate (MSG). The duration of taste loss and smell loss was defined by the time taken to return to normal baseline as subjectively assessed by the individual. Thus, partial recovery of some taste or smell was still considered an incomplete recovery. The duration of sensory loss was defined by continuous variables along with age, BMI and daily fruit and vegetable intake. Severity of taste and smell loss were ordinal variables, alongside severity of overall illness and severity of congestion, which were defined on an 11-point (0–10) scale, defined as 0 = no effect and 10 = total loss of sensation. Further ordinal variables were brushing frequency (1,2 or >2 times daily), alcohol consumption frequency (monthly, weekly, daily, never), smoking (never, former, current) and number of dental restorations (0, 1–5, 5–10, >10). Binary variables were biological sex, vitamin-D supplementation, antidepressant use, use of floss/interproximal cleaning, missing teeth (not lost due to trauma, orthodontics or impaction) and appliance wearing. Statistical analysis of ethnicity was precluded by low numbers of African and South Asian respondents.

2.3. Sample Size and Statistical Power

Based on a 95% confidence level, $p = 0.05$ and a precision of $\pm 5\%$, a sample size of 400 was deemed necessary as a representation of the study population [33]. Preliminary data exploration suggested a cut off of ~30 days would yield a sampling ratio of approximately 4:1 (recovery $\leq$ 28 days: recovery > 28 days). This distribution ratio was sufficient to detect effect sizes differing by 15–20% between groups with alpha = 0.05 and power = 0.8, based on a sample distribution of 229 participants (182 rapid recovery: 47 prolonged recovery).

2.4. Statistical Analyses

Python3 (Centrum Wiskunde & Informatica, Amsterdam, The Netherlands) and SPSS 27 (IBM, Armonk, NY, USA) were used to analyse and visualise data. Normality tests (QQ plots and Shapiro–Wilk test) were conducted on continuous data. The relationships between intensity of taste loss and intensity of smell loss and congestion severity were explored by Spearman's rank correlation. The timing of the recovery of smell and taste function was visualised. Differences between the degree of taste loss for the different taste sensations were analysed by Friedman test with Bonferroni-adjusted pairwise comparisons. Differences in the recovery time for smell and taste loss were explored. Differences between rapid recovery of taste ($\leq$28 days) and prolonged recovery (>28 days) were then explored for the remaining variables. Means were compared by two-tailed t-test or Mann–Whitney test where appropriate. Binary variables were compared using Fisher's exact test and categorical variables were compared by Pearson's chi-squared test and odds ratios calculated.

3. Results

3.1. Relationship between Resolution of Smell and Taste Loss

A total of 421 participants reported some degree of smell or taste disruption. The severity of these symptoms was highly significantly correlated, $\rho = 0.47$, $p < 0.0001$. Data are displayed in a bubble plot in Figure 2a. Both senses were most commonly reported as completely lost (rating of 10), although a tendency for smell loss to be rated as more severe than taste loss as evidenced when comparing the distribution of responses in the bottom right to the top left. Of these participants, 207 reported full recovery of both senses at the time of completing the survey. Duration of sensory recovery was also significantly correlated, $\rho = 0.83$, $p < 0.0001$. Figure 2b indicates that in 70% of cases individuals recovered both senses within a day of each other, although there were cases of either taste or smell recovering first by up to 90 days in a small number of cases. Recovery curves (Figure 2c) indicate that taste recovery was very similar to that of smell recovery. Within 14 days, 64% of cases had resolved and within 30 days, 87% had resolved, rising to 96% resolution within 90 days and only two cases (<1%) persisted beyond 120 days. No association was observed between congestion severity and taste loss intensity ($\rho = 0.04$, $p = 0.37$).

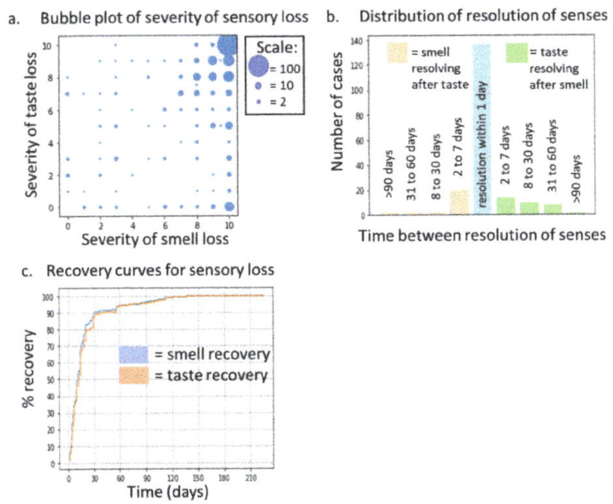

Figure 2. (**a**) Bubble plot showing the relationship between taste and smell loss severity, $n = 421$. (**b**) Plot indicating the differential time for resolution of taste and smell loss, $n = 207$. (**c**) Recovery curve for both taste and smell loss, $n = 207$.

3.2. *Differences between Severity of Loss of Different Taste Qualities*

The differences in the severity rating of each different taste quality were analysed for all individuals reporting some degree of taste loss. For all tastes the degree of effect ranged from 0 (no change) to 10 (complete inability to detect the taste). Data are shown in Figure 3, comparing individuals' ratings of each taste quality by Friedman test with Bonferroni-adjusted post hoc pairwise comparisons. Salt taste was significantly less affected than all other tastes ($p < 0.001$) and umami taste was significantly more severely affected than salty, sweet or sour tastes, which were all affected to a comparable degree.

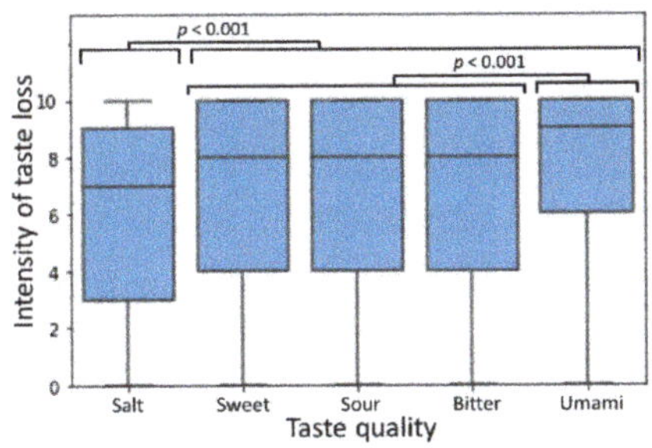

Figure 3. Comparison of intensity of taste sensation loss for the five primary taste modalities. p-values are for Friedman test with Bonferroni-adjusted post hoc pairwise comparisons between all groups, $n = 384$.

3.3. Differences between Rapid (≤28 Days) and Prolonged (>28 Days) Taste Recovery

At the time of completing the survey, 182 individuals reported a resolution of taste loss in ≤28 days and 47 individuals reported taste loss persisting >28 days. A full breakdown of the statistical analyses is presented in Table 1. Statistically significant differences between groups were found for age and the use of floss. Individuals with prolonged taste recovery were on average older than the rapid recovery group. Mean and 95% CI age for rapid taste recovery was 31.73 (30.50–32.96) years compared with 36.66 (33.07–40.25) for prolonged recovery, $p = 0.001$. A higher proportion of flossers was found in the rapid recovery groups compared with the prolonged recovery group. Distributions were 136/182 (75%) in the rapid taste recovery compared with 28/47 (60%) in the prolonged taste recovery, odds ratio (95% CI range) = 2.22 (1.15–4.25), $p = 0.047$. None of the other lifestyle and oral health parameters analysed differed significantly. A result approaching significance was found for illness severity when comparing rapid taste loss recovery, 4.42 (4.15–4.70) vs. prolonged taste loss recovery, 4.98 (4.42–5.54), $p = 0.061$.

Table 1. Comparison of short (≤28 days) and long (>28 days) taste loss. For Fisher's exact test and Chi^2 test observed values are shown followed by expected values in brackets. *—significant at $p < 0.05$, **—significant at $p < 0.01$.

Variable	Test	Short Smell Loss (≤28 Days) Mean ±95% CI		Long Smell Loss (>28 Days) Mean ±95% CI		Test Statistic	*p*-Value
Age	*t*-test	31.73 (30.50–32.96)		36.66 (33.07–40.25)		−3.23	0.001 **
BMI	*t*-test	26.74 (25.88–27.60)		26.16 (24.70–27.62)		0.62	0.54
Fruit/vegetable intake	*t*-test	2.98 (2.75–3.22)		3.20 (2.65–3.75)		−0.79	0.43
Illness severity	Mann–Whitney	4.42 (4.15–4.70)		4.98 (4.42–5.54)		−1.87	0.061
Smell loss severity	Mann–Whitney	8.46 (8.07–8.84)		8.36 (7.53–9.18)		−0.31	0.75
Taste loss severity	Mann–Whitney	7.79 (7.41–8.12)		7.56 (6.82–8.31)		−0.69	0.49
Sex	Fisher's exact	M	70 (65)	M	12 (17)	NA	0.13
		F	112 (117)	F	35 (30)		
Vitamin D	Fisher's exact	No	154 (157)	No	44 (41)	NA	0.15
		Yes	28 (25)	Yes	3 (6)		
Antidepressant	Fisher's exact	No	161 (161)	No	42 (42)	NA	1.00
		Yes	21 (21)	Yes	5 (5)		
Flossing	Fisher's exact	No	46 (52)	No	19 (13)	NA	0.047 *
		Yes	136 (130)	Yes	28 (34)		
Missing teeth	Fisher's exact	No	153 (153)	No	39 (39)	NA	0.81
		Yes	25 (25)	Yes	7 (7)		
Appliances	Fisher's exact	No	147 (147)	No	38 (38)	NA	1.00
		Yes	35 (35)	Yes	9 (9)		
Brushing freq.	Pearson's Chi^2	Daily	58 (53)	Daily	9 (14)	4.25	0.12
		2 × day	114 (116)	2 × day	32 (30)		
		>2 × day	9 (11)	>2 × day	5 (3)		

Table 1. *Cont.*

Variable	Test	Short Smell Loss (≤28 Days) Mean ±95% CI		Long Smell Loss (>28 Days) Mean ±95% CI		Test Statistic	*p*-Value
Alcohol freq.	Pearson's Chi^2	Never	35 (37)	Never	11 (9)	1.34	0.72
		Monthly	43 (43)	Monthly	11 (11)		
		Weekly	64 (65)	Weekly	18 (17)		
		Daily	40 (37)	Daily	7 (10)		
Smoking status	Pearson's Chi^2	Never	145 (142)	Never	34 (37)	1.19	0.55
		Former	12 (13)	Former	9 (7)		
		Current	25 (27)	Current	4 (3)		
No. of fillings	Pearson's Chi^2	None	44 (48)	None	16 (12)	2.93	0.40
		<5	84 (80)	<5	16 (21)		
		5–10	39 (40)	5–10	12 (11)		
		>10	13 (13)	>10	3 (3)		

4. Discussion

4.1. Relationship between Taste and Smell Loss

Whilst taste loss in COVID-19 infection is accepted to be closely linked to olfactory symptoms, few studies quantify the strength of the relationship. The present work finds a moderate yet highly significant correlation ($\rho = 0.47$, $p < 0.0001$) between the intensity of taste and smell loss. One study asked participants to rate their degree of taste and smell dysfunction from 0 to 10 using a Visual Analogue Scale (a similar approach to the present work) report a Pearson's correlation of $r = 0.91$ ($p < 0.0001$, $n = 162$). This reflects a stronger degree of relationship than is implied from our data, however fewer participants were used in that study [34]. Other findings suggest the correlation may be closer to the value reported in the present study (Pearson's $r = 0.53$), however the methodology used to assess taste and smell is not clear [35]. Further work in a larger sample confirms a weak but significant correlation between self-assessed smell and taste loss ($\rho = 0.25$, $p < 0.01$, $n = 1172$) [26].

Our results confirm that the correlation between the recovery time for smell and taste was stronger than the correlation between the severity of smell and taste loss ($\rho = 0.83$ vs. $\rho = 0.47$). Cecchetto et al., report that the recovery of smell and taste were both strongly associated with each other in multivariate analyses of sensory recovery, with a correlation coefficient between 0.86 and 0.91 [36]. Lee et al., imply a very close pattern of recovery between both senses, although it is not quantified [8]. Our observation that smell loss in the absence of taste loss appears more prevalent than the opposite is also supported by Lee et al., who observe this pattern of loss in 36% more cases than taste loss in the absence of smell loss. Our finding that smell and taste tend to resolve simultaneously (80% within one day of each other), with a small number of cases showing resolution of smell or taste first, with roughly equal prevalence, has not been reported elsewhere to our knowledge. We did not observe any significant relationship between congestion severity and taste loss severity. No link between congestion intensity and taste loss has been explored in the literature, although there are mixed reports of a link between the duration of smell loss and the presence of congestion in COVID-19 [23,37]. A significant link between symptom intensity has not been found [38]. The knowledge of the resolution time for COVID-19 is of key importance in making evidence-based guidelines for healthcare access in the post-pandemic world. International guidelines support deferring dental care in those with COVID-19 symptoms due to the risk of aerosol transmission [39]. Given that sensory symptoms can persist for weeks or months after an individual ceases to be able to transmit the infection, it is clearly not practical for dental care to be delayed this long.

4.2. Differences between Individual Taste Modalities

The majority of the literature on taste loss in COVID-19 treats taste as a single variable, rather than exploring the individual taste qualities [21]. Our study suggests that salt taste was less severely affected than sweet, sour, bitter and umami tastes and that umami taste was more severely affected than sour, sweet and bitter tastes. A recent objective study of taste thresholds in COVID-19 reported a decrease in salt threshold (i.e., greater ability to detect salt) in COVID-19 patients compared with regular controls. Sour, sweet and bitter taste thresholds all increased, and umami was not studied [40]. Other work finds that bitter and sour taste may be less affected than salt and sweet taste when participants rated intensity of these substances on a scale out of 100, however an appropriate control was absent [41]. Contrastingly, objective changes in sweet and salt taste have not been confirmed in separate works, with authors suggesting the taste losses are related to reduced retronasal olfaction in relation to smell loss [42,43].

4.3. Differences between Prolonged and Rapid Taste Recovery

Given the close relationship between taste and smell recovery that we observe, it is unsurprising that the associated differences between prolonged (>28 day) and rapid ($\leq$28 day) taste recovery are in line with our previous work on smell recovery [25]. The main difference was that illness severity was not significantly associated with recovery, although the relationship approached significance with $p = 0.06$. Age was positively associated with prolonged recovery of taste. Whilst some reports suggest age may be associated with the recovery of smell loss [37], systematic reviews suggest the majority of studies do not find an association between age and sensory recovery [44]. Regarding the association of flossing with taste recovery, it has been reported that poor periodontal health is associated with increased inflammation and poorer COVID-19 outcomes, although sensory symptoms were not specifically assessed [45,46]. Some of the oral health factors assessed, including brushing frequency and wearing of appliances, have been associated with taste sensitivity in healthy individuals [47,48]. These may arise from alterations in the oral environment and the biofilms that coat the tongue and the taste receptors [49]. While we observed a significant association with flossing, there is evidence that interdental brushing may be slightly better for periodontal health than flossing [50], thus this would represent an interesting avenue for future study. Tongue brushing, which has been shown to improve taste perception in the absence of disease, represents a further key variable that requires future study [51,52]. A targeted approach to recruitment would be indicated as it appears to be a relatively uncommon practice, with only 18% of people engaging in tongue brushing daily, which is necessary for optimal benefit [53,54].

Of the variables with no relationship with taste recovery, few have been explored previously. Smokers, whilst known to have diminished taste in health, have been observed to recover taste loss in COVID-19 infection faster than non-smokers [36]. The reason for this is not clear but may be related to short-term abstaining from smoking during illness causing a net increase in taste sensitivity. Alcohol consumption, antidepressant use and diet have not been directly studied in association with taste loss. Vitamin D levels have been found to be significantly different in those with or without taste loss in COVID-19 [55]. Regarding BMI, the duration of taste loss did not significantly differ between overweight/obese and normal weight participants, although those with higher BMI did appear to have a greater frequency of taste loss but not smell loss [56]. Sex is perhaps the most widely studied variable in associated with sensory disruption. A systematic review finds only four of seventeen articles found an association between sex and sensory symptoms [44]. Other studies find no relation between sex and recovery time for taste [23], although one study found an association (longer recovery in females) in a sub-group of their participants (Italian vs. British) [57].

Mechanistically, the loss of taste and smell in COVID-19 infection is still unclear. The role of ACE-2, which is expressed on the tongue and the taste receptors, is recognised in facilitating viral entry and is believed to have a pivotal role in the aetiology [18]. Recent work confirms that viral particles are detectable in the taste receptors of 75% of COVID-19 positive cadavers [58]. It has also been demonstrated in vitro that direct ACE-2 mediated viral entry into olfactory and gustatory neurones [59]. Salivary glands may present a further mechanism of viral entry and dissemination [60]. Collectively, these studies may imply there are multiple mechanisms by which SARS-CoV-2 can affect taste and may explain why the present study finds that some individuals suffer only loss of taste or smell independent of the other. The finding of flossing being associated with rapid taste recovery may also reflect a mechanistic link with viral entry. Flossing is linked to reduced plaque and bleeding, a clinical indicator of inflammation, as well as reduced bacteraemia [50,61,62]. Virion entry via inflamed periodontal pockets is a further source of COVID-19 infection [63], and raised inflammatory markers such as Interleukin-6 and C-reactive protein are implicated in sensory disruption in COVID-19 infection as well as gum disease [64,65]. Thus, flossing may reduce viral entry and dissemination in hosts as well as create a less inflammatory local environment that would predispose to sensory symptoms. Indeed, there is evidence from meta-analysis that flossing in combination with brushing confers gingival health benefits over brushing alone [50]. This is an effect that grows stronger from adopting the habit, up to a six-month follow-up. While infrequent brushing is associated with poor periodontal health, all participants in the present analysis brushed at least once a day, which is sufficient frequency not to affect periodontal health significantly [66,67].

4.4. *Limitations and Future Work*

The present work contains several limitations. Firstly, as it was conducted during the first wave of global lockdowns, mass testing was not readily available and thus participants with symptomatic diagnoses without PCR confirmation were included. Given the roughly equivalent specificity of sensory symptoms to PCR test and our analyses of individuals displaying sensory symptoms, this did not have much bearing on results when comparing PCR positive participants only [25]. A major challenge in the study of taste disorders in COVID-19 is the reliance of self-reported data rather than objective tests. Literature reviews suggest that the proportion of studies using self-assessed data is only about 8% [21,68]. The literature suggests that a reasonable correlation between self-reported and objectively tested smell function exists [34,69], however this is less clear for taste dysfunction in COVID-19. There is evidence that many individuals self-reporting taste dysfunction in COVID-19 display normal taste function when objectively tested [42], although subjective smell and taste scores do correlate significantly [42,70]. The present study made comparisons of self-assessed taste scores within individuals (i.e., paired comparisons), hence inter-individual variance in self-assessment should be negated by this. When considering between group differences, the primary outcome of taste recovery time is a more objective metric as individuals again report their sensation relative to their own baseline. Nevertheless, there is a clear need for future studies to undertake objective psychophysical assessments of taste and smell. As globally we are seeing increased cases of persisting sensory dysfunction in individuals who are no longer acutely infectious, these studies will become increasingly feasible [21]. Further challenges to the present work include the relatively uneven recovery, as the ratio of recovery before and after 28 days was about 3.9:1; therefore, it is possible that we may lack sufficient power to detect genuine differences between the groups with smaller effect sizes. This must be considered alongside the likely clinical and biological significance however, as this would be expected to be small in these circumstances. Finally, we must caution the lack of any causative associations that can be drawn from an observational study as this. For example, flossing cannot be claimed to be protective of long taste recovery in COVID-19 and may simply reflect an individual with greater health awareness who is engaging in other protective behaviours not assessed in this study. The p-value was only just below the 0.05 threshold and would not be significant following adjustment for multiple testing. As this work is primarily exploratory to identify potential relationships for further exploration, a high false discovery rate would be tolerable to mitigate the risk of Type I errors. Future prospective studies of a greater number, ideally clinically measuring periodontal pockets and bleeding, will aid confidence in this observed result. The observations of individuals with either only taste or smell loss in the absence of the other merits further investigation. A selective comparison between individuals experiencing only taste dysfunction versus only smell dysfunction would contribute to the mechanistic understanding of sensory dysfunction in COVID-19.

5. Conclusions

The present study suggests that taste dysfunction is closely correlated to smell dysfunction in COVID-19, both for intensity and duration of symptoms. The relationship was stronger for duration ($\rho = 0.83$) than intensity ($\rho = 0.47$), although both relationships were highly significant ($p < 0.0001$). There was a tendency for smell loss to occur more commonly in the absence of taste loss than taste loss to occur in the absence of smell loss. This knowledge can help target individuals for future study that may aid the understanding of the mechanistic effects of sensory loss in COVID-19. Salt taste was less affected than sweet, sour, bitter and umami taste and umami taste was more severely affected than bitter, sour and sweet taste. Future work involving the objective measurement of taste thresholds is indicated, as the current literature is heavily biased towards self-reported data. This will become more feasible in the future as taste disturbance can persist long after acute infection in some individuals. Persisting taste dysfunction >28 days was significantly associated with older age and reduced use of floss. Non-significant factors included sex, diet, BMI, vitamin-D, antidepressants, alcohol use, smoking, brushing frequency, missing teeth, appliances and number of restorations. Flossing may be an important marker of local inflammation and gingival pocketing, which may aid in viral entry and creation of a local environment triggering neurological dysfunction. Future study including clinical measurement of periodontal health is indicated to aid in the understanding of sensory dysfunction in COVID-19. The present results add to the growing literature that taste and smell dysfunction can persist for >28 days in approximately one quarter of COVID-19 infections. We would advise that guidelines created to advise the public and healthcare professionals about COVID-19 symptoms consider that taste and smell loss may persist beyond the transmissible stage of infection and thus should not automatically be a barrier to seeing a medical or dental professional.

Supplementary Materials: The following are available online at https://www.mdpi.com/article/10.3390/medicina58060715/s1, Figure S1: Information for participants and questionnaire.

Author Contributions: Conceptualization, A.G. and G.C.; methodology, A.G.; software, A.G. and G.C.; validation, A.G. and G.C.; formal analysis, A.G.; investigation, A.G. and G.C.; resources, A.G. and G.C.; data curation, G.C.; writing—original draft preparation, A.G. and G.C.; writing—review and editing, A.G. and G.C.; visualization, A.G.; supervision, A.G.; project administration, A.G.; funding acquisition, G.C. All authors have read and agreed to the published version of the manuscript.

Funding: This research was funded by the Tattersall foundation. The APC was funded by the University of Dundee Library and Learning Centre.

Institutional Review Board Statement: The study was conducted according to the guidelines of the Declaration of Helsinki and approved by The University of Dundee School of Health Sciences and Dentistry ethics committee (ref: UOD\SDEN\STAFF\2020\017).

Informed Consent Statement: Informed consent was obtained from all subjects involved in the study.

Data Availability Statement: The authors will make data available upon reasonable request.

Acknowledgments: The authors wish to thank the Tattersall Foundation for making this work possible.

Conflicts of Interest: The authors declare no conflict of interest.

References

1. Menni, C.; Valdes, A.M.; Freidin, M.B.; Ganesh, S.; El-Sayed Moustafa, J.S.; Visconti, A.; Hysi, P.; Bowyer, R.C.E.; Mangino, M.; Falchi, M.; et al. Loss of smell and taste in combination with other symptoms is a strong predictor of COVID-19 infection. *medRxiv* **2020**. [CrossRef]
2. Sudre, C.H.; Keshet, A.; Graham, M.S.; Joshi, A.D.; Shilo, S.; Rossman, H.; Murray, B.; Molteni, E.; Klaser, K.; Canas, L.D. Anosmia, ageusia, and other COVID-19-like symptoms in association with a positive SARS-CoV-2 test, across six national digital surveillance platforms: An observational study. *Lancet Digit. Health* **2021**, *3*, e577–e586. [CrossRef]
3. George, B.; McGee, J.; Giangrasso, E.; Finkelstein, S.; Wu, S.; Glatt, A.E. What Is the Predictive Value of a Single Nasopharyngeal SARS-CoV-2 PCR Swab Test in a Patient With COVID-Like Symptoms and/or Significant COVID-19 Exposure? *Open Forum Infect. Dis.* **2020**, *7*, ofaa399. [CrossRef] [PubMed]
4. Haehner, A.; Draf, J.; Dräger, S.; de With, K.; Hummel, T. Predictive Value of Sudden Olfactory Loss in the Diagnosis of COVID-19. *ORL J. Otorhinolaryngol. Relat. Spec.* **2020**, *82*, 175–180. [CrossRef]
5. Sedaghat, A.R.; Gengler, I.; Speth, M.M. Olfactory Dysfunction: A Highly Prevalent Symptom of COVID-19 With Public Health Significance. *Otolaryngol. Neck Surg.* **2020**, *163*, 12–15. [CrossRef]
6. Callejon-Leblic, M.A.; Moreno-Luna, R.; Del Cuvillo, A.; Reyes-Tejero, I.M.; Garcia-Villaran, M.A.; Santos-Peña, M.; Maza-Solano, J.M.; Martín-Jimenez, D.I.; Palacios-Garcia, J.M.; Fernandez-Velez, C.; et al. Loss of Smell and Taste Can Accurately Predict COVID-19 Infection: A Machine-Learning Approach. *J. Clin. Med.* **2021**, *10*, 570. [CrossRef]
7. Lechien, J.R.; Chiesa-Estomba, C.M.; Hans, S.; Barillari, M.R.; Jouffe, L.; Saussez, S. Loss of smell and taste in 2013 European patients with mild to moderate COVID-19. *Ann. Intern. Med.* **2020**, *173*, 672–675. [CrossRef]
8. Lee, Y.; Min, P.; Lee, S.; Kim, S.-W. Prevalence and Duration of Acute Loss of Smell or Taste in COVID-19 Patients. *J. Korean Med. Sci.* **2020**, *35*, e174. [CrossRef]
9. Boscolo-Rizzo, P.; Tirelli, G.; Meloni, P.; Hopkins, C.; Madeddu, G.; De Vito, A.; Gardenal, N.; Valentinotti, R.; Tofanelli, M.; Borsetto, D.; et al. Coronavirus disease 2019 (COVID-19)-related smell and taste impairment with widespread diffusion of severe acute respiratory syndrome-coronavirus-2 (SARS-CoV-2) Omicron variant. *Int. Forum Allergy Rhinol* **2022**. *Early View*. [CrossRef]
10. Gardner, A.; Carpenter, G.H. Anatomical stability of human fungiform papillae and relationship with oral perception measured by salivary response and intensity rating. *Sci. Rep.* **2019**, *9*, 9759. [CrossRef]
11. Roper, S.D.; Chaudhari, N. Taste buds: Cells, signals and synapses. *Nat. Rev. Neurosci.* **2017**, *18*, 485. [CrossRef] [PubMed]
12. Gilbertson, A.T.; Damak, S.; Margolskee, R.F. The molecular physiology of taste transduction. *Curr. Opin. Neurobiol.* **2000**, *10*, 519–527. [CrossRef]
13. Pinto, J.M. Olfaction. *Proc. Am. Thorac. Soc.* **2011**, *8*, 46–52. [CrossRef]
14. Kinnamon, S.C.; Margolskee, R. Mechanisms of taste transduction. *Curr. Opin. Neurobiol.* **1996**, *6*, 506–513. [CrossRef]
15. Rinaldi, A. The scent of life. The exquisite complexity of the sense of smell in animals and humans. *EMBO Rep.* **2007**, *8*, 629–633. [CrossRef]
16. Bushdid, C.; Magnasco, M.O.; Vosshall, L.B.; Keller, A. Humans Can Discriminate More than 1 trillion Olfactory Stimuli. *Science* **2014**, *343*, 1370–1372. [CrossRef]
17. Castro, J.B.; Ramanathan, A.; Chennubhotla, C.S. Categorical Dimensions of Human Odor Descriptor Space Revealed by Non-Negative Matrix Factorization. *PLoS ONE* **2013**, *8*, e73289. [CrossRef]
18. Eshraghi, A.A.; Mirsaeidi, M.; Davies, C.; Telischi, F.F.; Chaudhari, N.; Mittal, R. Potential Mechanisms for COVID-19 Induced Anosmia and Dysgeusia. *Front. Physiol.* **2020**, *11*, 1039. [CrossRef]
19. Lozada-Nur, F.; Chainani-Wu, N.; Fortuna, G.; Sroussi, H. Dysgeusia in COVID-19: Possible Mechanisms and Implications. *Oral Surg. Oral Med. Oral Pathol. Oral Radiol.* **2020**, *130*, 344–346. [CrossRef]
20. Tsuchiya, H. Oral Symptoms Associated with COVID-19 and Their Pathogenic Mechanisms: A Literature Review. *Dent. J.* **2021**, *9*, 32. [CrossRef]
21. Hannum, E.M.; Ramirez, A.V.; Lipson, S.J.; Herriman, R.D.; Toskala, A.K.; Lin, C.; Joseph, P.V.; Reed, D.R. Objective sensory testing methods reveal a higher prevalence of olfactory loss in COVID-19–positive patients compared to subjective methods: A systematic review and meta-analysis. *Chem. Senses* **2020**, *45*, 865–874. [CrossRef] [PubMed]
22. Risso, D.; Drayna, D.; Morini, G. Alteration, Reduction and Taste Loss: Main Causes and Potential Implications on Dietary Habits. *Nutrients* **2020**, *12*, 3284. [CrossRef] [PubMed]
23. Printza, A.; Katotomichelakis, M.; Valsamidis, K.; Metallidis, S.; Panagopoulos, P.; Panopoulou, M.; Petrakis, V.; Constantinidis, J. Smell and Taste Loss Recovery Time in COVID-19 Patients and Disease Severity. *J. Clin. Med.* **2021**, *10*, 966. [CrossRef]
24. Lechien, J.R.; Journe, F.; Hans, S.; Chiesa-Estomba, C.M.; Mustin, V.; Beckers, E.; Vaira, L.A.; De Riu, G.; Hopkins, C.; Saussez, S. Severity of anosmia as an early symptom of COVID-19 infection may predict lasting loss of smell. *Front. Med.* **2020**, *7*, 582802. [CrossRef] [PubMed]
25. Catton, G.; Gardner, A. Relationship between Recovery from COVID-19-Induced Smell Loss and General and Oral Health Factors. *Medicina* **2022**, *58*, 283. [CrossRef]
26. Song, J.; Deng, Y.-K.; Wang, H.; Wang, Z.-C.; Liao, B.; Ma, J.; He, C.; Pan, L.; Liu, Y.; Alobid, I.; et al. Self-reported Taste and Smell Disorders in Patients with COVID-19: Distinct Features in China. *Curr. Med. Sci.* **2021**, *41*, 14–23. [CrossRef]

27. Boscolo-Rizzo, P.; Guida, F.; Polesel, J.; Marcuzzo, A.V.; Antonucci, P.; Capriotti, V.; Sacchet, E.; Cragnolini, F.; D'Alessandro, A.; Zanelli, E.; et al. Self-reported smell and taste recovery in coronavirus disease 2019 patients: A one-year prospective study. *Eur. Arch. Oto-Rhino-Laryngol.* **2021**, *279*, 515–520. [CrossRef]
28. Nguyen, N.N.; Hoang, V.T.; Lagier, J.-C.; Raoult, D.; Gautret, P. Long-term persistence of olfactory and gustatory disorders in COVID-19 patients. *Clin. Microbiol. Infect.* **2021**, *27*, 931–932. [CrossRef]
29. Niklassen, A.S.; Draf, J.; Huart, C.; Hintschich, C.; Bocksberger, S.; Trecca, E.M.C.; Klimek, L.; Le Bon, S.D.; Altundag, A.; Hummel, T. COVID-19: Recovery from chemosensory dysfunction. a multicentre study on smell and taste. *Laryngoscope* **2021**, *131*, 1095–1100. [CrossRef]
30. Alwan, N.A.; Johnson, L. Defining long COVID: Going back to the start. *Medicine* **2021**, *2*, 501–504. [CrossRef]
31. Burges Watson, D.L.; Campbell, M.; Hopkins, C.; Smith, B.; Kelly, C.; Deary, V. Altered smell and taste: Anosmia, parosmia and the impact of long Covid-19. *PLoS ONE* **2021**, *16*, e0256998. [CrossRef] [PubMed]
32. Alshakhs, A.; AlMomen, A.; Alyaeesh, I.; AlOmairin, A.; Almutairi, A.A.; Alammar, Z.; AlMomen, H.; AlMomen, Z. The Association of Smell and Taste Dysfunction with COVID19, and Their Functional Impacts. *Indian J. Otolaryngol. Head Neck Surg.* **2021**, 1–6. [CrossRef] [PubMed]
33. Islam, M.R. Sample size and its role in Central Limit Theorem (CLT). *Comput. Appl. Math. J.* **2018**, *4*, 1–7.
34. Ciofalo, A.; Cavaliere, C.; Masieri, S.; Di Chicco, A.; Fatuzzo, I.; Re, F.L.; Baroncelli, S.; Begvarfaj, E.; Adduci, A.; Mezzaroma, I.; et al. Long-Term Subjective and Objective Assessment of Smell and Taste in COVID-19. *Cells* **2022**, *11*, 788. [CrossRef]
35. Ali, G.; Akhter, N.; Akram, R.; Kazmi, S.A.J.; Khan, M.S.; Iqbal, S. The Loss of Smell and Taste in the COVID-19 Outbreak, a Cross Sectional Study. *Haya Saudi J. Life Sci.* **2022**, *7*, 24–28. [CrossRef]
36. Cecchetto, C.; Di Pizio, A.; Genovese, F.; Calcinoni, O.; Macchi, A.; Dunkel, A.; Ohla, K.; Spinelli, S.; Farruggia, M.C.; Joseph, P.V.; et al. Assessing the extent and timing of chemosensory impairments during COVID-19 pandemic. *Sci. Rep.* **2021**, *11*, 17504. [CrossRef]
37. Coelho, D.H.; Reiter, E.R.; Budd, S.G.; Shin, Y.; Kons, Z.A.; Costanzo, R.M. Predictors of smell recovery in a nationwide prospective cohort of patients with COVID-19. *Am. J. Otolaryngol.* **2021**, *43*, 103239. [CrossRef]
38. Speth, M.M.; Singer-Cornelius, T.; Oberle, M.; Gengler, I.; Brockmeier, S.J.; Sedaghat, A.R. Olfactory dysfunction and sinonasal symptomatology in COVID-19: Prevalence, severity, timing, and associated characteristics. *Otolaryngol. Head Neck Surg.* **2020**, *163*, 114–120. [CrossRef]
39. D'Amico, C.; Bocchieri, S.; De Stefano, R.; Gorassini, F.; Surace, G.; Amoroso, G.; Scoglio, C.; Mastroieni, R.; Gambino, D.; Amantia, E.M.; et al. Dental Office Prevention of Coronavirus Infection. *Eur. J. Dent.* **2020**, *14*, S146–S151. [CrossRef]
40. Asadi, M.M.; Shankayi, Z.; Bahrami, F.; Mohammadzadeh, T.; Amini, H.; Naderi, M. Quantitative analysis of taste disorder in COVID-19 patients, the hypersensitivity to salty quality. *New Microbes New Infect.* **2021**, *43*, 100919. [CrossRef]
41. Konstantinidis, I.; Delides, A.; Tsakiropoulou, E.; Maragoudakis, P.; Sapounas, S.; Tsiodras, S. Short-Term Follow-Up of Self-Isolated COVID-19 Patients with Smell and Taste Dysfunction in Greece: Two Phenotypes of Recovery. *ORL J. Otorhinolaryngol. Relat. Spec.* **2020**, *82*, 295–303. [CrossRef] [PubMed]
42. Mazzatenta, A.; Neri, G.; D'Ardes, D.; De Luca, C.; Marinari, S.; Porreca, E.; Cipollone, F.; Vecchiet, J.; Falcicchia, C.; Panichi, V.; et al. Smell and Taste in Severe CoViD-19: Self-Reported vs. Testing. *Front. Med.* **2020**, *7*, 589409. [CrossRef] [PubMed]
43. Hintschich, C.A.; Niv, M.Y.; Hummel, T. The taste of the pandemic—Contemporary review on the current state of research on gustation in coronavirus disease 2019 (COVID-19). *Int. Forum Allergy Rhinol.* **2021**, *12*, 210–216. [CrossRef] [PubMed]
44. Santos, R.E.A.; da Silva, M.G.; Barbosa, D.A.M.; Gomes, A.L.D.V.; Galindo, L.C.M.; Aragão, R.D.S.; Ferraz-Pereira, K.N. Onset and duration of symptoms of loss of smell/taste in patients with COVID-19: A systematic review. *Am. J. Otolaryngol.* **2021**, *42*, 102889. [CrossRef] [PubMed]
45. Marouf, N.; Cai, W.; Said, K.N.; Daas, H.; Diab, H.; Chinta, V.R.; Hssain, A.A.; Nicolau, B.; Sanz, M.; Tamimi, F. Association between periodontitis and severity of COVID-19 infection: A case-control study. *J. Clin. Periodontol.* **2021**, *48*, 483–491. [CrossRef]
46. Kamel, A.H.M.; Basuoni, A.; Salem, Z.A.; AbuBakr, N. The impact of oral health status on COVID-19 severity, recovery period and C-reactive protein values. *Br. Dent. J.* **2021**, 1–7. [CrossRef]
47. Juzikis, E.; Klimenko, J.; Žilinskas, J.; Ivanauskienė, E. The effect of new acrylic full removable dentures on food taste. *Stomatologija* **2021**, *23*, 48–50.
48. Kaur, K.; Sculley, D.; Veysey, M.; Lucock, M.; Wallace, J.; Beckett, E.L. Bitter and sweet taste perception: Relationships to self-reported oral hygiene habits and oral health status in a survey of Australian adults. *BMC Oral Health* **2021**, *21*, 553. [CrossRef]
49. Neyraud, E.; Morzel, M. Biological films adhering to the oral soft tissues: Structure, composition, and potential impact on taste perception. *J. Texture Stud.* **2018**, *50*, 19–26. [CrossRef]
50. Worthington, H.V.; MacDonald, L.; Poklepovic Pericic, T.; Sambunjak, D.; Johnson, T.M.; Imai, P.; Clarkson, J.E. Home use of interdental cleaning devices, in addition to toothbrushing, for preventing and controlling periodontal diseases and dental caries. *Cochrane Database Syst. Rev.* **2019**, *4*, 1–159. [CrossRef]
51. Quirynen, M.; Avontroodt, P.; Soers, C.; Zhao, H.; Pauwels, M.; Van Steenberghe, D. Impact of tongue cleansers on microbial load and taste. *J. Clin. Periodontol.* **2004**, *31*, 506–510. [CrossRef]
52. Hyde, R.; Feller, R.; Sharon, I. Tongue Brushing, Dentifrice, and Age Effects on Taste and Smell. *J. Dent. Res.* **1981**, *60*, 1730–1734. [CrossRef]

53. Matsuda, S.; Saito, T.; Yoshida, H.; Yoshimura, H.; Sano, K. Prevalence of Tongue Cleaning Using a Toothbrush: A Questionnaire Survey in Fukui Prefecture, Japan. *BioMed Res. Int.* **2019**, *2019*, 6320261. [CrossRef] [PubMed]
54. Madiloggovit, J.; Chotechuang, N.; Trachootham, D. Impact of self-tongue brushing on taste perception in Thai older adults: A pilot study. *Geriatr. Nurs.* **2015**, *37*, 128–136. [CrossRef] [PubMed]
55. Elibol, E.; Baran, H. The relation between serum D-dimer, ferritin and vitamin D levels, and dysgeusia symptoms, in patients with coronavirus disease 2019. *J. Laryngol. Otol.* **2021**, *135*, 45–49. [CrossRef] [PubMed]
56. Cheng, W.A.; Turner, L.; Ruiz, C.J.M.; Tanaka, M.L.; Congrave-Wilson, Z.; Lee, Y.; Jumarang, J.; Perez, S.; Peralta, A.; Pannaraj, P.S. Clinical manifestations of COVID-19 differ by age and obesity status. *Influ. Other Respir. Viruses* **2021**, *16*, 255–264. [CrossRef] [PubMed]
57. Andrews, P.J.; Pendolino, A.L.; Ottaviano, G.; Scarpa, B.; Grant, J.; Gaudioso, P.; Bordin, A.; Marchese-Ragona, R.; Leoni, D.; Cattelan, A. Olfactory and taste dysfunction among mild-to-moderate symptomatic COVID-19 positive health care workers: An international survey. *Laryngoscope Investig. Otolaryngol.* **2020**, *5*, 1019–1028. [CrossRef] [PubMed]
58. Henin, D.; Pellegrini, G.; Carmagnola, D.; Attisano, G.C.L.; Lopez, G.; Ferrero, S.; Amendola, A.; De Angelis, D.; Tanzi, E.; Dellavia, C. Morphological and Immunopathological Aspects of Lingual Tissues in COVID-19. *Cells* **2022**, *11*, 1248. [CrossRef]
59. Lyoo, K.-S.; Kim, H.M.; Lee, B.; Che, Y.H.; Kim, S.-J.; Song, D.; Hwang, W.; Lee, S.; Park, J.-H.; Na, W. Direct neuronal infection of SARS-CoV-2 reveals cellular and molecular pathology of chemosensory impairment of COVID-19 patients. *Emerg. Microbes Infect.* **2022**, *11*, 406–411. [CrossRef]
60. Sinjari, B.; D'Ardes, D.; Santilli, M.; Rexhepi, I.; D'Addazio, G.; Di Carlo, P.; Chiacchiaretta, P.; Caputi, S.; Cipollone, F. SARS-CoV-2 and Oral Manifestation: An Observational, Human Study. *J. Clin. Med.* **2020**, *9*, 3218. [CrossRef]
61. Graves, R.C.; Disney, J.A.; Stamm, J.W. Comparative Effectiveness of Flossing and Brushing in Reducing Interproximal Bleeding. *J. Periodontol.* **1989**, *60*, 243–247. [CrossRef] [PubMed]
62. Carroll, G.C.; Sebor, R.J. Dental Flossing, and Its Relationship to Transient Bacteremia. *J. Periodontol.* **1980**, *51*, 691–692. [CrossRef] [PubMed]
63. Gupta, S.; Mohindra, R.; Chauhan, P.; Singla, V.; Goyal, K.; Sahni, V.; Gaur, R.; Verma, D.; Ghosh, A.; Soni, R. SARS-CoV-2 detection in gingival crevicular fluid. *J. Dent. Res.* **2021**, *100*, 187–193. [CrossRef] [PubMed]
64. Cazzolla, A.P.; Lovero, R.; Muzio, L.L.; Testa, N.F.; Schirinzi, A.; Palmieri, G.; Pozzessere, P.; Procacci, V.; Di Comite, M.; Ciavarella, D.; et al. Taste and Smell Disorders in COVID-19 Patients: Role of Interleukin-6. *ACS Chem. Neurosci.* **2020**, *11*, 2774–2781. [CrossRef]
65. Shimada, Y.; Komatsu, Y.; Ikezawa-Suzuki, I.; Tai, H.; Sugita, N.; Yoshie, H. The effect of periodontal treatment on serum leptin, interleukin-6, and C-reactive protein. *J. Periodontol.* **2010**, *81*, 1118–1123. [CrossRef]
66. Attin, T.; Hornecker, E. Tooth brushing and oral health: How frequently and when should tooth brushing be performed? *Oral Health Prev. Dent.* **2005**, *3*, 135–140.
67. Zimmermann, H.; Zimmermann, N.; Hagenfeld, D.; Veile, A.; Kim, T.-S.; Becher, H. Is frequency of tooth brushing a risk factor for periodontitis? A systematic review and meta-analysis. *Community Dent. Oral Epidemiol.* **2014**, *43*, 116–127. [CrossRef]
68. Saniasiaya, J.; Islam, A.; Abdullah, B. Prevalence and Characteristics of Taste Disorders in Cases of COVID-19: A Meta-analysis of 29,349 Patients. *Otolaryngol. Neck Surg.* **2020**, *165*, 33–42. [CrossRef]
69. Seok, J.; Shim, Y.J.; Rhee, C.-S.; Kim, J.-W. Correlation between olfactory severity ratings based on olfactory function test scores and self-reported severity rating of olfactory loss. *Acta Oto-Laryngol.* **2017**, *137*, 750–754. [CrossRef]
70. Le Bon, S.-D.; Payen, L.; Prunier, L.; Steffens, Y.; Horoi, M.; Vaira, L.A.; Hopkins, C.; Lechien, J.R.; Saussez, S. Making scents of loss of taste in COVID-19: Is self-reported loss of taste due to olfactory dysfunction? A prospective study using psychophysical testing. *Int. Forum Allergy Rhinol.* **2021**, *11*, 1504–1507. [CrossRef]

medicina MDPI

Article

Level of Anxiety Caused by the Coronavirus (COVID-19) Pandemic among Dentists in Poland

Ewa Rusyan [1], Agnieszka Mielczarek [1], Agnieszka Bogusławska-Kapała [2], Kamil Adamczyk [3], Robert Piec [4] and Barbara Szykuła-Piec [4,*]

1 Department of Conservative Dentistry, Warsaw Medical University, 02-097 Warsaw, Poland; erusyan@wum.edu.pl (E.R.); agnieszka.mielczarek@wum.edu.pl (A.M.)
2 Department of Comprehensive Dentistry, Warsaw Medical University, 02-097 Warsaw, Poland; aboguslawska@wum.edu.pl
3 Central Clinical Hospital of the Ministry of Interior and Administration in Warsaw, 02-507 Warsaw, Poland; kamil.adamczyk@cskmswia.gov.pl
4 The Main School of Fire Service, 01-629 Warsaw, Poland; rpiec@sgsp.edu.pl
* Correspondence: bpiec@sgsp.edu.pl

Abstract: *Background and Objectives*: The early information on both the speed and high morbidity rate and, above all, mortality triggered the symptoms of COVID-19-related panic and anxiety. Dentists were listed in the top five professions with the highest risk of transmission of the virus. The aim of the present study was to investigate the correlation between the fear level of COVID-19 and sociodemographic variables in Polish dentists. *Materials and Methods*: A cross-sectional study was conducted via an online survey questionnaire with seven statements in the COVID-19 Fear Scale (FCV-19S). The online questionnaire was completed by 356 dentists. The SPSS and PQStat were used to analyze, validate, and assess correlations and logistic regression. *Results*: In the studied population of dentists, the perceived level of anxiety associated with COVID-19 should be considered relatively low. When the respondents had children, lived with the elderly, or looked after them, the observed level of anxiety was higher, and physical symptoms, such as sweating palms and increased heart rate, occurred. *Conclusions*: Studies concerning the anxiety level related to COVID-19 carried out among Polish dentists ascertained that the tested level of anxiety among dentists was relatively low. The COVID-19 Fear Scale (FCV-19S) adjusted to the Polish language requirements is a reliable tool that can be used effectively for analyzing the impact of any pandemic on the Polish-speaking population.

Keywords: COVID-19; dentistry; anxiety; fear

Citation: Rusyan, E.; Mielczarek, A.; Bogusławska-Kapała, A.; Adamczyk, K.; Piec, R.; Szykuła-Piec, B. Level of Anxiety Caused by the Coronavirus (COVID-19) Pandemic among Dentists in Poland. *Medicina* **2022**, *58*, 415. https://doi.org/10.3390/medicina58030415

Academic Editors: Pier Paolo Poli and Cesare D'Amico

Received: 8 February 2022
Accepted: 7 March 2022
Published: 11 March 2022

1. Introduction

One of the global challenges that emerged worldwide at the end of 2019 was the coronavirus (COVID-19) pandemic. Early information on both the speed and high morbidity rate and, above all, mortality triggered the symptoms of COVID-19-related panic and anxiety [1]. Under these conditions, working in occupations exposed to infection has become particularly stressful. According to the New York Times analysis based on data of the U.S. Department of Labor [2], this group includes dentists listed in the top five professions with the highest risk of transmission of the virus. In the first phase of the spread of the disease, most clinics in Poland suspended their practice. At the beginning of the pandemic in Poland, only departments working in emergency provided services to patients with acute conditions [3]. Insufficient supply of personal protective equipment as well as the lack of clear legal interpretations in the field of civil and criminal liability caused anxiety as to the resumption of operations.

Anxiety and fear are universal basic emotions that a person can experience, especially in difficult, unpredictable situations, where common sense is replaced by fear and speculation, e.g., due to the lack of reliable and verified information about potential danger. As of 9 July 2020, nearly 12 million confirmed COVID-19 cases were reported to the WHO worldwide, including over 540,000 cases of deaths [4]. The rate of spread of the virus and the high global COVID-19 mortality rate may explain the fear of encountering potentially infected people [5]. Multiple studies confirm the strong impact that the threat of the new coronavirus disease (COVID-19) has on individuals [6,7]. Such strong emotions trigger both physiological and psychological reactions. At present, due to the prolonged state of the epidemic, it is important to pay attention to the psychological sphere [8], which is not insignificant for the transmission of the virus. Fear, defined as an "unclear, unpleasant emotional state characterized by experiencing fear, stress and annoyance, along with anxiety", says Taylor, is the main reaction that strongly influences the perception of the environment and individual behavior [9].

Pandemics are large-scale epidemics that spread around the world. In recent years, virologists have been outdoing each other in reports and predictions about future pandemics with probable, catastrophic consequences for humanity. In Poland, as of 9 July 2020, we had over 35,000 confirmed cases of COVID-19 with 1542 people who died due to complications from the coronavirus infection. With these statistics, most of the restrictions were lifted while concurrently maintaining imposing the necessity of wearing a mask in public places and keeping the required social distance. This study was generally aimed at investigating the association between the fear level of COVID-19 and sociodemographic variables in Polish dentists.

2. Materials and Methods

2.1. Study Design, Setting, Participants

In the study, a tool developed by the team of Ahorsu et al. was used, The COVID-19 Fear Scale (FCV-19S) [10], translated into Polish. The FCV-19S scale was validated for use as a reliable research tool in multiple studies [11–13]. The English version of the scale questionnaire was translated into Polish according to generally accepted rules by two independent translators. After comparing the received texts, a version was created on the basis that, according to an expert in the field of sociology, psychology, and medical science, best reflects the original version. In order to assess the impact of the pandemic on the level of fear in the study group, a decision was made to use the FCV-19S scale as a proven research tool. After this stage, the tool was used in accordance with the research assumptions.

Data obtained as a result of the study with the use of the scale questionnaire were subjected to statistical analysis in order to assess the reliability of the developed questionnaires. All the obtained results were statistically analyzed with the PQStat 18 for Windows Software. The entire statistical analysis was performed at the confidence level of $\alpha = 0.05$. The results in the case of the probability of making a type 1 error that involved rejecting the null (true) hypothesis lower than 0.05 were considered significant.

In this study, the internal consistency of the scales was tested using Lee Cronbach's alpha coefficient and by determining the correlation coefficients between the answers to individual questions and the total score of the scale. Internal consistency is assumed to be good if Lee Cronbach's alpha is at least 0.7—in the current study, the alpha is 0.9. The results are presented in Figure 1.

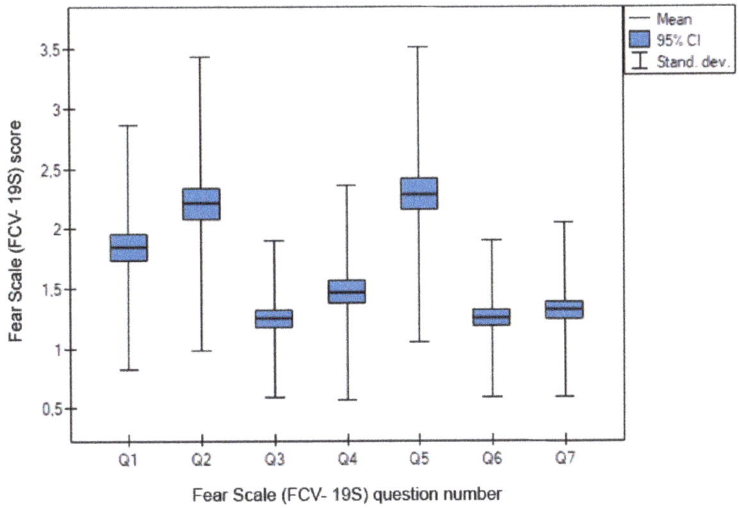

Figure 1. Distribution of responses in the COVID-19 Fear Scale questionnaire (FCV-19S) describing anxiety symptoms.

2.2. Variables

The variables were questions included in the questionnaire. The questionnaire consisted of demographic questions and were an essential part, in accordance with FCV-19S. These were 7 statements/questions meant to assess the perceived fear of COVID-19. The questions were closed ended. The level of anxiety was evaluated on a five-point scale, where the value of 1 means that a respondent did not have a given symptom, and 5 means that a respondent felt it strongly.

Patients' fear of COVID-19 was measured by questions and statements:

1. I am afraid of coronavirus (COVID-19) more than anything else.
2. Thinking about coronavirus (COVID-19) makes me uncomfortable.
3. My palms sweat when I think about coronavirus.
4. I am worried that I will die from the coronavirus infection.
5. When I hear about coronavirus (COVID-19) in the media and on the Internet, I get nervous and worried.
6. I cannot sleep because of coronavirus.
7. My heart starts to beat faster when I think about coronavirus.

New variables were created: factor 1, emotional fear reactions (questions 1, 2, 4, and 5); factor 2, symptomatic expressions of fear (questions 3, 6, and 7); and factor 3, the general level of anxiety, consisting of all 7 symptoms of anxiety (questions 1–7).

A cross-sectional study was conducted in the period from 26 May 2020 to 18 June 2020, with the use of an online survey questionnaire. Data were collected based on social media. In this period in Poland (from 26 May to 18 June), there were 22,000 active coronavirus cases to 30,000, with an average of 400 cases per day. The sample consisted of dentists from clinical and academic centers in Warsaw and Gdańsk, Poland. Those dentists were active professionally with available good technical support, with assured personal protective equipment and with current knowledge arising, among others, from academic lectures. Participants accessed the final questionnaire via a link in the emails and information in the Messenger application as well as via a link shared in two closed Facebook groups whose members are dentists only. Data were collected using a specially prepared Google Forms questionnaire. Consent was implied upon completion and submission of the questionnaire. Submitted surveys were collated in a directory and de-identified prior to analysis. The research has been approved by the Bioethics Committee at Medical University of Warsaw—

approval number AKBE/143/2020. Written informed consent was obtained from all the participants.

2.3. Study Size

According to the Supreme Medical Chamber, which is a professional self-government of dentists, 37,773 people practiced this profession in Poland in 2020, including 28,458 (75%) women and 9315 (25%) men [14]. Three hundred and fifty-six people completed the online questionnaire, and three hundred and forty-seven questionnaires were classified for further analysis after the correctness of the entered data was assessed, including 71% women and 29% men. In the studied group, the proportions of men and women were similar to the general distribution characterizing the gender distribution among dentists in Poland. Only the questionnaires in which the respondent answered all questions and the marked internship was in the range from 1 to 60 were allowed for further analysis.

For the entire population of dentists, assuming a significance level 0.05 and a margin of error of 0.05, the required number of people taking the tests is 380. The collected number of questionnaires was slightly smaller, and consequently, a margin of error was calculated. For the following data:

- Confidence level (α) 95%
- Sample size (n) 1000
- Proportion percentage (p) 50
- Population size (N) 37,773

the obtained margin of error was: ±5.237%.

The study population and the statistical methods are shown in Figure 2.

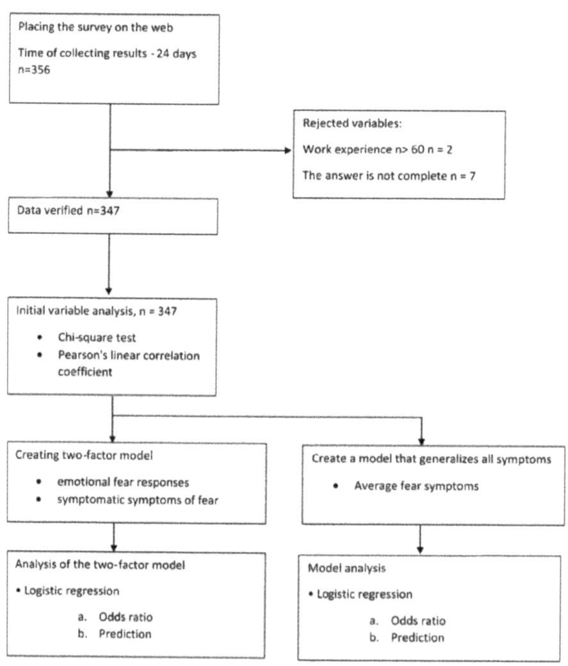

Figure 2. Flow diagram—the study population (respondents) and the statistical methods using.

2.4. Statistical Methods

SPSS Statistics version 21.0 and PQStat were used to carry out statistical analyses, and to correlate and assess the relation of responses, among others, the chi-square test and

Pearson's correlation coefficient were used. Logistic regression analysis was performed for the newly created variables.

A two-factor model of the COVID-19 measure was built. New variables were created: factor 1, emotional fear reactions (questions 1, 2, 4, and 5), and factor 2, symptomatic expressions of fear (questions 3, 6, and 7). It was established that if the average is less than 2.5, the respondent is not afraid, and the variable takes the value 0; if the average is greater than 2.51, the respondent is afraid, and the variable takes the value 1. Additionally, a model was created to generalize all symptoms—the general level of anxiety, consisting of all 7 symptoms of anxiety (questions 1–7); analogous values were adopted if the average is less than 2.5, indicating the respondent is not afraid, and the variable takes the value 0; if the average is greater than 2.51, the respondent is afraid, and the variable takes the value 1. After constructing new variables, a logistic regression analysis was performed.

2.5. *Quantitative Variables*

The answers were coded from 1 for "definitely not" to 5 for "definitely yes", with the possibility of marking "3" for imprecise definition of one's opinion. The applied Likert scale allows for averaging responses in two groups of statements: 1 and 2—general low level of anxiety, 4 and 5—general high level of anxiety. In the new variables constructed based on the obtained responses, it was established that if the average is less than 2.5, the respondent is not afraid, and then, the variable acquires the value 0; if the average is greater than 2.51, the respondent is afraid, and the variable acquires the value 1.

2.6. *Bias*

The survey was voluntary and anonymous but distributed via the Internet and social media. Currently, most educated people use the Internet and social media, and yet, it cannot be ruled out that there are dentists who use the Internet very rarely. Large, renowned clinical and academic centers in Warsaw (the largest city in Poland) and Gdańsk (6th city in terms of the number of inhabitants in Poland) were used to collect the data, where even in the first wave of the COVID-19 pandemic, there was relatively high availability of personal protective equipment in comparison to small centers.

3. Results

Participants

Three hundred and fifty-six people completed the online questionnaire, and three hundred and forty-seven questionnaires were classified for further analysis after the correctness of the entered data was assessed, including 71% women and 29% men. The questionnaire was completed by dentists with very little 1-year work experience and very experienced dentists with 49 years of work experience (mean 12.48 years). Detailed data are presented in Table 1.

Table 1. Demographic information.

Demographics	Group	n (%)
Gender	Female	245 (70.6%)
	Male	102 (29.4%)
Relationship status	Single	15 (4.3%)
	Divorced or widowed	52 (15.0%)
	In a relationship, living apart together	15 (4.3%)
	In a relationship, living together	38 (11.0%)
Having children	No	145 (41.8%)
	Yes	202 (58.2%)
Elderly care	No	297 (85.6%)
	Yes	50 (14.4%)

In the studied population of dentists, the perceived level of anxiety associated with COVID-19 should be considered relatively low. When the respondents had children, lived with the elderly, or looked after them, the observed level of anxiety was higher, and physical symptoms, such as sweating palms and increased heart rate, occurred. Detailed data are presented in Table 2.

Table 2. Distribution of answers to individual questions of The COVID-19 Fear Scale.

Questionnaire Item	Group	Frequency	Percent	Mean	Std. Dev.
I am most afraid of COVID-19.	1	173	49.9	1.85	1.016
	2	85	24.5		
	3	63	18.2		
	4	21	6.1		
	5	5	1.4		
It makes me uncomfortable to think about COVID-19.	1	133	38.3	2.22	1.224
	2	85	24.5		
	3	68	19.6		
	4	43	12.4		
	5	18	5.2		
My hands become clammy when I think about COVID-19.	1	290	83.6	1.25	0.652
	2	36	10.4		
	3	14	4.0		
	4	5	1.4		
	5	2	0.6		
I am afraid of losing my life because of COVID-19.	1	250	72.0	1.47	0.897
	2	55	15.9		
	3	24	6.9		
	4	12	3.5		
	5	6	1.7		
When watching news and stories about COVID-19 on social media, I become nervous or anxious.	1	124	35.7	2.29	1.229
	2	87	25.1		
	3	64	18.4		
	4	57	16.4		
	5	15	4.3		
I cannot sleep because I'm worrying about getting COVID-19.	1	289	83.3	1.25	0.653
	2	37	10.7		
	3	14	4.0		
	4	5	1.4		
	5	2	0.6		
My heart races or palpitates when I think about getting COVID-19.	1	276	79.5	1.32	0.728
	2	44	12.7		
	3	18	5.2		
	4	6	1.7		
	5	3	0.9		

In the next step, which combined all the aforementioned symptoms, both physiological and psychological, the risk of increased anxiety was found in 8.2% of the research sample (indications 4 and 5) (Table 3).

Table 3. Average percentage distribution of general anxiety defined by all marked feelings.

Level of Fear	Percent	Mean
1—Fear low	63.2	
2	17.7	
3	10.9	1.66
4	6.1	
5—Fear extremely high	2.1	

The results presented in Table 4 indicate that gender did not have a statistically significant influence on the level of anxiety in the respondents. Nor can it be said that seniority affects the level of anxiety. However, the level of anxiety seems to be significantly influenced by having children.

Analyses of the distribution of indications and test results allow the statistically significant assumption that people with children are afraid of coronavirus more than anything else. The statement "I'm afraid of coronavirus more than anything else", in the Polish version implies undefined fear without necessity compared with any point of reference. People with children feel more often uncomfortable when they think about the coronavirus (COVID-19). They are also significantly more worried about dying from COVID-19 infection, and they get upset when they hear about coronavirus in the media and on the Internet. The situation is similar when the respondents live with older people. The distribution of answers indicates that the respondents also experience physical symptoms that indicate anxiety, such as sweating palms.

Odds ratios were determined by regression analysis for the dependent variable emotional fear responses. The variables of gender, seniority, and relationship status are statistically insignificant.

Table 4. Statistical significance of the chi-square test and values and statistical significance of Pearson's correlation coefficient.

Questionnaire Item	Gender	Work Experience	Relationship Status	Having Children	Eldery Care
I am most afraid of COVID-19.	0.28	Pearson Correlation R = 0.12 Sig. = 0.03	0.42	0.00	0.01
It makes me uncomfortable to think about COVID-19.	0.08	Pearson Correlation R = 0.05 Sig. = 0.31	0.21	0.00	0.16
My hands become clammy when I think about COVID-19.	0.46	Pearson Correlation R = 0.01 Sig. = 0.83	0.58	0.41	0.00
I am afraid of losing my life because of COVID-19.	0.18	Pearson Correlation R = 0.12 Sig. = 0.03	0.38	0.02	0.26
When watching news and stories about COVID-19 on social media, I become nervous or anxious.	0.69	Pearson Correlation R = 0.10 Sig. = 0.08	0.36	0.00	0.00
I cannot sleep because I'm worrying about getting COVID-19.	0.28	Pearson Correlation R = 0.12 Sig. = 0.03	0.42	0.00	0.01
My heart races or palpitates when I think about getting COVID-19.	0.08	Pearson Correlation R = 0.05 Sig. = 0.31	0.21	0.00	0.16

For respondents who have children, we have determined a 2.4 odds ratio of an increase in the chance of a high level of anxiety (Table 5).

Table 5. Model of logistic regression analysis of the variables emotional fear reactions and having children.

	b Coeff.	b Error	−95% CI	+95% CI	Wald Stat.	*p*-Value	Odds Ratio	−95% CI	+95% CI
Intercept	−2.36	0.45	−3.24	−1.47	27.32	<0.001	0.09	0.04	0.23
Having children	0.88	0.26	0.38	1.39	11.65	<0.001	2.42	1.46	4.02

For the variable determining whether the tested person lives with the elderly, the odds ratios are statistically significant, and there is a 3-fold higher risk of emotional symptoms if one lives with an elderly person (Table 6). The multiple model, which takes into account the simultaneous variable of having children and living with the elderly, is also statistically significant, but the odds ratios change very little. For all variants of the model, the absence of emotional symptoms is predicted, while the highest probability of occurrence of emotional symptoms has been ascertained for the situation when the examined person has children and lives with an elderly person.

Table 6. Model of logistic regression analysis of the variables emotional fear reactions and person lives with the elderly.

	b Coeff.	b Error	−95% CI	+95% CI	Wald Stat.	*p*-Value	Odds Ratio	−95% CI	+95% CI
Intercept	−2.20	0.39	−2.97	−1.44	32.02	<0.001	0.11	0.05	0.24
Person lives with the elderly	1.10	0.31	0.49	1.72	12.42	<0.001	3.01	1.63	5.57

The logistic regression model taking into account the physical variables and all seven anxiety symptoms did not show a statistically significant effect.

4. Discussion

In view of the strong influence of anxiety on individual and collective behavior, a scale for measuring fear was developed by a team of scientists to diagnose its level among people living in different parts of the globe. This study was conducted to assess the anxiety and fear of contracting the disease among dentists in Poland while working during the COVID-19 epidemic. It is very important because they are at a great risk of SARS-CoV-2 transmission via respiratory droplets [15,16]. Having defined a number of feelings which, according to the authors of the scale, make up the general characteristics of the level of anxiety, it can be concluded that the tested group was not subject to strong anxiety associated with COVID-19.

On average, the level of anxiety characterizing the studied population was 1.66 (ranging from 1—very low to 5—high). The obtained results are not consistent with the results of the study conducted in Poland on a group of 875 dentists, the aim of which was to assess the attitudes of dentists and their professional approach when confronted with the COVID-19 pandemic. In that study, more than half of the surveyed dentists expressed concerns about their own and their families' health [17]. In this paper, over 70% of the respondents have suspended their practice, which was an effect resulting from insufficient availability of professional protective means, but it also resulted from the feelings of anxiety, uncertainty, and fear of the infection.

One of the main reasons for the discrepancy in anxiety levels among the population of Polish dentists between this study and the study conducted by Tysiąc-Miśta [17] could be the time when the survey was carried out. In this study, the survey-response period falls within the third month since the WHO announcement of the pandemic on 11 March 2020 (May–June 2020). In the case of the Tysiąc-Miśta study, it was the first month of the pandemic (April 2020). As indicated by Ferrara et al. in their study [18], the impact of the pandemic on anxiety, depression, and stress was highest in the first weeks of the pandemic and changed with time.

This is at variance with the limited professional activity that took place in the first months of the pandemic in Poland, when the vast majority of offices were closed. In April, a still rather high percentage of jobs did not resume work, and as late as in May, about 50% of private offices restarted their activity. It is also possible that the study was conducted at a time when the population managed to adapt better to the new situation, which to a lesser extent, reflects the primary emotions associated with the coronavirus. Undoubtedly, the dentists were dealing with adaptation to new working conditions that allow reducing the risk of transmission by using appropriate personal protective equipment (PPE) and complying with sanitary regulations. Moreover, a clear definition of the legal situation as to the potential risk of infection in the conditions of a dentist's office appeared to have considerably calmed both the doctors and the patients themselves. As the study had been carried out among persons living in large cities, which are concurrently academic centers, we may assume that the relatively low anxiety level could arise among others from good access of the studied group of dentists to knowledge based on professional research. Good accessibility to library bases, direct information exchange between physicians, as well as contacts via professional online discussions make it possible for those persons to obtain reliable data quickly and easily, which as a consequence, helps minimize their anxiety. Furthermore, in large urban centers, dentists tend to work together in larger teams, which could also be considered to contribute to lower stress levels. It may also be assumed that mutual psychological support of fellow workers as well as the above-mentioned exchange of latest knowledge concerning the virus and ways of staying protected from the infection also minimized their anxiety. Additionally, dentists working in major clinics find it easier to organize work in a way that allows more convenient distribution of tasks (e.g., by adopting a shift system), which concurrently minimizes work overload and concerns. A further analysis of this issue appears to be quite an interesting venture.

Based on information obtained from the questionnaire, the concern about the health of the people for whom the respondents are responsible remains unchanged. Having children and caring for the elderly who are more susceptible to infections raises the level of anxiety in the respondents. It would seem that the presented attitude is irrelevant to the practiced profession, but it indicates the importance of basic family relations, especially in the period of danger. Results of studies published among physicians in Pakistan imply that there was a particularly high anxiety level found in women. According to the authors, this fact arises, apart from cultural reasons, from the responsibility for the family associated with their social functions of wives and mothers [19]. A similar dependence is observed in our own studies even though, without differentiation by gender, persons responsible for family members are exposed to anxiety and stress connected with the pandemic to a much greater extent. Perhaps medical education and knowledge in the field of epidemiology have a positive effect on the mental health of dentists. According to De Kock et al., systemic support, adequate knowledge, and resilience were identified as factors protecting against adverse mental health outcomes [20]. Additionally, results of answers given to the question concerning nervousness, namely "when I hear about the coronavirus in the media and the Internet", seem to be quite interesting. In the situation of a virus that is invisible, we can deal with reactions intensified by the lack of proven knowledge and information chaos, as has been confirmed by our research. One in five respondents becomes nervous and anxious when they hear about the coronavirus (COVID-19) in the media and on the Internet. This can be further triggered by the frustration of being unable to divert attention away from the topic of the pandemic and the flood of information. Due to the scale of the problem, the World Health Organization (WHO) has added a "mythbusters" section to its website, where coronavirus-related advice is posted in order to debunk a large number of "fake news". The study used a previously validated tool that has so far carried out thousands of assessments of anxiety levels around the world.

The Limitations of the Study

The limitations of this study are that the data were collected within a short time period and, given the strong impact of the epidemic on the psychophysical sphere, it may be assumed that attitudes may evolve with the emerging new reports related to COVID-19. The examined sample corresponds to 0.9% of the total number of dentists, which is a relatively low percentage and may not be fully representative of the whole community. Moreover, the sampling method for the questionnaire was non-probabilistic. It was addressed to people from large academic centers, who have better access to both information and personal protective equipment. The use of social media could have also limited access to the study for elderly people who do not use a computer.

Additionally, the tool used does not take into account the current/active background for the study, which strongly affects the respondents' responses. Depending on the emotional state in which they are examined and on objective circumstances, specific physiological reactions have been identified. Hence, statements concerning physiological responses, such as sweating of palms, sleeping problems, and an increased heart rate, are difficult to identify in a generalized perception of behavior-realistic information during catastrophic events [21]. In the event of a pandemic, the factors of anxiety are difficult to capture, which is another significant limitation for the obtained research results.

5. Conclusions

Studies concerning the anxiety level related to COVID-19 carried out among the Polish dentists ascertained that the tested level of anxiety among dentists was relatively low. However, the mindset, which is not easy to change, and the reaction to a continuous information flow concerning COVID-19 had a significant impact on the level of declared anxiety.

The COVID-19 Fear Scale (FCV- 19S), adjusted to the Polish language requirements, is a reliable tool that can be used effectively for analyzing the impact of any pandemic on the Polish-speaking population.

Author Contributions: Each author is made substantial contributions to the work. E.R., A.M. and A.B.-K., data acquisition; R.P. and B.S.-P., analysis and interpretation of data; K.A., R.P. and B.S.-P., drafting the work; E.R., A.M. and A.B.-K., substantively revising the work. All authors have read and agreed to the published version of the manuscript.

Funding: This research received no external funding.

Institutional Review Board Statement: The study was conducted according to the guidelines of the Declaration of Helsinki and approved by the Bioethics Committee at Medical University of Warsaw—approval number AKBE/143/2020.

Informed Consent Statement: Informed consent was obtained from all subjects involved in the study.

Data Availability Statement: Data sharing not applicable No new data were created or analyzed in this study. Data sharing is not applicable to this article.

Conflicts of Interest: The authors declare no conflict of interest.

References

1. Lancet, T. COVID-19: Fighting panic with information. *Lancet* **2020**, *395*, 537. [CrossRef]
2. Gamio, L. The Workers Who Face the Greatest Coronavirus Risk—The New York Times. Available online: https://www.nytimes.com/interactive/2020/03/15/business/economy/coronavirus-worker-risk.html (accessed on 16 December 2021).
3. Karwowska, A. Coronavirus Has Restricted Our Access to Medical Care. Here Is the Breakdown of How Hospitals, Clinics and Private Practice Now Operate. Available online: https://wyborcza.pl/7,173236,25964988,coronavirus-has-restricted-our-access-to-medical-care-here.html (accessed on 16 December 2021).
4. World Health Organization. WHO Coronavirus (COVID-19) Dashboard | WHO Coronavirus (COVID-19) Dashboard with Vaccination Data. Available online: https://covid19.who.int/ (accessed on 16 December 2021).
5. Lin, C.-Y. Social reaction toward the 2019 novel coronavirus (COVID-19). *Soc. Health Behav.* **2020**, *3*, 1. [CrossRef]

6. Bhuiyan, A.K.M.I.; Sakib, N.; Pakpour, A.H.; Griffiths, M.D.; Mamun, M.A. COVID-19-Related Suicides in Bangladesh Due to Lockdown and Economic Factors: Case Study Evidence from Media Reports. *Int. J. Ment. Health Addict.* **2020**, *19*, 2110–2115. [CrossRef] [PubMed]
7. Qiu, J.; Shen, B.; Zhao, M.; Wang, Z.; Xie, B.; Xu, Y. A nationwide survey of psychological distress among Chinese people in the COVID-19 epidemic: Implications and policy recommendations. *Gen. Psychiatry* **2020**, *33*, e100213. [CrossRef]
8. Pappas, G.; Kiriaze, I.; Giannakis, P.; Falagas, M. Psychosocial consequences of infectious diseases. *Clin. Microbiol. Infect.* **2009**, *15*, 743–747. [CrossRef]
9. Taylor, S. *The Psychology of Pandemics: Preparing for the Next Global Outbreak of Infectious Disease*; Cambridge Scholars Publishing: Newcastle upon Tyne, UK, 2019; pp. 23–39.
10. Ahorsu, D.K.; Lin, C.-Y.; Imani, V.; Saffari, M.; Griffiths, M.D.; Pakpour, A.H. The Fear of COVID-19 Scale: Development and Initial Validation. *Int. J. Ment. Health Addict.* **2020**, 1–9. [CrossRef] [PubMed]
11. Sakib, N.; Bhuiyan, A.K.M.I.; Hossain, S.; Al Mamun, F.; Hosen, I.; Abdullah, A.H.; Sarker, A.; Mohiuddin, M.S.; Rayhan, I.; Hossain, M.; et al. Psychometric Validation of the Bangla Fear of COVID-19 Scale: Confirmatory Factor Analysis and Rasch Analysis. *Int. J. Ment. Health Addict.* **2020**, *11*, 1–12. [CrossRef]
12. Satici, B.; Gocet-Tekin, E.; Deniz, M.E.; Satici, S.A. Adaptation of the Fear of COVID-19 Scale: Its Association with Psychological Distress and Life Satisfaction in Turkey. *Int. J. Ment. Health Addict.* **2020**, *19*, 1980–1988. [CrossRef]
13. Soraci, P.; Ferrari, A.; Abbiati, F.A.; Del Fante, E.; De Pace, R.; Urso, A.; Griffiths, M.D. Validation and Psychometric Evaluation of the Italian Version of the Fear of COVID-19 Scale. *Int. J. Ment. Health Addict.* **2020**, *4*, 1–10. [CrossRef]
14. Polish Supreme Medical Council. Statistical Information of the Polish Supreme Medical Council, on 3 July 2020. Available online: https://nil.org.pl/rejestry/centralny-rejestr-lekarzy/informacje-statystyczne (accessed on 16 December 2021).
15. Ather, A.; Patel, B.; Ruparel, N.B.; Diogenes, A.; Hargreaves, K.M. Coronavirus Disease 19 (COVID-19): Implications for Clinical Dental Care. *J. Endod.* **2020**, *46*, 584–595. [CrossRef]
16. Meng, L.; Hua, F.; Bian, Z. Coronavirus Disease 2019 (COVID-19): Emerging and Future Challenges for Dental and Oral Medicine. *J. Dent. Res.* **2020**, *99*, 481–487. [CrossRef]
17. Tysiąc-Miśta, M.; Dziedzic, A. The Attitudes and Professional Approaches of Dental Practitioners during the COVID-19 Outbreak in Poland: A Cross-Sectional Survey. *Int. J. Environ. Res. Public Health* **2020**, *17*, 4703. [CrossRef]
18. Ferrara, M.; Langiano, E.; Falese, L.; De Marco, A.; De Vito, E. Quality of Life and Psychosocial Impacts of the Different Restrictive Measures during One Year into the COVID-19 Pandemic on Patients with Cancer in Italy: An Ecological Study. *Int. J. Environ. Res. Public Health* **2021**, *18*, 7161. [CrossRef] [PubMed]
19. Mahmood, Q.K.; Jafree, S.R.; Mukhtar, S.; Fischer, F. Social Media Use, Self-Efficacy, Perceived Threat, and Preventive Behavior in Times of COVID-19: Results of a Cross-Sectional Study in Pakistan. *Front. Psychol.* **2021**, *12*, 2354. [CrossRef] [PubMed]
20. De Kock, J.H.; Latham, H.A.; Leslie, S.J.; Grindle, M.; Munoz, S.A.; Ellis, L.; Polson, R.; O'Malley, C.M. A rapid review of the impact of COVID-19 on the mental health of healthcare workers: Implications for supporting psychological well-being. *BMC Public Health* **2021**, *21*, 1–18. [CrossRef] [PubMed]
21. Jerusalem, M.; Schwarzer, R. Self-efficacy as a resource factor in stress appraisal processes. In *Self-Efficacy: Thought Control of Action*; Hemisphere Publishing Corp.: Washington, DC, USA, 1992; pp. 195–213.

medicina

MDPI

Article

Title Cross-Sectional Study to Evaluate Knowledge and Attitudes on Oral Hygiene of Romanian Students

Catalina Iulia Saveanu, Cosmin Constantin Cretu *, Irina Bamboi *, Alexandra Ecaterina Săveanu * and Daniela Anistoroaei

Department of Dent-Alveolar and Maxillo-Facial Surgery, Faculty of Dental Medicine, University of Medicine and Pharmacy Grigore T Popa, 700115 Iasi, Romania; cisaveanu@prevod.umfiasi.ro (C.I.S.); daniulia05@yahoo.com (D.A.)

* Correspondence: cosmincretu01@gmail.com (C.C.C.); irina.bamboi@umfiasi.ro (I.B.); alexandra-ecaterina.dd.saveanu@students.umfiasi.ro (A.E.S.)

Abstract: *Background and Objectives:* the purpose of this study was to evaluate students' level of knowledge and attitude towards oral hygiene. *Materials and Methods:* the evaluation was carried out by a questionnaire, with 30 Q (questions) as follows: demographic data (Q1–Q5), oral hygiene knowledge data (Q6–Q23) and oral hygiene attitude data (Q24–Q30). The study included students from Romanian schools and the selection of the study group was made following selection criteria in accordance with ethical issues. A descriptive statistical analysis was performed and a value of $p \leq 0.05$ was considered statistically significant. *Results:* the study included a number of 718 subjects with a mean age of 14.54 (±2.22), male 250 (34.8%) and female 468 (65.2%), MS (middle school students) 354 (49.4%) and HH (high school students) 364 (50.6%). Most of the subjects 292 (MS = 160; HS = 132) know a toothbrushing technique, $p = 0.009$, r = 0.091 and 587 (MS = 278; HS = 309) know that brushing removes the bacterial plaque $p = 0.027$, r = −0.082 but only 147 (MS = 71; HS = 76) know that (by) brushing can re-mineralize hard dental structures. The duration of the toothbrushing is variable, for 2- or 3-min $p = 0.058$, r = 0.043. Criteria for choosing the toothbrush were based mainly on the indications of the dentist, respectively, for toothpaste on its properties. The frequency of toothbrushing is mainly twice a day 428 (MS = 234; HS = 248), $p = 0.079$, r = 0.037, 73 (MS = 33; HS = 40) after every meal. $p = 0.099$, r = 0.095. Mouthwash is used by 421 (MS = 199; HS = 222) $p = 0.111$, r = −0.048, and 228 (MS = 199; HS = 222) after each brushing. Dental floss is used by 240 (MS = 106; HS = 134), $p = 0.031$, r = −0.073 and only 74 (MS = 41; HS = 33) after each brushing. *Conclusions:* there are differences in the level of knowledge and attitudes regarding the determinants of oral hygiene depending on the level of education.

Keywords: oral hygiene; toothbrushing; toothpaste; dental floss

Citation: Saveanu, C.I.; Cretu, C.C.; Bamboi, I.; Săveanu, A.E.; Anistoroaei, D. Title Cross-Sectional Study to Evaluate Knowledge and Attitudes on Oral Hygiene of Romanian Students. *Medicina* **2022**, *58*, 406. https://doi.org/10.3390/medicina58030406

Academic Editors: Cesare D'Amico and Pier Paolo Poli

Received: 20 February 2022
Accepted: 3 March 2022
Published: 9 March 2022

1. Introduction

Prevention is becoming increasingly important because most diseases that affect the oral cavity can be deterred by appropriate prevention measures. Generally, understanding the factors that influence oral health can help dental professionals to implement an effective strategy. The Center of Disease Control on Oral Prevention recommendations require a sustained education about food hygiene, oral hygiene as well as the importance of both general and local fluoridation, and sealing [1–4]. The long-term implications of oral health will be found in adult oral health, a health issue that affects both carious lesions and periodontal lesions or even cancer [5–11]. The results of specialized studies have highlighted the need to establish educational methods designed to improve the determinants of oral health [12–15]. In addition, numerous studies address the socio-economic and behavioral aspects of children and adolescents in order to highlight their knowledge, attitudes and practices regarding oral health [10,16,17].

Oral hygiene is found in the primary prevention recommendations of the World Health Organization (WHO). In order to change certain behaviors and attitudes, oral hygiene must be evaluated on different population categories, as well as in different regions [6]. In conformity with the results obtained, dental professionals will establish an appropriate therapy that can aim to improve the parameters of oral health. Oral health is a key indicator of overall health, well-being and quality of life. According to WHO reports, more than 530 million children suffer from dental caries of primary teeth and severe periodontal disease, almost 10% of the global population being affected. The Global Burden of Disease Study 2017 estimated that oral diseases affect 3.5 billion people worldwide [18]. According to WHO specifications, improving oral health requires a reform of oral health systems to shift the focus from invasive dental treatment to prevention and as many minimally invasive treatments as possible. WHO has identified key strategies for improving oral health, including prevention through education.

Oral health education aims to inform and develop, among the population, a concept and a hygienic behavior, in order to defend general health, dental and periodontal health, harmonious development and strengthening the body, its adaptation to environmental conditions. Health education can be defined as the sum of all the influences that, together, determine knowledge, concepts and behaviors related to the promotion, maintenance and recovery of health individually and collectively.

These influences include the formative education in the family, school and society, respectively, in the special context of the activity of the health services.

Health education is a communication activity, aimed at improving health and preventing or reducing disease, individually or collectively, by influencing their conceptions, attitudes and behavior, with the help of power and community.

Bacterial plaque is the determining factor in the appearance of tooth decay and periodontal disease. In this context, poor hygiene due to lack of knowledge can lead to compromising the integrity of the tooth. The choice of a toothbrush taking into account its characteristics and a toothpaste taking into account its properties are also very important aspects reported in other specialized studies [19–21]. Fluoride is a key agent in reducing the prevalence and severity of dental caries [21–25].

Brushing twice a day with fluoride toothpaste is more efficient, as it maintains adequate fluoride around the teeth for a greater part of the day [26]. In addition, in many countries toothbrushing is part of school routines aimed at improving health [21,25]. Community programs aiming to improve the determinants of oral health should also include nurses from school health services or support staff who can initiate toothbrushing exercises. Thus, these personnel must include oral health education in their regular activities. Teachers, with appropriate guidance, can also motivate and guide students in their toothbrushing. These aspects have long been highlighted in a specialized guide [27]. In this context, oral hygiene is a continuous concern for researchers in the field and must be performed properly by each individual daily at least twice a day [12–17].

The negative economic impact through lack of resources will affect the individual from this point of view, but lack of knowledge will affect him even more. Even if, in some situations, the aspects of achieving oral hygiene and the long-term implications in its absence are known, there will always be a number of subjects not sensibilized from this point of view.

The null hypothesis for this study is that there are no differences in the level of knowledge and attitudes of the students regarding oral hygiene depending on the level of education.

The testable hypothesis was that there are differences in the level of knowledge and attitudes towards oral hygiene depending on the level of education.

The study aimed to evaluate the level of knowledge of students between 10–19 years old regarding oral hygiene. The objectives of this study were to assess the level of knowledge of the students about: toothbrushing technique, choosing the type of toothbrush, choosing toothpaste, the attitudes towards toothbrushing conditions, the use of mouthwash and dental floss.

2. Materials and Methods

2.1. Study Design and Setting

This is a cross-sectional survey designed to monitor the level of knowledge and attitudes of the student population. The applied questionnaire followed the formative level of the students in terms of oral hygiene. This can help in the future in the design of education programs. This cross-sectional study was carried out according to the formal approval of the research center of the University of Medicine and Pharmacy. For the purpose of the study, seven areas (Iasi, Botosani, Suceava, Prahova, Neamt, Bucuresti, Bacau) of the Romanian region were listed. The state schools were considered in the study based on ease of access.

2.2. Study Sample

A preliminary semi-structured questionnaire was originally developed in Romanian translated into English by a professional translator and translated back into Romanian to ensure accuracy. The questionnaire was iteratively tested, with both English and Romanian speakers, to assess the length of the questions, the respondent's understanding of the questions, to follow the relevance and order of the questions. The final changes to the questionnaire were translated into Romanian by a bilingual staff member and independently reviewed by two other bilingual employees. Many topics were included to understand oral hygiene knowledge and attitudes about students' daily oral hygiene habits. So, this study included students from 5th to 12th (aged between 10–19 years) grade male and female gender randomly selected from state schools. Sample size estimation was based on the alpha error probability = 0.05, power = 0.95. Thus for 614,767, students in high school education for an error of 5% the sample size is 384 students. The chosen sample is representative for Romania. Our study included 718 students. Survey participants sampling was unlikely. The selection of the study group was made following the selection criteria. The inclusion criteria were as follows: schools where teachers received the information and agreed to distribute the student questionnaire; students who agreed to complete the questionnaire; middle school or high school students. The exclusion criteria were as follows: schools in which teachers did not receive information to send the questionnaire to students; parents who did not agree to have the child complete the questionnaire; problems with the teenager's desire not to complete the questionnaire; students from another level of study. Completion recommendations were sent to the class guidance teacher and the parents were completely informed by the teachers, through meetings. The agreement to complete the questionnaire was supported by the class teacher, the person under whose supervision this action was possible. The teacher explained it to the parents during the class work sessions. Subjects considered eligible were those who wished to complete this questionnaire after reading its contents.

2.3. Study Instrument Development and Validation

The level of knowledge and attitudes of the students regarding oral hygiene was assessed. The questionnaire method was applied for this evaluation. The questionnaire was evaluated by a panel of experts from the Faculty of Dentistry, following a qualitative pretesting of the content, followed by its validation. The questionnaire was pilot tested with a sample of fifty students to ensure that it was brief and straightforward. In addition, the questionnaire was field-tested to determine its ease of use and accuracy in knowledge items.

2.4. Questionnaire Contents

The questionnaire consisted of 30 multiple choice questions with a single correct answer to each question. The oral hygiene knowledge and attitudes of the students were assessed using a structured, questionnaire openly applied and uploaded online on the google docs platform. The questionnaire items included demographic information (Q1–Q5), followed by questions on the level of knowledge of oral hygiene (Q6–Q23) and data on the attitude of the students regarding oral hygiene (Q24–Q30) Table 1.

Table 1. The questions applied in the questionnaire and the possible answers.

Q 1 = How old are you?
Q 2 = What is your gender? (F = female; M = male).
Q 3 = What is the county where you study? (IS = Iasi; BT = Botosani; SV = Suceava; PH = Prahova; NT = Neamt; B = Bucharest; BC = Bacau).
Q 4 = What is the class level? (MS = middle school/HS = high school).
Q 5 = What class grade are you in? (5-th; 6-th; 7-th; 8-th; 9-th; 10-th; 11-th; 12-th).
Q 6 = Do you know a special dental brushing technique? (Yes/No).
Q 7 = Do you think that dental brushing is done to remove dental bacterial plaque? (Yes/No).
Q 8 = Do you think that dental brushing is done to remove food? (Yes/No).
Q 9 = Do you think that dental brushing is done to have whiter teeth? (Yes/No).
Q 10 = Do you think that dental brushing aims to remineralizers your teeth? (Yes/No).
Q 11 = How long do you think dental brushing should last? 1 = 1 min; 2 = 2 min; 3 = 3 min; 4 = 4 min.
Q 12 = Is the design important when choosing a toothbrush? (Yes/No).
Q 13 = Is the price important when choosing a toothbrush? (Yes/No).
Q 14 = Is the manufacturer company important when buying a toothbrush? (Yes/No).
Q 15 = Is age important when choosing a toothbrush? (Yes/No).
Q 16 = Is it important to follow dental professional recommendations when choosing a toothbrush? (Yes/No).
Q 17 = Is it important to consider advertising when choosing a toothbrush? (Yes/No).
Q 18 = Is it important to take into account the design when choosing toothpaste? (Yes/No).
Q 19 = Is it important to take into account the price when choosing toothpaste? (Yes/No).
Q 20 =Is it important to take the manufacturer company into account when choosing toothpaste? (Yes/No).
Q 21 = Is it important to take into account the fluoride content when choosing toothpaste? (Yes/No).
Q 22 = Is it important to take into account the properties of paste when choosing your toothpaste? (Yes/No).
Q 23 = It is important to take into account advertising when choosing your toothpaste? (Yes/No).
Q 24 = How much toothpaste do you use when you brush your teeth? (1 = the length of the toothbrush; 2 = as much as a pea; 3 = less than a pea).
Q 25 = What is the frequency of brushing? (1 = once a day; 2 = twice a day; 3 = three times a day; 4 = after each meal; 5 = when I feel the need).
Q 26 = When do you brush your teeth? (1 = in the morning; 2 = in the evening; 3 = both morning and evening; 4 = after each meal; 5 = when I feel the need).
Q 27 = Do you use mouthwash? (Yes/No).
Q 28 = When do you use mouthwash? (1 = after each brushing; 2 = when I feel the need; 3 = in the morning; 4 = in the evening; 5 = I don't use).
Q 29 = Do you floss for dental cleaning? (Yes/No).
Q 30 When do you use dental floss for interdental cleaning? (1 = after each brushing; 2 = when I feel the need; 3 = in the morning; 4 = in the evening; 5 = I do not use).

2.5. *Assessment of the Oral Hygiene Knowledge and Attitudes*

All the multiple-choice questions had a single best response. Every correct answer in the questionnaire received a score of zero, while every incorrect response received a score of one.

2.6. *Statistical Analysis*

The data was collected and introduced into a database. Descriptive statistics of frequency distribution, percentages, and mean knowledge scores were calculated for oral hygiene education. A descriptive statistic of the study was performed by applying crosstabs to all the aspects analyzed according to MS and HH. The processing of statistical data was performed with the program SPSS version 26.00 for Windows, (IBM, Armonk, NY, USA) establishing a threshold of statistical significance of $p \leq 0.05$. The development of the codebook was based on codes recorded in the interview guide. The codes were grouped into preliminary topics and discussed with the research team to reach a thematic consensus. A member of the team with experience and expertise in qualitative research methods and oral health also reviewed all transcripts, codes and final thematic interpretation. The Chi-square test was used for the comparative analysis in function by study level. The correlation of overall knowledge and attitudes between students was performed using Pearson's correlation test.

3. Results

3.1. *Demographic Data*

The study included a number of 718 students with a mean age of 14.54 (±2.22) the youngest being 10 years old and the oldest being 19 years old, male 250 (34,8%) and female 468 (65.2%), middle school students 354 (49.4%) and high school 364 (50.6%). The distribution of subjects according to class, gender and county is presented in Table 2.

Table 2. Demographic data -distribution of subjects according to class, gender and county.

Count		Study Level		Gender		County							Total
		Ms	Hs	M	F	IS	BT	SV	PH	NT	B	BC	
Class	5th	60	-	21	39	48	0	2	1	0	5	4	60
	6th	116	-	39	77	104	0	7	0	1	3	1	116
	7th	135	-	55	80	38	0	15	2	35	14	31	135
	8th	43	-	20	23	7	0	14	2	16	3	1	43
	9th	-	76	18	58	69	0	3	1	0	3	0	76
	10th	-	86	26	60	59	0	1	19	0	6	1	86
	11th	-	135	38	97	91	2	9	23	1	9	0	135
	12th	-	67	33	34	42	6	5	11	0	3	0	67
Total		354	364	250	468	458	8	56	59	53	46	38	718

3.2. *Criteria for Choosing Toothbrush and Toothpaste*

The answers regarding the questions related to the criteria used when choosing the toothbrush were in descending order depending on: the indications of the dentist; by age; the design of the toothbrush; the manufacturing company; the price and advertisements Table 3.

Table 3. Answers to questions about the criteria used when choosing a toothbrush and toothpaste.

	Questions	Yes	MS	HS	*p*	R
	Criteria for choosing a toothbrush:					
Q12	Is design important?	231	84	147	0 *	−0.178
Q13	Is price important?	140	52	88	0.001 *	0.12
Q14	Is the manufacturer company important?	213	82	131	0 *	−0.14
Q15	Is age important?	247	160	87	0 *	0.224
Q16	Are dental professional recommendations important?	372	202	170	0.003 *	0.104
Q17	Is advertising important?	45	18	27	0.128	−0.048
	Criteria for choosing a tube of toothpaste:					
Q18	Is design important?	66	33	33	0.341	0.02
Q19	Is price important?	107	49	58	0.431	−0.029
Q20	Is the manufacturer company important?	220	92	128	0.005 *	−0.1
Q21	Is the fluoride content important?	173	83	90	0.689	−0.015
Q22	Are the properties important?	550	275	275	0.282	0.025
Q23	Is advertising important?	55	20	35	0.031 *	−0.074

* Significance level $p \leq 0.05$.

The answers to the questions related to the criteria when choosing a tube of toothpaste were in descending order according to: its properties; the manufacturing company; the amount of fluoride; the price; design and advertising Table 3.

3.3. The Attitude towards the Amount of Toothpaste Used, the Frequency of Toothbrushing Use

Regarding the question on how much toothpaste you use when brushing your teeth, an approximately equal number of students apply toothpaste over its entire length of the brush 373 (MS = 178; HS = 195) or as much as a pea 340 (MS = 173; HS = 167). $p = 0.0625$, r = −0.035. The frequency of toothbrushing is variable, with most students performing it twice a day for 428 (MS = 234; HS = 248), after each meal for 53 (MS = 25; HS = 28) and once a day for 92 (MS = 55; HS = 37) with $p = 0.079$, establishing a very low positive correlation depending on the level of study r = 0.037. As a time of day, most of the subjects brush their teeth both in the morning and in the evening 508 (MS = 246; HS = 262) and only a small number of subjects, respectively, 73 (MS = 33; HS = 40) brush their teeth after every meal. From this point of view, the results are not significant $p = 0.099$ and correlate very poorly depending on the level of study r = 0.095 Table 4.

Table 4. Answers to questions about the attitude towards the amount of toothpaste used, the frequency of toothbrushing use.

	Questions	MS	HS	Total	*p*	R
Q24	How much toothpaste do you use when brushing your teeth?				0.625	−0.035
	1 = the length of the toothbrush	178	195	373		
	2 = as much as a pea	173	167	340		
	3 = less than a pea	3	2	5		

Table 4. *Cont.*

	Questions	MS	HS	Total	*p*	R
Q25	What is the frequency of brushing?				0.079	0.037
	1 = once a day	55	37	92		
	2 = twice a day	234	248	482		
	3 = three times a day	21	36	57		
	4 = after each meal	25	28	53		
	5 = when I feel the need	19	15	34		
Q26	When do you brush your teeth?				0.099	0.095
	1 = in the morning	36	24	60		
	2 = in the evening	25	15	40		
	3 = both morning and evening	246	262	508		
	4 = after each meal	33	40	73		
	5 = when I feel the need	11	21	32		
	6 = I don't use	3	2	5		

Most of the subjects 292 (MS = 160; HS = 132) know a toothbrushing technique, $p = 0.009$, r = 0.091. In addition, the majority 587 (MS = 278; HS = 309), know that brushing removes the bacterial plaque $p = 0.027$, r = −0.082 and the remaining food on the dental surfaces 521 (MS = 264; HS = 257), $p = 0.233$, r = 0.045. About half of the 353 subjects (MS = 183; HS = 170) consider that by applying the brushing they will have whiter teeth $p = 0.181$, r = 0.050 and 147 (MS = 71; HS = 76) know that brushing can remineralize hard dental structures.

3.4. *The Attitude towards the Time of Toothbrushing*

The duration of the toothbrushing is variable, for most of the students being 2 min for 335 (MS = 182; HS = 153) of the students and 3 min for 209 of the students (MS = 89; HS = 120), $p = 0.058$, r = 0.043 of the students (Figure 1).

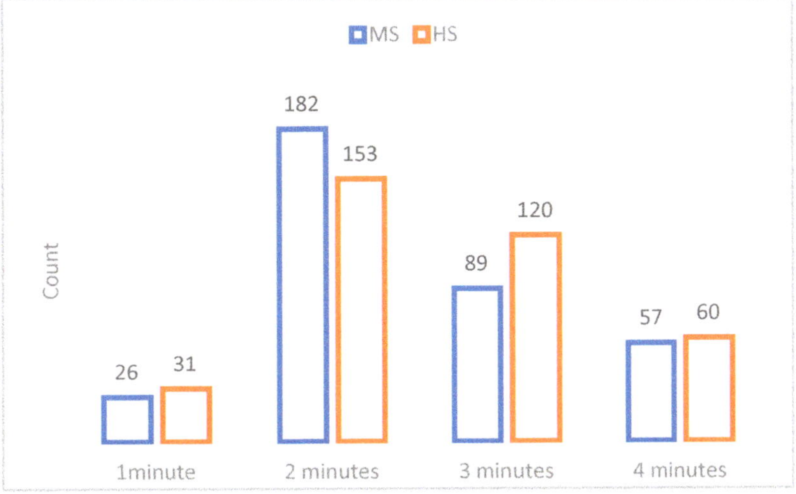

Figure 1. Frequency (count) of time allocated for each dental brushing (count) in function of study level, respectively, MS and HS.

3.5. The Attitude towards the Mouthwash and Dental Floss

More than half of the students use mouthwash 421 (MS = 199; HS = 222) $p = 0.111$, r = −0.048, after each brushing 228 of the students (MS = 199; HS = 222), followed by the situation when the students feel the need 139 (MS = 56; HS = 83), then by those who use the mouthwash in the morning 42 (MS = 20; HS = 22) and in the evening 31 (MS = 19; HS = 12). Dental floss is used by about a third of students 240 (MS = 106; HS = 134), $p = 0.031$, r = −0.073. Of these, 132 students (MS = 52; HS = 80) use it when they feel the need, 74 (MS = 41; HS = 33) after each brushing, and the rest in the evening, $p = 0.091$, r = −0.038 Table 5.

Table 5. Data on the attitude towards the mouthwash and dental floss.

	Questions	MS	HS	Total	*p*	R
	Do you use mouthwash?					
Q27	Yes	199	222	421	0.194	−0.048
	No	155	142	297		
	When do you use mouthwash?					
	1 = after each brushing	109	119	228		
Q28	2 = when I feel the need	56	83	139	0.062	−0.078
	3 = in the morning	20	22	42		
	4 = in the evening	19	12	31		
	5 = I don't use	150	128	278		
	Do you floss for dental cleaning?					
Q29	Yes	106	134	240	0.051	−0.073
	No	248	230	478		
	When do you use dental floss for interdental cleaning?					
	1 = after each brushing	41	33	74		
Q30	2 = when I feel the need	52	80	132	0.091	−0.038
	3 = in the morning	1	0	1		
	4 = in the evening	19	21	40		
	5 = I do not use	241	230	471		

4. Discussion

There are numerous studies in the specialized literature that analyze the relationship between the level of knowledge of the students and the attitude towards oral health [28–33]. This study aimed at students' level of knowledge about oral hygiene. According to Zhu et al., preventive measures are more effective than curative measures [34]. Thus, the information obtained about the students' level of knowledge will contribute to the improvement of oral health education programs. As female subjects had a higher share in the study 65.18% (468) we did not follow the comparative analysis of knowledge by gender [35]. Oral hygiene is a determining factor in general health [31,36]. According to a specialized study, the number of people with untreated oral conditions increased from 2.5 billion in 1990 to 3.5 billion in 2015 [37]. Therefore, the primary prevention of dental caries should be a priority for both the specialist and the health decision-makers [38–40]. The World Health Organization supports the promotion of oral health through educating students [33,39]. Thus, individualized education regarding oral hygiene can provide better premises for oral health, a fact supported by other specialized studies [41–44]. Other studies show that primary prevention cannot be achieved only by implementing knowledge of oral hygiene with diet being an equally important factor to consider [45,46]. The results of a study show that training courses are needed for hygienic nurses in terms of knowledge about brushing.

In this context, the need for educational programs designed to develop oral hygiene skills among students should be emphasized once again.

The most important factor to consider when choosing a toothbrush, for 51.81% of students, was the opinion of a dental professional. The fact that dental professionals are the main source of information about oral hygiene issues is confirmed in other specialized studies [47–49]. Other studies suggest that the media is the main source of information [50–52]. Choosing the electric brushing technique is an option to achieve better results of oral hygiene monitoring indices [53]. Although 76.60% of the subjects know that when choosing the toothpaste they must take into account its properties, they do not correlate this aspect with the remineralization capacity of the toothpaste a fact highlighted in another specialized study [54]. Only about 20.47% of MH and HH students know about the beneficial effect of fluoride in toothpaste and its role in mineralizing hard dental tissues. The fact that students do not know the properties of fluoride and its beneficial effects has also been highlighted by other authors in the literature [48,49,55]. One study found that the proportion of Australian preschoolers using non-fluoridated toothpaste was higher than in other world regions [56]. A Cochrane Review study supports the benefits of using fluoride toothpaste in preventing tooth decay when compared to non-fluoride toothpaste because a dose-response effect was observed for D (M) FS in children and adolescents [57]. The attitude towards the amount of toothpaste used is generally based on the recommendation to use a pea-sized amount of toothpaste. These is the optimal amount of toothpaste which is considered to be the best, in terms of reduced risk of ingestion and fluoride benefit [58]. Using a larger amount of toothpaste is not so important, the recommendations are to us a pea size amount According to Hu S et al., it is important to control the amount of toothpaste used in order to reduce the risk of fluorosis [59]. The results of a meta-analysis showed that using as much pea as a pea will minimize the risk of fluorosis in children while maximizing the caries-prevention benefit for all age groups [60].

The frequency of brushing is known by only 67.1% of students. The fact that a significant percentage of the students do not know the amount of toothpaste and the frequency with which the brushing should be performed is also highlighted in other specialized studies [48,50–52,54,55,61]. The fact that more than half of the students brush their teeth twice a day is beneficial, but it is necessary to improve the level of knowledge about the frequency of oral hygiene, as well as the time of day when it should be performed. In addition, 73 students declared that they brush after each meal as a time of day, but in terms of frequency, only 53 answered that they brush after each meal. This can lead to some variations and lack of credibility regarding the students' answers. The results of a meta-analysis study showed that the frequency of brushing between more than 2 times a day and less than twice a day does not influence the incidence of carious lesions in general, but they pointed out that incidence and increment of carious lesions was higher in deciduous (OR: 1.75; 95% CI: 1.49 to 2.06) than permanent dentition (OR: 1.39; 95% CI: 1.29 to 1.49) [62]. These results have been highlighted in other specialized studies [63–66]. Another study showed that the strongest evidence related to caries in the 12-year-old group was found in the frequency of toothbrushing and dental plaque. A study that analyzed the oral health status of adolescents in Shandong province highlighted the importance of visiting a dental practitioner and performing regular oral hygiene to prevent dental caries and gingivitis [67]. The same aspect has been highlighted in other studies that have analyzed the risk factors for dental caries and periodontal disease [68].

Knowing a brushing technique is the first step in increasing the efficiency of oral hygiene. The results of our study indicate that most of the subjects 292 (MS = 160; HS = 132) know a toothbrushing technique. A study on the efficiency of the brushing technique and the importance of knowing a brushing technique, pointed out that the Bass brushing technique is much more efficient both in terms of removing bacterial plaque and in terms of maintaining the verticality of the brush bristles for a while longer time [69]. Globally, dental caries and periodontal disease still have a high prevalence rate [70]. Bacterial plaque is one of the determining factors present both in the etiology of carious lesions and in the etiology of periodontal disease [47,71]. Our study shows that about half of the students know a brushing technique, but 81.75% know that brushing removes bacterial plaque, the results obtained being similar to the results of other specialized studies [34,50,54]. In order to receive individualized information on oral hygiene, it is recommended to take into account the provision of access to specialized dental services [44,72].

The attitude towards the mouthwash and dental floss was presented in many studies [73–95]. The use of toothbrush adjuvants is necessary to remove plaque from inaccessible spaces. A study that looked at whether or not motivational interviewing promotes oral health in adolescents found that prevailing health education was less effective than motivational interviewing in evoking favorable changes in the oral health patterns of adolescents and preventing dental caries [73].

The fact that 31.75% of the subjects use mouthwash after brushing is a good attitude, but because only 20.47% of the students know the remineralization capacity, we can say that the difference of 11.28% of the subjects cannot select a mouthwash with remineralization potential. One study found that the use of mouthwash into the size of the caries-preventive effect is less clear [74]. Although some studies do not show the effect of mouthwash in the prevention of tooth decay, the results of a review study that included 37 trials involving 15,813 children and adolescents found that supervised regular use of oral fluoride by children and adolescents is associated with a large reduction in tooth decay of permanent teeth [75]. In addition, the effect of reducing the bacterial plaque of chlorhexidine rinsing solutions is still highlighted in studies, chlorhexidine plays a key role in dentistry and is used to treat or prevent periodontal disease, and has earned its eponymous gold standard [76,77]. The beneficial role of mouthwashes containing cetylpyridinium chloride in the prevention of tooth decay, has also been demonstrated [78,79]. The antibacterial effect of Listerine has also been shown in both in vitro and in vivo studies [80,81].

Flossing is an alternative to plaque removal, but it is carried out by only 33.42% of subjects and only 10.3% of them do this consistently. The results obtained are in accordance with the data obtained in certain studies conducted and published in the literature [48,50,82–85]. In general, according to specialized studies, regardless of the adjuvants used, when they are used, an improvement in oral hygiene indices, plaque indices and bleeding indices is obtained [86–91]. Use of dental floss was not a daily behavior for most teenagers, as indicated by other specialized studies [92,93]. Students should be trained by dental practitioners regarding the use of dental floss, a fact highlighted in other specialized studies [94,95].

This study has some limitations that need to be considered: year of study or specialization was uneven, the subjects were randomly selected and the bias of any analyzed group was not followed.

5. Conclusions

Within the limits of this study, we can draw the following conclusions: The testable hypothesis is true, there are different attitudes regarding oral hygiene depending on the level of education. Students have a deficient level of knowledge regarding the principles and rules of oral hygiene promoted through health education. Most students have a minimum, basic knowledge of the frequency of brushing, the purpose and time when it should be carried out. About half of the subjects do not know the recommended amount of toothpaste to be used during brushing. Only a quarter of the subjects take into account the fluoride content when choosing their toothpaste. About half of the subjects do not know a brushing technique and choose their brush according to other criteria than the dental practitioner instructions. About one-third of students do not use mouthwash or dental floss. Education programs are needed to improve students' level of knowledge and attitudes toward oral hygiene.

Author Contributions: Conceptualization, C.I.S. and C.C.C.; data curation, C.I.S., C.C.C., A.E.S.; formal analysis, C.I.S.; investigation, C.C.C.; methodology, C.I.S. and C.C.C.; supervision, C.I.S., D.A. and I.B.; visualization; C.I.S., C.C.C., D.A., I.B. and A.E.S.; writing—original draft, C.I.S., C.C.C. and A.E.S.; writing—review and editing, C.I.S., D.A., I.B. All authors have read and agreed to the published version of the manuscript.

Funding: This research received no external funding.

Institutional Review Board Statement: "Ethical review and approval were waived for this study due to REASON—The questionnaire was uploaded to the google docs platform. The link of the questionnaire was sent to the coordinating teachers of the class and they distributed the questionnaire to the students. Subjects were informed that the study did not record personal data. The subjects were invited to participate in research that aimed to establish the level of knowledge about oral hygiene, were informed that the research did not involve any risk, the data on the electronic devices from which they would l complete the questionnaire were not highlighted in any way. It was specified that the data collected did not involve any risk and no reward would be obtained. The legislation in force regarding the ownership, use and protection of personal data—GDPR (Regulation 679/2016) has been complied with". From an ethical point of view, this study was carried out in accordance with Research Law no. 206 of 27 May 2004 on good conduct in scientific research, technological development and innovation, the Integrity Guide in Scientific Research (published by the National Council for Ethics in Scientific Research, Technological Development and Innovation on 12 November 2020) and current European legislation. Ethical acceptance for these questions was given in No. 144/30 January 2022.

Informed Consent Statement: Informed consent was obtained from all subjects involved in the study after initial information before completion and by sending the questionnaire after completion. Subjects included in the study could not be identified, therefore no written consent was required for publication.

Data Availability Statement: The data that support the findings of this study are available on request from the corresponding author.

Conflicts of Interest: The authors declare no conflict of interest.

References

1. Ahovuo-Saloranta, A.; Forss, H.; Walsh, T.; Hiiri, A.; Nordblad, A.; Mäkelä, M.; Worthington, H.V. Sealants for preventing dental decay in the permanent teeth. *Cochrane Database Syst. Rev.* **2013**, *3*, CD001830. [CrossRef]
2. Dye, B.A.; Li, X.; Beltran-Aguilar, E.D. Selected oral health indicators in the United States, 2005–2008. *NCHS Data Brief.* **2012**, *27*, 1–8.
3. Marinho, V.C.; Higgins, J.P.; Sheiham, A.; Logan, S. Fluoride toothpastes for preventing dental caries in children and adolescents. *Cochrane Database Syst. Rev.* **2003**, *1*, CD002278. [CrossRef] [PubMed]
4. Marinho, V.C.; Worthington, H.V.; Walsh, T.; Clarkson, J.E. Fluoride varnishes for preventing dental caries in children and adolescents. *Cochrane Database Syst. Rev.* **2013**, *7*, CD002279. [CrossRef]
5. Kappenberg-Nitescu, D.C.; Luchian, I.; Martu, I.; Solomon, S.M.; Martu, S.; Pasarin, L.; Marțu, A.; Sioustis, I.A.; Goriuc, A.; Tatarciuc, M. Periodontal effects of two innovative oral rinsing substances in oncologic patients. *Exp. Ther. Med.* **2021**, *21*, 98. [CrossRef]
6. Centers for Disease Control and Prevention. *Oral Health Surveillance Report: Trends in Dental Caries and Sealants, Tooth Retention, and Edentulism, United States, 1999–2004 to 2011–2016*; Centers for Disease Control and Prevention, US Department of Health and Human Services: Atlanta, GA, USA, 2019; pp. 4–8.
7. Dye, B.A.; Tan, S.; Smith, V.; Lewis, B.G.; Barker, L.K.; Thornton-Evans, G.; Eke, P.I.; Beltrán-Aguilar, E.D.; Horowitz, A.M.; Li, C.H. *Trends in oral health status: United States, 1988–1994 and 1999–2004. Vital and Health Statistic. Series 11, Data from the National Health Survey*; Centers for Disease Control and Prevention: Atlanta, GA, USA, 2007; Volume 248, pp. 1–92.
8. Eke, P.I.; Thornton-Evans, G.O.; Wei, L.; Borgnakke, W.S.; Dye, B.A.; Genco, R.J. Periodontitis in US Adults: National Health and Nutrition Examination Survey 2009–2014. *J. Am. Dent. Assoc.* **2018**, *149*, 576–588.e6. [CrossRef] [PubMed]
9. Griffin, S.O.; Barker, L.K.; Griffin, P.M.; Cleveland, J.L.; Kohn, W. Oral health needs among adults in the United States with chronic diseases. *J. Am. Dent. Assoc.* **2009**, *140*, 1266–1274. [CrossRef]
10. Kumar, S.; Tadakamadla, J.; Kroon, J.; Johnson, N.W. Impact of parent-related factors on dental caries in the permanent dentition of 6–12-year-old children: A systematic review. *J. Dent.* **2016**, *46*, 1–11. [CrossRef]
11. National Cancer Institute. Surveillance, Epidemiology, and End Results (SEER) Program. (N.D.) SEER Stat Fact Sheets: Oral Cavity and Pharynx Cancer website. Available online: http://seer.cancer.gov/statfacts/html/oralcav.htmlexternalicon (accessed on 5 July 2016).

12. Saveanu, C.I.; Forna, N.C.; Mohamed, D.; Bobu, L.; Anistoroaei, D.; Bamboi, I.; Balcos, C.; Cheptea, C.; Saveanu, A.E.; Tanculescu-Doloca, O. Study on dietary habits of first grade schoolchildren in Iasi, Romania. *RJDME* **2020**, *9*, 62–68.
13. Saveanu, C.I.; Gheorghiu-Rusu, T.; Balcos, C.; Bamboi, I.; Bobu, L.; Saveanu, A.E.; Anistoroaei, D.; Golovcencu, L.; Tanculescu-Doloca, O. Comparative study of assessment of educational level high school students in Suceava, Romania. *RJDME* **2020**, *9*, 6–14.
14. Saveanu, C.I.; Bobu, L.; Mohamed, D.; Balcos, C.; Bamboi, I.; Golovcencu, L.; Săveanu, A.E.; Anistoroaei, D.; Melian, A. Study on oral health attitudes and behaviors of first grade schoolchildren in Iasi, Romania. *RJOR* **2019**, *11*, 223–227.
15. Saveanu, C.I.; Anistoroaei, D.; Golovcencu, L.; Saveanu, A.E. Assessing the level of knowledge and attitudes about oral health behaviors of preschoolers. *RJDME* **2019**, *8*, 71–78.
16. Gupta, T.; Sequeira, P.; Achary, S. Oral health knowledge, attitude and practices of a 15-year-old adolescent population in Southern India and their social determinants. *Oral. Health Prev. Dent.* **2012**, *10*, 345–354.
17. Traebert, J.Y.; De Lacerda, J.T. Association between maternal schooling and caries prevalence: A cross-sectional study in southern Brazil. *Oral. Health Prev. Dent.* **2011**, *9*, 47–52. [PubMed]
18. Institute for Health Metrics and Evaluation (IHME). *Findings from the Global Burden of Disease Study 2017*; Institute for Health Metrics and Evaluation (IHME): Seattle, WA, USA, 2018.
19. Peres, M.A.; Macpherson, L.; Weyant, R.J.; Daly, B.; Venturelli, R.; Mathur, M.R.; Listl, S.; Celeste, R.K.; Guarnizo-Herreño, C.C.; Kearns, C.; et al. Oral diseases: A global public health challenge. *Lancet* **2019**, *394*, 249–260. [CrossRef]
20. Hosseinpoor, A.R.; Itani, L.; Petersen, P.E. Socio-economic inequality in oral healthcare coverage: Results from the World Health Survey. *J. Dent. Res.* **2012**, *91*, 275–281. [CrossRef] [PubMed]
21. *Ending Childhood Dental Caries: WHO Implementation Manual*; World Health Organization: Geneva, Switzerland, 2019.
22. O'Mullane, D.M.; Baez, R.J.; Jones, S.; Lennon, M.A.; Petersen, P.E.; Rugg-Gunn, A.J.; Whelton, H.; Whitford, G.M. Fluoride and Oral Health. *Comm. Dent. Health* **2016**, *33*, 69–99.
23. WHO Expert Committee on Oral Health Status and Fluoride Use & World Health Organization. *Fluorides and Oral Health: Report of a WHO Expert Committee on Oral Health Status and Fluoride Use [Meeting Held in Geneva from 22 to 28 November 1993]*; World Health Organization: Geneva, Switzerland, 1994. Available online: https://apps.who.int/iris/handle/10665/39746 (accessed on 18 July 2021).
24. Resolution WHA 60.17. Oral health: Action plan for promotion and integrated disease prevention. In *Sixtieth World Health Assembly, Geneva, 23 May 2007*; World Health Organization: Geneva, Switzerland, 2007. Available online: http://apps.who.int/iris/bitstream/handle/10665/22590/A60_R17-en.pdf (accessed on 21 August 2021).
25. Petersen, P.E.; Ogawa, H. Prevention of dental caries through the use of fluoride-the WHO approach. *Comm. Dent. Health* **2016**, *33*, 66–68.
26. Marinho, V.C.; Higgins, J.P.; Logan, S.; Sheiham, A. Topical fluoride (toothpastes, mouthrins, gels or varnishes) for preventing dental caries in children and adolescents. *Cochrane Database Syst. Rev.* **2003**, *4*, CD002782. [CrossRef]
27. Sharon, E.M.; Barmes, D.E.; Bailey, K.V.; Sundram, C.J. *Guidelines on Oral Health*; A manual for health personnel Dental Health. Unit; Penang Printed and distributed by the Regional Office for the Western Pacific of the World Health Organization: Penang, Malaysia, 1971; pp. 15–20.
28. Smyth, E.; Caamano, F.; Fernández-Riveiro, P. Oral health knowledge, attitudes and practice in 12-year-old schoolchildren. *Med. Oral Patol. Oral Cir. Bucal.* **2007**, *12*, 614–620.
29. Singh, A.; Gambhir, R.S.; Singh, S.; Kapoor, V.; Singh, J. Oral health: How much do you know?-A study on knowledge, attitude and practices of patients visiting a North Indian dental school. *Eur. J. Dent.* **2014**, *8*, 63–67. [CrossRef]
30. Carneiro, L.; Kabulwa, M.; Makyao, M.; Mrosso, G.; Choum, R. Oral Health Knowledge and Practices of Secondary School Students, Tanga, Tanzania. *Int. J. Dent.* **2011**, *2011*, 806258. [CrossRef] [PubMed]
31. Duangthip, D.; Chu, C.H. Challenges in Oral Hygiene and Oral Health Policy. *Front. Oral. Health* **2020**, *1*, 575428. [CrossRef] [PubMed]
32. Ghaffari, M.; Rakhshanderou, S.; Ramezankhani, A.; Noroozi, M.; Armoon, B. Oral Health Education and Promotion Programmes: Meta-Analysis of 17-Year Intervention. *Int. J. Dent. Hyg.* **2018**, *16*, 59–67. [CrossRef] [PubMed]
33. Ghaffari, M.; Rakhshanderou, S.; Ramezankhani, A.; Buunk-Werkhoven, Y.; Noroozi, M.; Armoon, B. Are educating and promoting interventions effective in oral health? A systematic review. *Int. J. Dent. Hyg* **2018**, *16*, 48–58. [CrossRef] [PubMed]
34. Zhu, L.; Petersen, P.E.; Wang, H.Y.; Bian, J.Y.; Zhang, B.X. Oral health knowledge, attitudes and behaviour of children and adolescents in China. *Int. Dent. J.* **2003**, *53*, 289–298. [CrossRef] [PubMed]
35. Shaheen, R.; Al Shulayyi, M.; Baseer, M.A.; Saeed Bahamid, A.A.; Al Saffan, A.D.; Al Herbisch, R. Self-Reported Basic Oral Health Knowledge of Primary School Students and Teachers in Rural Areas of Saudi Arabia. *Clin. Cosmet. Investig. Dent.* **2021**, *13*, 521–529. [CrossRef]
36. Genco, R.J.; Sanz, M. Clinical and public health implications of periodontal and systemic diseases: An overview. *Periodontology* **2020**, *83*, 7–13. [CrossRef]
37. Kassebaum, N.J.; Smith, A.G.C.; Bernabé, E.; Fleming, T.D.; Reynolds, A.E.; Vos, T.; Murray, C.; Marcenes, W.; GBD 2015 Oral Health Collaborators (2017). Global, Regional, and National Prevalence, Incidence, and Disability-Adjusted Life Years for Oral Conditions for 195 Countries, 1990–2015: A Systematic Analysis for the Global Burden of Diseases, Injuries, and Risk Factors. *J. Dent. Res.* **2017**, *96*, 380–387. [CrossRef]

38. Shaghaghian, S.; Zeraatkar, M. Factors Affecting Oral Hygiene and Tooth Brushing in Preschool Children, Shiraz/Iran. *J. Dent. Biomater.* **2017**, *4*, 394–402.
39. Sharma, A.S.; Sheth, S.A.; Dhaduk, P.J.; Chovateeya, S.R.; Mistry, B.J.; Jogi, M.R. Oral Hygiene Practices and Factors Affecting Oral Health Service Utilization among Children (11–14 Years) of Government School of Nikol Ward of East Zone of Ahmedabad, Gujarat, India. *Contemp. Clin. Dent.* **2019**, *10*, 299–303. [CrossRef] [PubMed]
40. Beyene, D.H.; Beyene, B.S.; Digesa, L.E.; Tariku, E.Z. Oral Hygiene Practices and Associated Factors among Patients Visiting Private Dental Clinics at Hawassa City, Southern Ethiopia, 2018. *Int. J. Dent.* **2021**, *2021*. [CrossRef] [PubMed]
41. Muller-Bolla, M.; Courson, F. Toothbrushing methods to use in children: A systematic review. *Oral. Health Prev. Dent.* **2013**, *11*, 341–347. [CrossRef] [PubMed]
42. Rajwani, A.R.; Hawes, S.N.D.T.A.; Quaranta, A.; Rincon Aguilar, J.C. Effectiveness of Manual Toothbrushing Techniques on Plaque and Gingivitis: A Systematic Review. *Oral. Health Prev. Dent.* **2020**, *18*, 843–854. [CrossRef]
43. Jackson, S.L.; Vann, W.F.; Jr Kotch, J.B.; Pahel, B.T.; Lee, J.Y. Impact of poor oral health on children's school attendance and performance. *Am. J. Public Health* **2011**, *101*, 1900–1906. [CrossRef]
44. Tachalov, V.V.; Orekhova, L.Y.; Kudryavtseva, T.V.; Isaeva, E.R.; Loboda, E.S. Manifestations of personal characteristics in individual oral care. *EPMA J.* **2016**, *7*, 8. [CrossRef]
45. Skafida, V.; Chambers, S. Positive association between sugar consumption and dental decay prevalence independent of oral hygiene in pre-school children: A longitudinal prospective study. *J. Public Health* **2018**, *40*, e275–e283. [CrossRef]
46. Nazarianpirdosti, M.; Janatolmakan, M.; Andayeshgar, B.; Khatony, A. Assessment of Knowledge, Attitude, and Practice of Iranian Nurses towards Toothbrush Maintenance and Use. *Nurs. Res. Pract.* **2021**, 3694141. [CrossRef]
47. Marsh, P.D. Dental plaque as a biofilm and a microbial community–Implications for health and disease. *BMC Oral Health* **2006**, *6*, S14. [CrossRef]
48. Al-Qahtani, S.M.; Razak, P.A.; Khan, S.D. Knowledge and Practice of Preventive Measures for Oral Health Care among Male Intermediate Schoolchildren in Abha, *Saudi Arabia. Int. J. Environ. Res. Public Health* **2020**, *17*, 703. [CrossRef]
49. Hou, R.; Mi, Y.; Xu, Q.; Wu, F.; Ma, Y.; Xue, P.; Xiao, G.; Zhang, Y.; Wei, Y.; Yang, W. Oral health survey and oral health questionnaire for high school students in Tibet, China. *Head Face Med.* **2014**, *10*, 17. [CrossRef] [PubMed]
50. Ogunrinde, T.J.; Oyewole, O.E.; Dosumu, O.O. Dental care knowledge and practices among secondary school adolescents in Ibadan North Local Government Areas of Oyo State, Nigeria. *Eur. J. Gen. Dent.* **2015**, *4*, 68–73. [CrossRef]
51. Graça, S.R.; Albuquerque, T.S.; Luis, H.S.; Assunção, V.A.; Malmqvist, S.; Cuculescu, M.; Johannsen, A. Oral Health Knowledge, Perceptions, and Habits of Adolescents from Portugal, Romania, and Sweden: A Comparative Study. *J. Int Soc. Prev Community Dent.* **2019**, *9*, 470–480. [CrossRef]
52. Gao, J.; Ruan, J.; Zhao, L.; Zhou, H.; Huang., R.; Tian, J. Oral health status and oral health knowledge, attitudes and behavior among rural children in Shaanxi, western China: A cross-sectional survey. *BMC Oral Health* **2014**, *14*, 144. [CrossRef]
53. Kulkarni, P.; Singh, D.K.; Jalaluddin, M. Comparison of Efficacy of Manual and Powered Toothbrushes in Plaque Control and Gingival Inflammation: A Clinical Study among the Population of East Indian Region. *J. Int. Soc. Prev. Community Dent.* **2017**, *7*, 168–174. [CrossRef]
54. Wyne, A.H.; Chohan, A.N.; Al-Dosari, K.; Al-Dokheil, M. Oral health knowledge and sources of information among male Saudi school children. *Odontostomatol. Trop.* **2004**, *27*, 22–26. [PubMed]
55. Wahengbam, P.P.; Kshetrimayum, N.; Wahengbam, B.S.; Nandkeoliar, T.; Lyngdoh, D. Assessment of oral health knowledge, attitude and self-care practice among adolescents—A state wide cross- sectional study in Manipur, North Eastern India. *J. Clin. Diagn. Res.* **2016**, *10*, ZC65–ZC70. [CrossRef]
56. Buckeridge, A.; King, N.; Anthonappa, R. Relationships between parental education, choice of child dentifrice, and their children's caries experience. *Int. J. Ped. Dent.* **2021**, *31*, 115–121. [CrossRef]
57. Walsh, T.; Worthington, H.V.; Glenny, A.M.; Marinho, V.C.; Jeroncic, A. Fluoride toothpastes of different concentrations for preventing dental caries. *Cochrane Database Syst. Rev.* **2019**, *3*, CD007868. [CrossRef]
58. Creeth, J.; Bosma, M.L.; Govier, K. How much is a 'pea-sized amount'? A study of dentifrice dosing by parents in three countries. *Int. Dent. J.* **2013**, *63*, 25–30. [CrossRef]
59. Nordström, A.; Birkhed, D. Attitudes and behavioural factors relating to toothbrushing and the use of fluoride toothpaste among caries-active Swedish adolescents-A questionnaire study. *Acta Odontol. Scand.* **2017**, *75*, 483–487. [CrossRef] [PubMed]
60. Wright, J.T.; Hanson, N.; Ristic, H.; Whall, C.W.; Estrich, C.G.; Zentz, R.R. Fluoride toothpaste efficacy and safety in children younger than 6 years: A systematic review. *J. Am. Dental Assoc.* **2014**, *145*, 182–189. [CrossRef] [PubMed]
61. Fernandes, F.I.; Groisman, S.; Toledo, E.; Sampaio, F.H.; Verbicario, R.J.; Ricardo, H.; Olival, R. Habits and Knowledge about Toothpaste of Students from Legiao da Boa Vontade (LBV). *J. Dent. Health Oral. Disord. Ther.* **2015**, *3*, 00076. [CrossRef]
62. Kumar, S.; Tadakamadla, J.; Johnson, N.W. Effect of Toothbrushing Frequency on Incidence and Increment of Dental Caries: A Systematic Review and Meta-Analysis. *J. Dent. Res.* **2016**, *95*, 1230–1236. [CrossRef] [PubMed]
63. Holmes, R.D. Tooth brushing frequency and risk of new carious lesions. *Evid. Based Dent.* **2016**, *17*, 98–99. [CrossRef] [PubMed]
64. Gudipaneni, R.K.; Patil, S.R.; Assiry, A.A.; Karobari, M.I.; Bandela, V.; Metta, K.K.; Almuhanna, R. Association of oral hygiene practices with the outcome of untreated dental caries and its clinical consequences in pre- and primary school children: A cross-sectional study in a northern province of Saudi Arabia. *Clin. Exp. Dent. Res.* **2021**, *7*, 968–977. [CrossRef]

65. Prasai Dixit, L.; Shakya, A.; Shrestha, M.; Shrestha, A. Dental caries prevalence, oral health knowledge and practice among indigenous Chepang school children of Nepal. *BMC Oral Health* **2013**, *13*, 20. [CrossRef]
66. Obregón-Rodríguez, N.; Fernández-Riveiro, P.; Piñeiro-Lamas, M.; Smyth-Chamosa, E.; Montes-Martínez, A.; Suárez-Cunqueiro, M.M. Prevalence and caries-related risk factors in schoolchildren of 12-and 15-year-old: A cross-sectional study. *BMC Oral Health* **2019**, *19*, 120. [CrossRef]
67. Zhang, M.; Lan, J.; Zhang, T.; Sun, W.; Liu, P.; Wang, Z. Oral health and caries/gingivitis-associated factors of adolescents aged 12–15 in Shandong province, China: A cross-sectional Oral Health Survey. *BMC Oral Health* **2021**, *21*, 288. [CrossRef]
68. Folayan, M.O.; El Tantawi, M.; Chukwumah, N.M.; Alade, M.; Oginni, O.; Mapayi, B.; Arowolo, O.; Sam-Agudu, N.A. Individual and familial factors associated with caries and gingivitis among adolescent's resident in a semi-urban community in South-Western Nigeria. *BMC Oral Health* **2021**, *21*, 166. [CrossRef]
69. Ausenda, F.; Jeong, N.; Arsenault, P.; Gyurko, R.; Finkelman, M.; Dragan, I.F.; Levi, P.A., Jr. The Effect of the Bass Intrasulcular Toothbrushing Technique on the Reduction of Gingival Inflammation: A Randomized Clinical Trial. *J. Evid. Based Dent. Pract.* **2019**, *19*, 106–114. [CrossRef] [PubMed]
70. GBD 2016 Diseases and Injury Incidence and Prevalence Collaborators. Global, regional, and national incidence, prevalence, and years lived with disability for 328 diseases and injuries for 195 countries, 1990–2016: A Systematic Analysis for the Global Burden of Disease Study. *Lancet* **2017**, *390*, 1211–1259. [CrossRef]
71. Seneviratne, C.J.; Zhang, C.F.; Samaranayake, L.P. Dental plaque biofilm in oral health and disease. *Chin. J. Dent. Res.* **2011**, *14*, 87–94.
72. Zareban, I.; Karimy, M.; Araban, M.; Delaney, D. Oral self-care behavior and its influencing factors in a sample of school children from Central Iran. *Arch. Public Health* **2021**, *79*, 175. [CrossRef] [PubMed]
73. Hawrot, H. Does motivational interviewing promote oral health in adolescents? *Evid. Based Dent.* **2021**, *22*, 134–135. [CrossRef]
74. Shahid, M. Regular supervised fluoride mouthrinse use by children and adolescents associated with caries reduction. *Evid. Based Dent.* **2017**, *18*, 11–12. [CrossRef]
75. Marinho, V.C.; Chong, L.Y.; Worthington, H.V.; Walsh, T. Fluoride mouthrinses for preventing dental caries in children and adolescents. *Cochrane Database Syst. Rev.* **2016**, *7*, CD002284. [CrossRef] [PubMed]
76. Thangavelu, A.; Kaspar, S.S.; Kathirvelu, R.P.; Srinivasan, B.; Srinivasan, S.; Sundram, R. Chlorhexidine: An Elixir for Periodontics. *J. Pharm. Bio Allied Sci.* **2020**, *12*, S57–S59. [CrossRef]
77. Fernandez, M.; Guedes, M.; Langa, G.; Rösing, C.K.; Cavagni, J.; Muniz, F. Virucidal efficacy of chlorhexidine: A systematic review. *Odontology* **2021**, *2021*, 1–17. [CrossRef]
78. Rösing, C.K.; Cavagni, J.; Gaio, E.J.; Muniz, F.; Ranzan, N.; Oballe, H.; Friedrich, S.A.; Severo, R.M.; Stewart, B.; Zhang, Y.P. Efficacy of two mouthwashes with cetylpyridinium chloride: A controlled randomized clinical trial. *Braz. Oral Res.* **2017**, *31*, 47. [CrossRef]
79. Williams, M.I. The antibacterial and antiplaque ef.ffectiveness of mouthwashes containing cetylpyridinium chloride with and without alcohol in improving gingival health. *J. Clin. Dent.* **2011**, *22*, 179–182. [PubMed]
80. Pelino, J.; Passero, A.; Martin, A.A.; Charles, C.A. In vitro effects of alcohol-containing mouthwashes on human enamel and restorative materials. *Braz. Oral Res.* **2018**, *32*, e25. [CrossRef] [PubMed]
81. Vlachojannis, C.; Al-Ahmad, A.; Hellwig, E.; Chrubasik, S. Listerine® Products: An Update on the Efficacy and Safety. *Phytother. Res. PTR* **2016**, *30*, 367–373. [CrossRef] [PubMed]
82. Hu, S.; Lai, W.P.B.; Lim, W.; Yee, R. Recommending 1000 ppm fluoride toothpaste for caries prevention in children. *Proc. Singap. Healthcare* **2021**, *30*, 250–253. [CrossRef]
83. Blaggana, A.; Grover, V.; Anjali, A.K.; Blaggana, V.; Tanwar, R.; Kaur, H.; Haneet, R.K. Oral health knowledge, attitudes and practice behaviour among secondary school children in Chandigarh. *J. Clin. Diagn. Res.* **2016**, *10*, ZC01–ZC06. [CrossRef]
84. Togoo, R.A.; Yaseen, S.; Zakirulla, M.; Nasim, V.S.; Al Zamzami, M. Oral hygiene knowledge and practices among school children in a rural area of southern Saudi Arabia. *Int. J. Contemp. Dent.* **2012**, *3*, 57–62.
85. Amarlal, D.; Devdas, K.; Priya, M.; Venkatachalapathy, A. Oral health attitudes, knowledge and practice among school children in Chennai, India. *J. Educ. Ethic Dent.* **2013**, *3*, 26. [CrossRef]
86. NHS–Why Should I use Interdental Brushes? 2021. Available online: https://www.nhs.uk/common-health-questions/dental-health/why-should-i-use-interdental-brushes (accessed on 15 July 2021).
87. Rosenauer, T.; Wagenschwanz, C.; Kuhn, M.; Kensche, A.; Stiehl, S.; Hannig, C. The Bleeding on Brushing Index: A novel index in preventive dentistry. *Int. Dent. J.* **2017**, *67*, 299–307. [CrossRef]
88. Silva, C.; Albuquerque, P.; De Assis, P.; Lopes, C.; Anníbal, H.; Lago, M.; Braz, R. Does flossing before or after brushing influence the reduction in the plaque index? A systematic review and meta-analysis. *Int. J. Dent. Hyg.* **2022**, *20*, 18–25. [CrossRef]
89. Marchetti, G.; Assunção, L.R.D.S.; Soares, G.M.S.; Fraiz, F.C. Are Information Technologies Capable of Stimulating the Use of Dental Floss by Adolescents? A Cluster Randomized Clinical Trial. *Oral. Health Prev. Dent.* **2020**, *18*, 427–432. [CrossRef]
90. Worthington, H.V.; MacDonald, L.; Poklepovic Pericic, T.; Sambunjak, D.; Johnson, T.M.; Imai, P.; Clarkson, J.E. Home use of interdental cleaning devices, in addition to toothbrushing, for preventing and controlling periodontal diseases and dental caries. *Cochrane Database Syst. Rev.* **2019**, *4*, CD012018. [CrossRef] [PubMed]
91. Gallie, A. Home use of interdental cleaning devices and toothbrushing and their role in disease prevention. *Evid. Based Dent.* **2019**, *20*, 103–104. [CrossRef] [PubMed]

92. Wigen, T.I.; Wang, N.J. Characteristics of teenagers who use dental floss. *Comm. Dental Health* **2021**, *38*, 10–14. [CrossRef]
93. Baumgartner, C.S.; Wang, N.J.; Wigen, T.I. Oral health behaviors in 12-year-olds. Association with caries and characteristics of the children? *Acta Odontol. Scand.* **2022**, *80*, 15–20. [CrossRef]
94. Pandey, N.; Koju, S.; Khapung, A.; Gupta, S.; Aryal, D.; Dhami, B. Dental Floss Prescription Pattern among the Dental Interns of Nepal. *JNMA J. Nepal Medical Assoc.* **2020**, *58*, 580–586. [CrossRef]
95. Akhionbare, O.; Ehizele, A.O. Use of dental floss: Opinion of present and future oral health workers. *Odonto-Stomatol. Trop. Trop. Dent. J.* **2016**, *39*, 40–48.

medicina

MDPI

Article

Orthodontic Adolescent Patients' Attitudes toward Protective Face Mask Wearing during the COVID-19 Pandemic

Jessica Olivia Chereches [1], Luminița Ligia Vaida [1,*], Abel Emanuel Moca [1,*], Raluca Dima [1], Gabriela Ciavoi [1] and Marius Bembea [2]

[1] Department of Dentistry, Faculty of Medicine and Pharmacy, University of Oradea, 10 Piața 1 Decembrie Street, 410073 Oradea, Romania; chereches_jessica@yahoo.com (J.O.C.); razdima@gmail.com (R.D.); gciavoi@uoradea.ro (G.C.)

[2] Department of Preclinical Disciplines, Faculty of Medicine and Pharmacy, University of Oradea, 10 Piața 1 Decembrie Street, 410073 Oradea, Romania; bembea13@yahoo.com

* Correspondence: ligia_vaida@yahoo.com (L.L.V.); abelmoca@yahoo.com (A.E.M.)

Citation: Chereches, J.O.; Vaida, L.L.; Moca, A.E.; Dima, R.; Ciavoi, G.; Bembea, M. Orthodontic Adolescent Patients' Attitudes toward Protective Face Mask Wearing during the COVID-19 Pandemic. *Medicina* **2022**, *58*, 393. https://doi.org/10.3390/medicina58030393

Academic Editor: Cesare D'Amico

Received: 30 December 2021
Accepted: 3 March 2022
Published: 6 March 2022

Abstract: *Background and Objectives:* The COVID-19 pandemic led to restrictive measures, which aimed to limit the spread of the SARS-CoV-2 virus. These restrictions impacted all areas of life, including the activity of dental offices. For patients with orthodontic appliances, closing the dental offices was a major issue, as most orthodontic treatments last for more than a year and require regular checkups. The aim of this research was to assess the impact that the restrictive measures that were imposed during the COVID-19 pandemic, and, especially, wearing a face mask had on a sample of Romanian teenagers undergoing fixed orthodontic treatment. *Material and Methods:* The study group consisted of 277 orthodontic patients, with ages between 12 and 17.9 years, from North-Western Romania. They completed a 9-item questionnaire. The control group consisted of 231 participants, with ages between 12 and 17.9 years. They completed an 8-item questionnaire. *Results:* Most patients from the study group were not worried that wearing a protective face mask would hide their braces (never—49.5%; rarely—26.7%), and their desire to undergo an orthodontic treatment was not affected by the compulsoriness of face mask wearing (never—51.6%; rarely—26%). In contrast to that, in the control group, more than 50% of the participants were worried to some degree that wearing a protective face mask would hide their smile (occasionally—29.9%; frequently—18.2%; very frequently—2.2%). The majority of the participants from the study group did not consider interrupting the orthodontic treatment due to the COVID-19 pandemic (62.5%), and the majority of the participants from the control group did not consider not going to the dentist due to the COVID-19 pandemic (70.6%). Most of the participants from the study group were not happy that they had to wear a face mask, which covered their orthodontic appliances, during the orthodontic treatment (68.6%). The attitude was similar to that of the participants from the control group, who were not happy that they had to wear a face mask, that covered their smile (51.1%). In the study group, most patients did not want face mask wearing to continue to be compulsory, given the fact that their orthodontic appliances were no longer visible (52%). In the control group, the attitude was similar, with 48.1% of the participants not wanting face mask compulsoriness to be maintained. *Conclusions*: In conclusion, although, most patients would not like to continue wearing a face mask as a mandatory regulation, they were not concerned or negatively affected by wearing a protective face mask, even though face masks hid their braces.

Keywords: COVID-19; protective face mask; orthodontic patients; adolescents

1. Introduction

The identification of a new type of coronavirus at the end of 2019, outlined the scenario that announced the beginning of a major public health crisis worldwide [1]. The disease, a form of severe acute respiratory syndrome, caused by SARS-CoV-2 and called COVID-19, has been described by the World Health Organization as being a viral pneumonia [2]. The symptoms are numerous, and include dry cough, fever, shortness of breath, sore throat, headache, myalgia, fatigue, diarrhea [3], and radiological signs of lung damage [4].

The transmission rate of COVID-19 is high, as it spreads easily from person to person [5]. Coughing, sneezing, or talking can generate aerosols [6], which through close contact with infected people are safe sources of contamination [5]. The virus can enter the body by air and attaches to the mucous membranes of the oral cavity, nose, or eyes [6,7].

As a result of the increase in the number of cases with COVID-19 disease, a pandemic was declared, and worldwide, in an attempt to limit the spread of the virus, quarantine was instated in all countries [8]. Among other restrictions, a safe distance of 1–2 m had to be maintained between people [9]. For dental professionals, this distance was impossible to maintain, as dental work requires close contact with the patient's oropharyngeal and nasal region, increasing the risk of contamination [9,10]. The activity of dental offices was suspended, which affected all patients [11]. Emergency dental treatments consisting of pain, swelling, bleeding, infections, and trauma were permitted in certain authorized dental offices [12,13].

For patients with orthodontic appliances, closing the dental offices was a major issue, as most orthodontic treatments last for more than a year [12], and require regular check-ups [14]. During this period of disruption, treatments could no longer be supervised and were negatively affected, with patients reaching high levels of anxiety caused by the new situation [12].

Face mask wearing became mandatory in many countries as it is considered an important preventive measure during the COVID-19 pandemic [15]. Face masks are considered beneficial since wearing a mask in areas where the advised social distance cannot be properly maintained lowers the spread of virus-loaded droplets [16]. As they cover the nose and mouth of the patients, and the area around them [17], protective face masks also cover the fixed orthodontic appliances bonded on the buccal surface of the teeth, which are visible in smile and speech. For some patients this aspect could potentially cause frustration, since the desire for orthodontic treatment among teenagers has been proven to be high [18], and patients are usually satisfied with their facial aspect during the orthodontic treatment [19]. The question was raised whether the necessity to cover the orthodontic appliance with a face mask could cause teenagers to be less interested in undergoing a necessary orthodontic treatment, especially because often braces are perceived as being an elective luxury and a symbol of status, wealth, and style [20], or whether it could nurture a disobedience towards the mandatory wearing of face masks.

The aim of this research was to assess the attitude that a sample of Romanian teenagers undergoing orthodontic treatment with fixed appliances, during the COVID-19 pandemic, had regarding wearing protective face masks, considering the fact that they covered the orthodontic appliances. Their attitude towards the suspension of dental activity, as orthodontic patients, was investigated as well.

2. Materials and Methods

2.1. Ethical Considerations

The study was conducted in accordance with the 1964 Declaration of Helsinki and its later amendments and was approved by the Research Ethics Committee of the University of Oradea (No. 23/25.02.2021). Before filling in the questionnaires, all parents, caregivers, and participants gave their consent for taking part in this study.

2.2. Sample Size Calculation

Sample size estimation was made using GPower 3.1.9.7 software. By the design of the study, it was considered that the measured items (in Likert scale format) would be mostly compared between genders, using Mann–Whitney U tests (for items with 5 answers) or contingency tables (for items with 3 answers), and the ideal allocation ratio of the genders should be 1:1. Therefore, it was estimated using a medium effect size of $d = 0.5$, with a minimum power of 0.8 and an $\alpha = 0.05$, that the minimum sample size should be of 74 patients in each group for Mann–Whitney U tests (a total of 168). For contingency tables, considering a medium effect size of w = 0.3 with Df = 2, a minimum power of 0.8 and an $\alpha = 0.05$, the minimum total sample size should be equal to 108. Using these values, an estimation was made that a minimum of 74 patients in each gender (with a total of 168 patients) should exist in the study for a minimum power of 0.8 for most tests.

2.3. Participants and Data Collection

The study design was a cross-sectional survey. It was carried out in the period between November 2020 and February 2022. A pilot study was not conducted prior to this research. During the period in which this study was conducted, restrictive measures regarding the mandatory wearing of face masks and social distancing were active.

For the study group, the authors designed a questionnaire consisting of 9 items. For the control group, only 8 items were used, since Item 9 referred strictly to orthodontic patients. The questionnaires were printed on paper and applied in two private orthodontic practices from the city of Oradea, North-Western Romania, which offer treatments to patients who come from families with various incomes (from low to high). They were distributed to adolescents, aged between 12 and 17.9 years. In the study group, the respondents were orthodontic patients, undergoing an orthodontic treatment with fixed appliances. In the control group, the respondents were non-orthodontic patients, who came to the office for a clinical examination. Before filling in the questionnaire, all patients and their parents (or caregivers) were informed that they were being applied for research purposes, and that by filling in the questionnaires, they confirmed their willingness to participate anonymously in this study. The names of the participants were not mentioned on the survey form, and the authors did not know how patients answered. Patients had the possibility to withdraw from the research with no consequences, and no financial incentives were promised to the respondents. No time limit was imposed. The language used for the questionnaires was Romanian.

A Likert-type scale was used for Items 1, 2, 3, 4, and 8. The options included were "never", "rarely", "occasionally", "frequently", and "very frequently". For Items 5, 6, 7, and 9, participants had to choose from three options, these being "no", "yes", and "maybe". Items are translated and detailed in Table 1.

Table 1. Items.

	Number of Item	Question
Study group	Item 1	"Are you worried that wearing a protective face mask will hide your braces?"
	Item 2	"Does the compulsoriness of wearing a protective face mask affect your desire to undergo the orthodontic treatment, given the fact that it covers your braces?"
	Item 3	"Were you affected by the suspension of dental offices' activity, as a patient undergoing an orthodontic treatment with fixed appliances?"
	Item 4	"Were you worried that you won't be able to continue the orthodontic treatment due to the COVID-19 pandemic?"
	Item 5	"Did you consider interrupting the orthodontic treatment because of the COVID-19 pandemic?"
	Item 6	"Are you happy that you have to wear a face mask during the orthodontic treatment, considering the fact that it covers your braces?"
	Item 7	"Do you want face masks to continue being mandatory, given the fact that they cover your braces?"
	Item 8	"Do you consider that wearing a face mask that hides your orthodontic appliance causes you stress?"
	Item 9	"Do you still want to continue with the orthodontic treatment while wearing a face mask, even though your orthodontic appliance is not visible?"

Table 1. *Cont.*

	Number of Item	Question
Control group	Item 1	"Are you worried that wearing a protective face mask will hide your smile?"
	Item 2	"Does the compulsoriness of wearing a protective face mask affect you, given the fact that is covers your smile?"
	Item 3	"Were you affected by the suspension of dental offices' activity?"
	Item 4	"Were you worried that you won't be able to go to the dentist due to the COVID-19 pandemic?"
	Item 5	"Did you consider not going to the dentist because of the compulsoriness of face mask wearing?"
	Item 6	"Are you happy that you have to wear a face mask, considering the fact that it covers your smile?"
	Item 7	"Do you want face masks to continue to be mandatory, given the fact that they cover your smile?"
	Item 8	"Do you consider that wearing a face mask that hides your smile causes you stress?"

For the study group, the inclusion criteria were that the participants had to be patients wearing a metallic or ceramic fixed orthodontic appliance (bonded on the buccal surface of teeth, and visible in smile and speech), with ages between 12 and 17.9 years, and to live in Romania. The control group consisted of participants who were not wearing and did not wear orthodontic appliances (fixed or removable), with ages between 12 and 17.9 years, and were living in Romania. Patients who were in the contention phase of the orthodontic treatment, as well as questionnaires that were incomplete or incorrectly completed were excluded from this study. Incorrectly completed questionnaires were those where the patients offered more than one answer for the same item.

2.4. Statistical Analysis

Statistical analysis was performed by using IBM SPSS software, version 25 (IBM, Chicago, IL, USA). Quantitative variables were tested for distribution using the Shapiro–Wilk test and were expressed as mean values with standard deviations or medians with interpercentile intervals. The independent quantitative variables with a non-parametric distribution were tested with the Mann–Whitney U or Kruskal–Wallis H tests, and all correlations between them were verified with Spearman's rho correlation coefficient. Qualitative variables were expressed as absolute numbers or percentages and were tested with Fisher's exact test.

3. Results

In the study group, the questionnaires were handed out to 320 orthodontic patients, but only 290 agreed to take part in this research and filled in the survey forms. After applying the exclusion criteria, 277 valid questionnaires remained in the study. In the control group, the questionnaires were handed out to 260 participants, but only 251 agreed to take part in this research and filled in the survey forms. After applying the exclusion criteria, 231 valid questionnaires remained in the study (Figure 1).

3.1. Socio-Demographic Data

The study group consisted of 173 (62.5%) girls and 104 (37.5%) boys. Regarding the living environment of the participants, 93 (33.6%) came from a rural environment, while 184 (66.5%) came from an urban environment. The mean age of the respondents was 14.91 ± 1.49 years, with a median of 15 years, and a range between 12 and 17.9 years.

The control group consisted of 134 (58%) girls and 97 (42%) boys. Regarding the living environment of the participants, 92 (39.8%) came from a rural environment, while 139 (60.2%) came from an urban environment. The mean age of the respondents was 14.77 ± 1.64 years, with a median of 15 years and a range between 12 and 17.9 years.

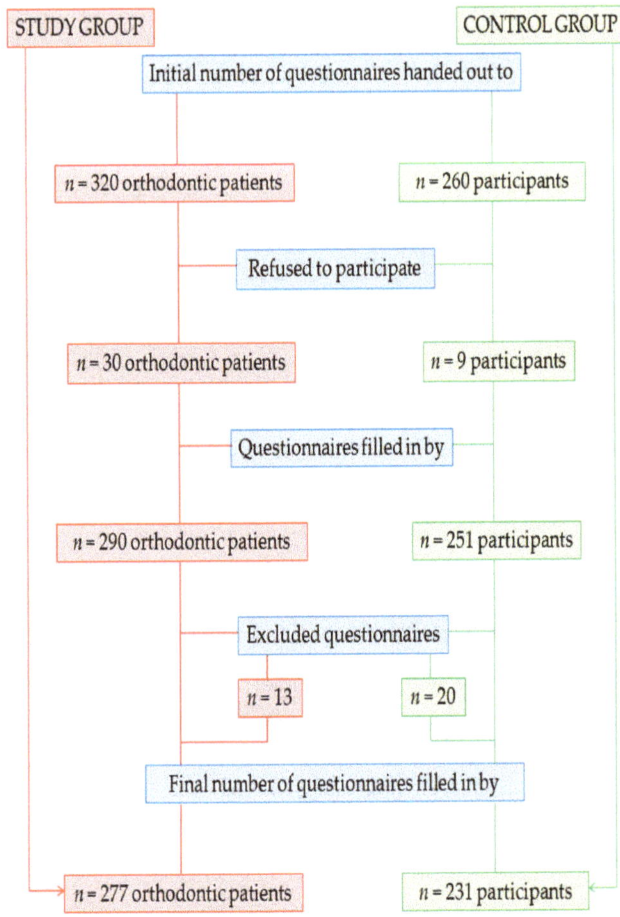

Figure 1. Study flowchart.

Data in Table 2 shows the comparison of participants' ages in relation to the living environment. According to the Shapiro–Wilk test, in the study sample, age distribution was non-parametric in both groups, and the Mann–Whitney U test showed that age differences were significant. Participants living in an urban environment had a higher age than those living in a rural environment. In the control sample the age difference was not significant between the groups.

Table 2. Comparison of participants' ages in relation to the living environment.

Living Environment	Mean Value ± SD (Years)	Median (IQR) (Years)	Medium Rank	p *
		Study group		
Rural ($p < 0.001$ **)	14.68 ± 1.52	15 (14–15)	123.05	0.016
Urban ($p < 0.001$ **)	15.03 ± 1.47	15 (14–16)	147.06	
		Control group		
Rural ($p = 0.002$ **)	14.8 ± 1.68	15 (14–16)	117.47	0.783
Urban ($p < 0.001$ **)	14.76 ± 1.61	15 (13–16)	115.03	

SD—standard deviation; IQR—interquartile range; * Mann–Whitney U test; ** Shapiro–Wilk test.

The Mann–Whitney U test showed that the age of the participants was not statistically significant between the study group and the control group ($p = 0.346$). The living environment of the participants was, also, not statistically significant between the study group and the control group ($p = 0.165$).

3.2. *Attitude towards Protective Face Mask Wearing and Treatment Interruption*

Data in Table 3 shows the distribution of the patients according to the answers given for all 9 items (study group) and 8 items (control group). In the study group, most patients were not worried that wearing a protective face mask would hide their braces (Item 1), and their desire to undergo an orthodontic treatment was not affected by the compulsoriness of face mask wearing (Item 2). The majority of the participants did not consider interrupting the orthodontic treatment due to the COVID-19 pandemic (Item 5), but most of them were not happy that they had to wear a face mask, which covered their orthodontic appliances, during the orthodontic treatment (Item 6), and did not want face mask wearing to continue to be compulsory, given the fact that their orthodontic appliances were no longer visible (Item 7). In the control group, more than half of the participants were worried to some degree (occasionally, frequently, very frequently) that wearing a protective face mask would hide their smile (Item 1) and were affected by the compulsoriness of face mask wearing (Item 2). The majority of the participants did not consider not going to the dentist due to the COVID-19 pandemic (Item 5).

Table 3. Distribution of the patients according to the answers provided.

5 Option Items					
Answer (No., %)	**Never**	**Rarely**	**Occasionally**	**Frequently**	**Very Frequently**
			Study group		
Item 1	137 (49.5%)	74 (26.7%)	21 (7.6%)	26 (9.4%)	19 (6.9%)
Item 2	143 (51.6%)	72 (26%)	29 (10.5%)	25 (9%)	8 (2.9%)
Item 3	130 (46.9%)	44 (15.9%)	33 (11.9%)	39 (14.1%)	31 (11.2%)
Item 4	66 (23.8%)	69 (24.9%)	64 (23.1%)	40 (14.4%)	38 (13.7%)
Item 8	143 (51.6%)	47 (17%)	63 (22.7%)	14 (5.1%)	10 (3.6%)
			Control group		
Item 1	71 (30.7%)	44 (19%)	69 (29.9%)	42 (18.2%)	5 (2.2%)
Item 2	41 (17.7%)	35 (15.2%)	42 (18.2%)	92 (39.8%)	21 (9.1%)
Item 3	48 (20.8%)	99 (42.9%)	17 (7.4%)	63 (27.3%)	4 (1.7%)
Item 4	116 (50.2%)	38 (16.5%)	57 (24.7%)	18 (7.8%)	2 (0.9%)
Item 8	57 (24.7%)	42 (18.2%)	76 (32.9%)	45 (19.5%)	11 (4.8%)

3 Option Items			
	No	**Maybe**	**Yes**
		Study group	
Item 5	173 (62.5%)	78 (28.2%)	26 (9.4%)
Item 6	190 (68.6%)	63 (22.7%)	24 (8.7%)
Item 7	144 (52%)	102 (36.8%)	31 (11.2%)
Item 9	65 (23.5%)	30 (10.8%)	182 (65.7%)
		Control group	
Item 5	163 (70.6%)	57 (24.7%)	11 (4.8%)
Item 6	118 (51.1%)	32 (13.9%)	81 (35.1%)
Item 7	111 (48.1%)	51 (22.1%)	69 (29.9%)

No.—number; %—percentage.

3.3. *Correlational Results*

In the study group, statistically significant correlations were found between respondents' age and answers provided for Items 1, 3 and 8. As such, patients with higher ages were less concerned about the fact that wearing a protective face mask would hide their braces and were less affected by the suspension of dental offices' activity, as patients undergoing an orthodontic treatment with fixed appliances. However, younger patients were less stressed about wearing a protective face mask that hid the orthodontic appliances (Table 4). In the control group, there were no statistically significant correlations identified between respondents' age and answers provided for Items 1, 3, and 8.

Table 4. Correlations between age and Items 1, 3, and 8.

Correlations	p *
Study group	
Age ($p < 0.001$ **) x Item 1 Score ($p < 0.001$ **)	0.001, R = −0.204
Age ($p < 0.001$ **) x Item 3 Score ($p < 0.001$ **)	<0.001, R = −0.223
Age ($p < 0.001$ **) x Item 8 Score ($p < 0.001$ **)	0.001, R = 0.195
Control group	
Age ($p < 0.001$ **) x Item 1 Score ($p < 0.001$ **)	0.255, R = 0.075
Age ($p < 0.001$ **) x Item 3 Score ($p < 0.001$ **)	0.244, R = 0.077
Age ($p < 0.001$ **) x Item 8 Score ($p < 0.001$ **)	0.853, R = 0.012

* Spearman's rho correlation coefficient, ** Shapiro–Wilk test.

In the study group, patients' gender influenced the answers received for Items 6 and 7. As such, boys were unhappier with wearing a protective face mask during the orthodontic treatment, while indecisive patients were more frequently girls. Boys were, also, less eager to continue wearing a face mask as a mandatory regulation, considering the fact that face masks covered the braces. The answers received for Items 5, 7, and 9 were significantly influenced by participants' living environment. Patients living in an urban environment were less prone to considering interrupting the orthodontic treatment as a result of the COVID-19 pandemic, and were more eager to maintain the compulsoriness of face mask wearing, even though face masks covered the orthodontic appliances. Patients living in a rural environment were more frequently indecisive about interrupting the orthodontic treatment during the COVID-19 pandemic, were less eager to maintain the compulsoriness of face mask wearing during the orthodontic treatment, and were more frequently indecisive about interrupting the orthodontic treatment while wearing a face mask (Table 5). In the control group, only the answers received for Item 7 were influenced by patients' gender. As such, girls were unhappier than boys about the fact that they have to wear a protective face mask that would cover their smile. The answers received for Item 5 were significantly influenced by participants' living environment. As such, patients living in a rural environment were more frequently indecisive than patients living in an urban environment about not going to the dentist due to the COVID-19 pandemic (Table 5).

Other significant correlations were found between answers provided for some items. As such, in the study group, participants who were more concerned that wearing a face mask would hide their orthodontic appliance (Item 1) considered that the compulsoriness of face mask wearing affected their desire to undergo an orthodontic treatment, because face masks covered their braces (Item 2) ($p < 0.001$, R = 0.300), and were more affected by the suspension of dental offices' activity, as patients undergoing an orthodontic treatment with fixed orthodontic appliances (Item 3) ($p = 0.001$, R = 0.194).

Patients who did not want protective face masks to continue being mandatory, given the fact that they covered the braces (Item 7) were more frequently indecisive about their willingness to continue the orthodontic treatment while wearing a protective face mask (Item 9) (Table 6).

Table 5. Patients' distribution according to gender, living environment, and answers provided for different items.

Gender/Answer (No., %)	Girls	Boys	*p* *
	Study group		
	Item 6		
No	110 (63.6%)	80 (76.9%)	
Maybe	48 (27.7%)	15 (14.4%)	0.031
Yes	15 (8.7%)	9 (8.7%)	
	Item 7		
No	76 (43.9%)	68 (65.4%)	
Maybe	73 (42.2%)	29 (27.9%)	0.002
Yes	24 (13.9%)	7 (6.7%)	
	Control group		
	Item 6		
No	73 (54.5%)	45 (46.4%)	
Maybe	19 (14.2%)	13 (13.4%)	0.376
Yes	42 (31.3%)	39 (40.2%)	
	Item 7		
No	76 (56.7%)	35 (36.1%)	
Maybe	32 (23.9%)	19 (19.6%)	<0.001
Yes	26 (19.4%)	43 (44.3%)	
Living Environment/Answer (No., %)	**Rural**	**Urban**	*p* *
	Study group		
	Item 5		
No	49 (52.7%)	124 (67.4%)	
Maybe	39 (41.9%)	39 (21.2%)	0.001
Yes	5 (5.4%)	21 (11.4%)	
	Item 7		
No	59 (63.4%)	85 (46.2%)	
Maybe	30 (32.3%)	72 (39.1%)	0.005
Yes	4 (4.3%)	27 (14.7%)	
	Item 9		
No	15 (16.1%)	50 (27.2%)	
Maybe	17 (18.3%)	13 (7.1%)	0.007
Yes	61 (65.6%)	121 (65.8%)	
	Control group		
	Item 5		
No	62 (67.4%)	101 (72.7%)	
Maybe	30 (32.6%)	27 (19.4%)	0.002
Yes	0 (0%)	11 (7.9%)	
	Item 7		
No	47 (51.1%)	64 (46%)	
Maybe	25 (27.2%)	26 (18.7%)	0.065
Yes	20 (21.7%)	49 (35.3%)	

No.—number; %—percentage; * Fisher's exact test.

Table 6. Patients' distribution according to answers provided for Items 7 and 9.

Answer (No., %)	Correction neg.	Indecisive	Correction pos.	*p* *
Compulsoriness neg.	27 (41.5%)	22 (73.3%)	95 (52.2%)	
Indecisive	25 (38.5%)	7 (23.3%)	70 (38.5%)	0.020
Compulsoriness pos.	13 (20%)	1 (3.3%)	17 (9.3%)	

No.—number; %—percentage; neg.—negative; pos.—positive; * Fisher's exact test.

3.4. Comparative Results

Comparisons were made between participants considering their age, gender, and living environment. Although significant differences were found for some items in relation to age and gender, no significant differences were found in relation to the living environment. Regarding age, in the study group, significant differences were found for Item 9. A comparison of age in relation to patients' desire to continue the orthodontic treatment while wearing a face mask was made. Age distribution was non-parametric in most groups according to the Shapiro–Wilk test ($p < 0.05$). The differences between groups were statistically significant according to the Kruskal–Wallis H test ($p = 0.002$), and post-hoc tests showed that indecisive patients had a lower age than patients who said they do not want to continue the orthodontic treatment while wearing a face mask, given the fact that the orthodontic appliances were no longer visible ($p = 0.044$) or than patients who said they want to continue the orthodontic treatment while wearing a face mask, despite the fact that the orthodontic appliances were no longer visible ($p = 0.001$).

Regarding patients' gender, in the study group significant differences were identified for Items 2 and 4. The results obtained showed that boys' desires to undergo orthodontic treatment were less affected by the compulsoriness of a face mask that covers the braces, in comparison with girls, and they were less worried about the possibility of the orthodontic treatment suspension than girls (Table 7). In the control group, significant differences were identified for Item 4. The results were similar to the study group. Girls were more worried that they would not be able to go to the dentist due to the COVID-19 pandemic (Table 7).

Table 7. Comparison of answers provided for Items 2 and 4 in relation to gender.

Gender	Mean Value ± SD	Median (IQR)	Medium Rank	p *
		Study group		
		Item 2		
Girls ($p < 0.001$ **)	1.94 ± 1.07	2 (1–3)	147.58	0.012
Boys ($p < 0.001$ **)	1.71 ± 1.15	1 (1–2)	124.74	
		Item 4		
Girls ($p < 0.001$ **)	2.86 ± 1.27	3 (2–4)	149.42	0.004
Boys ($p < 0.001$ **)	2.42 ± 1.41	2 (1–4)	121.66	
		Control group		
		Item 2		
Girls ($p < 0.001$ **)	3.05 ± 1.26	3 (2–4)	114.77	0.732
Boys ($p < 0.001$ **)	3.1 ± 1.29	3 (2–4)	117.70	
		Item 4		
Girls ($p < 0.001$**)	2.04 ± 1.05	2 (1–3)	123.31	0.034
Boys ($p < 0.001$ **)	1.77 ± 1.06	1 (1–3)	105.90	

SD—standard deviation; IQR—interquartile range; * Mann–Whitney U test, ** Shapiro–Wilk test.

Other significant differences were found between answers provided for some items. In the study group, significant differences were identified between Items 1 and 9, Items 2 and 5, Items 3 and 5, and Items 3 and 7. In the control group, significant differences were identified between Items 3 and 5 and Items 3 and 7. They are detailed in Table 8, which shows the results of the Kruskal–Wallis H test and Shapiro–Wilk test.

Tables 9 and 10 show the comparisons of answers provided for Item 1 to Item 8, according to the analyzed groups (study group and control group). Statistically significant differences were identified for most items. As such, participants undergoing an orthodontic treatment with fixed appliances (study group) were less affected by the compulsoriness of face mask wearing, in comparison to the participants from the control group (Item 2) and were worried that they would not be able to continue the orthodontic treatment (Item 4). In comparison with the study group, participants from the control group were more worried about the fact that they had to wear a protective face mask (Item 1) and were more stressed that they had to wear a protective face mask (Item 8).

Table 8. Comparisons between various items.

Comparison	Answer	Mean Value ± SD	Median (IQR)	Medium Rank	p *
	Study group				
Item 1 and Item 9	No ($p < 0.001$ **)	2.26 ± 1.35	2 (1–3)	157.08	0.014
	Maybe ($p = 0.005$ **)	1.67 ± 0.77	1.5 (1–2)	128.67	
	Yes ($p < 0.001$ **)	1.84 ± 1.19	1 (1–2)	129.55	
Item 2 and Item 5	No ($p < 0.001$ **)	1.98 ± 1.12	2 (1–2)	149.32	0.009
	Maybe ($p < 0.001$ **)	1.59 ± 0.98	1 (1–2)	119.13	
	Yes ($p < 0.001$ **)	1.85 ± 1.25	1 (1–3)	129.94	
Item 3 and Item 5	No ($p < 0.001$ **)	2.12 ± 1.34	2 (1–3)	132.34	0.025
	Maybe ($p < 0.001$ **)	2.33 ± 1.5	2 (1–4)	141.79	
	Yes ($p < 0.001$ **)	3.08 ± 1.69	3 (1–5)	174.94	
Item 3 and Item 7	No ($p < 0.001$ **)	2.51 ± 1.61	2 (1–4)	149.19	0.041
	Maybe ($p < 0.001$ **)	1.95 ± 1.18	1 (1–3)	124.51	
	Yes ($p < 0.001$ **)	2.16 ± 1.21	2 (1–3)	139.34	
	Control group				
Item 3 and Item 5	No ($p < 0.001$ **)	2.5 ± 1.15	2 (2–4)	118.22	0.009
	Maybe ($p < 0.001$ **)	2.19 ± 1.1	2 (1–2)	100.78	
	Yes ($p = 0.001$ **)	3.27 ± 0.9	4 (2–4)	162.00	
Item 3 and Item 7	No ($p < 0.001$ **)	2.25 ± 1.08	2 (2–3)	104.69	0.007
	Maybe ($p < 0.001$ **)	2.41 ± 1.06	2 (2–4)	114.56	
	Yes ($p < 0.001$ **)	2.84 ± 1.23	3 (2–4)	135.26	

SD—standard deviation; IQR—interquartile range; * Kruskal–Wallis H test, ** Shapiro–Wilk test.

Table 9. Comparison of answers provided for Items 1, 2, 3, 4, and 8 according to the analyzed groups.

Groups	Mean Value ± SD	Median (IQR)	Medium Rank	p *
		Item 1		
Control ($p < 0.001$ **)	2.42 ± 1.16	3 (1–3)	286.69	<0.001
Study ($p < 0.001$ **)	1.97 ± 1.25	2 (1–2)	227.65	
		Item 2		
Control ($p < 0.001$ **)	3.07 ± 1.27	3 (2–4)	324.51	<0.001
Study ($p < 0.001$ **)	1.86 ± 1.1	1 (1–2)	196.11	
		Item 3		
Control ($p < 0.001$ **)	2.46 ± 1.15	2 (2–4)	274.97	0.003
Test ($p < 0.001$ **)	2.27 ± 1.44	2 (1–4)	237.43	
		Item 4		
Control ($p < 0.001$ **)	1.93 ± 1.06	1 (1–3)	209.61	<0.001
Test ($p < 0.001$ **)	2.69 ± 1.34	3 (2–4)	291.94	
		Item 8		
Control ($p < 0.001$ **)	2.61 ± 1.18	3 (2–3)	300.39	<0.001
Test ($p < 0.001$ **)	1.92 ± 1.12	1 (1–3)	216.23	

SD—standard deviation; IQR—interquartile range; * Mann–Whitney U test, ** Shapiro–Wilk test.

Table 10. Comparison of answers provided for Items 5, 6, and 7 according to the analyzed groups.

Groups	No	Maybe	Yes	p *
		Item 5		
Control	163 (48.5%)	57 (42.2%)	11 (29.7%)	0.064
Test	173 (51.5%)	78 (57.8%)	26 (70.3%)	
		Item 6		
Control	118 (38.3%)	32 (33.7%)	81 (77.1%)	<0.001
Test	190 (61.7%)	63 (66.3%)	24 (22.9%)	
		Item 7		
Control	111 (43.5%)	51 (33.3%)	69 (69%)	<0.001
Test	144 (56.5%)	102 (66.7%)	31 (31%)	

No.—number; %—percentage; * Fisher's exact test.

4. Discussion

The COVID-19 pandemic has had a strong impact on the global healthcare system, affecting both the economy of health systems [21] and the way patients have accessed healthcare services. During the pandemic, the use of healthcare fell by about a third among patients [22]. Dental practices have also been affected by the restrictions imposed during the pandemic. Restrictive measures maintained for a longer period of time could lead to financial distress, the most affected being dental practices with high operational costs [23]. Withholding dental care led to the progression of undiagnosed and untreated oral diseases [24], and orthodontic treatments were suspended during the lockdown period, with orthodontists being unable to sustain ongoing treatments. In Romania, a state of lockdown was established for a period of two months, between March 16 and May 16, 2020 [25].

It is important to determine patients' attitudes towards restrictive measures and, especially, towards wearing a protective mask, during the orthodontic treatment, keeping in mind that face masks cover the orthodontic appliances. For this purpose, we designed a short questionnaire, comprising only 9 items (8 items for the control group), to which patients can easily answer in the waiting room, before completing their regular checkup. The use of questionnaires is an accessible method for collecting data from patients, in order to conduct a statistical study [26]. Although most research in the field of dentistry investigating different attitudes during the COVID-19 pandemic is based on questionnaires applied on online platforms [27,28], websites [29], e-mail addresses of dentists [30] or patients, or both online and on paper [31], in the present study the paper printed version of the questionnaire was used for a better selection of patients and for an easier application of the inclusion and exclusion criteria. Additionally, by completing the questionnaires in the dental office after a longer period of wearing a face mask, patients were given clarifications about any questions they could not comprehend. However, completing the questionnaires in the dental office could make participants feel obligated to respond in a manner that would positively represent an orthodontic treatment. In order to reduce this possibility, patients were encouraged to answer freely and honestly, and were assured that the questionnaires will remain anonymous.

Although there are other studies that have examined the impact of the pandemic on orthodontic patients, they have attempted to determine the challenges that patients had and the solutions proposed by them [1]. Our study focused mainly on finding out information about the patients' attitudes towards wearing a protective mask during the orthodontic treatment. We selected adolescent patients because, generally, they are the main population group receiving orthodontic treatment [32]. The protective mask covers the middle and lower third of the face, thus covering the teeth in smile and speech. In this way, the orthodontic appliance is no longer visible. In our study, although the desire of most patients to undergo the orthodontic treatment was not negatively affected by wearing a face mask, even though face masks covered their braces, most patients were not happy to wear a face mask while wearing the orthodontic appliance. In our view, a potential reason for the unhappiness caused by face mask wearing during the orthodontic treatment could be that adolescent patients, for the most part, want to have the orthodontic appliance visible in smile and speech, since they can be viewed as a fashion statement [20]. A type of fixed braces called "fashion braces" has been developed, with the unique purpose of imitating an orthodontic treatment, but having no therapeutic effect [20]. In other studies, however, there is a preference of young patients for less visible appliances, such as clear aligners [33], while adult patients prefer aesthetic orthodontic appliances [34]. It would be beneficial to find out if face mask wearing could increase patients' preferences towards less esthetic orthodontic appliances, given the fact that they would not be visible while wearing the protective face mask. Nonetheless, teenagers require further support and stimulation for continuing to respect the COVID-19 mandatory regulations. They should be involved in educational programs that help other people understand the benefits of face mask wearing during the COVID-19 pandemic.

Most teenagers in this study did not consider that it would be necessary to interrupt the treatment due to the COVID-19 pandemic. The lack of concern about the fact that wearing a protective face mask would cover the orthodontic appliance increased with the age of the respondents, so that patients with higher ages were less concerned about the fact that wearing a mask would cover the orthodontic appliances (p = 0.001, R = −0.204). This suggests that younger patients were more eager to have their orthodontic appliance visible. Generally, people are not concerned about wearing a protective face mask, and although there is an impression that the anti-mask sentiment is widespread [35], most studies show that people are willing to follow the authorities' recommendations and wear a face mask [35].

Regarding the living environment of the respondents and their attitude towards wearing a protective mask, it can be emphasized that patients living in an urban environment were more eager to maintain the compulsoriness of face mask wearing, even though the face mask covered the orthodontic appliances, while patients living in a rural environment were less eager to maintain the compulsoriness of face mask wearing (p = 0.005). This may be due to the fact that the rural population engages less in preventive health behaviors than the urban population [36,37], as other studies suggested.

Regarding the sample size estimation, it is important to highlight the fact that when the sample size was estimated, an ideal gender allocation ratio of 1:1 was taken into consideration. The main goal was to determine the minimum number of questionnaires that had to be completed for each gender. However, more questionnaires than initially planned were distributed, and we did not want to lose the information obtained through these forms. We do not consider that the final distribution of patients could influence the obtained results.

The COVID-19 pandemic and the restrictions connected to it have changed the lives of patients [38]. Despite some inconveniences caused by wearing protective masks [39], wearing protective face masks should be encouraged, because they offer a high protection against the spread of the SARS-CoV-2 virus [40]. Protective face masks, along with proper ventilation, social distancing [41], and vaccination, are the safest methods to combat the COVID-19 pandemic [42].

The limitations of this study are related, first of all, to the number of items. It would be useful to extend the questionnaires and add more items, investigating the attitudes toward orthodontic appliances, oral health, self-esteem, and the main purpose for wearing orthodontic appliances. Extending the questionnaire to the adult population would be beneficial, since it would offer an even more comprehensive view of face mask wearing during the orthodontic treatment. The application of online questionnaires could allow a multicenter, national approach of this topic. In this way, data could be collected from several orthodontic practices from across Romania. However, given the restrictive circumstances in which this survey was conducted, during the COVID-19 pandemic, we consider it to be a solid starting point for future research. Even though mask policies are temporary, the COVID-19 pandemic is still actively causing infections [43], meaning that face masks may remain useful for an indefinite amount of time. Moreover, there are still areas at risk of impactful spillover, which could be the starting point of future pandemics [44]. Under these conditions, face masks could become the new normal.

5. Conclusions

Adolescents wearing fixed orthodontic appliances had a generally positive attitude towards protective face masks, despite the fact that they covered their orthodontic appliances, most of them not being bothered by the fact that face mask wearing was mandatory and not being concerned that they must wear a protective mask that would cover their orthodontic appliances. Usually, boys were less affected by the compulsoriness of face mask wearing, during the orthodontic treatment, in comparison with girls, and they were less worried about the possibility of orthodontic treatment suspension than girls. Wearing a face mask remains one of the key measures in the prevention of the SARS-CoV-2 virus spread and should be encouraged. Non-orthodontic patients were more worried about the fact that they had to wear a protective face mask and more stressed about this issue.

Author Contributions: Conceptualization, J.O.C. and A.E.M.; methodology, J.O.C., L.L.V. and A.E.M.; software, R.D.; validation, J.O.C., G.C. and R.D.; formal analysis, L.L.V. and R.D.; investigation, J.O.C. and G.C.; resources, L.L.V. and R.D.; data curation, A.E.M.; writing—original draft preparation, J.O.C.; writing—review and editing, L.L.V. and A.E.M.; visualization, R.D. and G.C.; supervision, M.B.; project administration, G.C. and R.D.; funding acquisition, J.O.C. and G.C. All authors have read and agreed to the published version of the manuscript.

Funding: This research was funded through the Project 123008, entitled "SmartDoct—High quality programs for doctoral students and postdoctoral researchers from the University of Oradea for growth of the relevance of research and innovation in the context of regional economy", project financed through the Human Capital Operation Program 2014–2020.

Institutional Review Board Statement: The study was conducted according to the guidelines of the Declaration of Helsinki and approved by the Ethics Committee of the University of Oradea (No. 23/25.02.2021).

Informed Consent Statement: Informed consent was obtained from all subjects involved in the study.

Data Availability Statement: The data presented in this study are available on request from the corresponding authors. The data are not publicly available due to privacy reasons.

Conflicts of Interest: The authors declare no conflict of interest.

References

1. Bustati, N.; Rajeh, N. The impact of COVID-19 pandemic on patients receiving orthodontic treatment: An online questionnaire cross-sectional study. *J. World Fed. Orthod.* **2020**, *9*, 159–163. [CrossRef] [PubMed]
2. Bahramian, H.; Gharib, B.; Baghalian, A. COVID-19 Considerations in Pediatric Dentistry. *JDR Clin. Trans. Res.* **2020**, *5*, 307–311. [CrossRef] [PubMed]
3. Yüce, M.; Filiztekin, E.; Özkaya, K.G. COVID-19 diagnosis—A review of current methods. *Biosens. Bioelectron.* **2021**, *172*, 112752. [CrossRef] [PubMed]
4. Lei, S.; Jiang, F.; Su, W.; Chen, C.; Chen, J.; Mei, W.; Zhan, L.Y.; Jia, Y.; Zhang, L.; Liu, D.; et al. Clinical characteristics and outcomes of patients undergoing surgeries during the incubation period of COVID-19 infection. *E. Clin. Med.* **2020**, *21*, 100331. [CrossRef]
5. Huang, C.; Wang, Y.; Li, X.; Ren, L.; Zhao, J.; Hu, Y.; Zhang, L.; Fan, G.; Xu, J.; Gu, X.; et al. Clinical features of patients infected with 2019 novel coronavirus in Wuhan, China. *Lancet* **2020**, *395*, 497–506. [CrossRef]
6. Malekshoar, M.; Javanshir, B. Challenges, limitations, and solutions for orthodontists during the coronavirus pandemic: A review. *Am. J. Orthod. Dentofac. Orthop.* **2021**, *159*, e59–e71. [CrossRef]
7. Belser, J.A.; Rota, P.A.; Tumpey, T.M. Ocular tropism of respiratory viruses. *Microbiol. Mol. Biol. Rev.* **2013**, *77*, 144–156. [CrossRef]
8. Kharroubi, S.; Saleh, F. Are Lockdown Measures Effective Against COVID-19? *Front. Public Health* **2020**, *8*, 549692. [CrossRef]
9. Turkistani, K.A. Precautions and recommendations for orthodontic settings during the COVID-19 outbreak: A review. *Am. J. Orthod. Dentofac. Orthop.* **2020**, *158*, 175–181. [CrossRef]
10. Derruau, S.; Bouchet, J.; Nassif, A.; Baudet, A.; Yasukawa, K.; Lorimier, S.; Prêcheur, I.; Bloch-Zupan, A.; Pellat, B.; Chardin, H.; et al. On Behalf Of Task Force Covid-Collège National des EnseignantS En Biologie Orale Cnesbo-France. COVID-19 and Dentistry in 72 Questions: An Overview of the Literature. *J. Clin. Med.* **2021**, *10*, 779. [CrossRef]
11. Peloso, R.M.; Pini, N.I.P.; Sundfeld Neto, D.; Mori, A.A.; Oliveira, R.C.G.; Valarelli, F.P.; Freitas, K.M.S. How does the quarantine resulting from COVID-19 impact dental appointments and patient anxiety levels? *Braz. Oral Res.* **2020**, *34*, e84. [CrossRef] [PubMed]
12. Alharbi, A.; Alharbi, S.; Alqaidi, S. Guidelines for dental care provision during the COVID-19 pandemic. *Saudi Dent. J.* **2020**, *32*, 181–186. [CrossRef] [PubMed]
13. Suri, S.; Vandersluis, Y.R.; Kochhar, A.S.; Bhasin, R.; Abdallah, M.N. Clinical orthodontic management during the COVID-19 pandemic. *Angle Orthod.* **2020**, *90*, 473–484. [CrossRef] [PubMed]
14. Umeh, O.D.; Utomi, I.L.; Isiekwe, I.G.; Aladenika, E.T. Impact of the coronavirus disease 2019 pandemic on orthodontic patients and their attitude to orthodontic treatment. *Am. J. Orthod. Dentofac. Orthop.* **2021**, *159*, e399–e409. [CrossRef] [PubMed]
15. Zhao, X.; Knobel, P. Face mask wearing during the COVID-19 pandemic: Comparing perceptions in China and three European countries. *Transl. Behav. Med.* **2021**, *11*, 1199–1204. [CrossRef]
16. Matuschek, C.; Moll, F.; Fangerau, H.; Fischer, J.C.; Zänker, K.; van Griensven, M.; Schneider, M.; Kindgen-Milles, D.; Knoefel, W.T.; Lichtenberg, A.; et al. Face masks: Benefits and risks during the COVID-19 crisis. *Eur. J. Med. Res.* **2020**, *25*, 32. [CrossRef]

17. Kisielinski, K.; Giboni, P.; Prescher, A.; Klosterhalfen, B.; Graessel, D.; Funken, S.; Kempski, O.; Hirsch, O. Is a Mask That Covers the Mouth and Nose Free from Undesirable Side Effects in Everyday Use and Free of Potential Hazards? *Int. J. Environ. Res. Public Health* **2021**, *18*, 4344. [CrossRef]
18. Feldens, C.A.; Nakamura, E.K.; Tessarollo, F.R.; Closs, L.Q. Desire for orthodontic treatment and associated factors among adolescents in Southern Brazil. *Angle Orthod.* **2015**, *85*, 224–232. [CrossRef]
19. Mihailescu, A.; Labunet, A.; Muntean, A.; Kui, A.; Campian, R.S. Psycho-social impact of orthodontic treatment in Romanian teenagers and young adults. *Clujul Med.* **2018**, *91*, 336–341. [CrossRef]
20. Hakami, Z.; Chung, H.S.; Moafa, S.; Nasser, H.; Sowadi, H.; Saheb, S.; Bokhari, A.M.; Anderson, N.K. Impact of fashion braces on oral health related quality of life: A web-based cross-sectional study. *BMC Oral Health* **2020**, *20*, 236. [CrossRef]
21. Kaye, A.D.; Okeagu, C.N.; Pham, A.D.; Silva, R.A.; Hurley, J.J.; Arron, B.L.; Sarfraz, N.; Lee, H.N.; Ghali, G.E.; Gamble, J.W.; et al. Economic impact of COVID-19 pandemic on healthcare facilities and systems: International perspectives. *Best Pract. Res. Clin. Anaesthesiol.* **2021**, *35*, 293–306. [CrossRef] [PubMed]
22. Moynihan, R.; Sanders, S.; Michaleff, Z.A.; Scott, A.M.; Clark, J.; To, E.J.; Jones, M.; Kitchene, E.; Fox, M.; Johansson, M.; et al. Impact of COVID-19 pandemic on utilisation of healthcare services: A systematic review. *BMJ Open* **2021**, *11*, e045343. [CrossRef] [PubMed]
23. Schwendicke, F.; Krois, J.; Gomez, J. Impact of SARS-CoV2 (Covid-19) on dental practices: Economic analysis. *J. Dent.* **2020**, *99*, 103387. [CrossRef] [PubMed]
24. Coulthard, P.; Thomson, P.; Dave, M.; Coulthard, F.P.; Seoudi, N.; Hill, M. The COVID-19 pandemic and dentistry: The clinical, legal and economic consequences—Part 2: Consequences of withholding dental care. *Br. Dent. J.* **2020**, *229*, 801–805. [CrossRef]
25. Vancea, F.; Apostol, M.Ş. Changes in mental health during the COVID-19 crisis in Romania: A repeated cross-section study based on the measurement of subjective perceptions and experiences. *Sci. Prog.* **2021**, *104*, 368504211025873. [CrossRef]
26. Sekulic, D.; Ostojic, D.; Decelis, A.; Castro-Piñero, J.; Jezdimirovic, T.; Drid, P.; Ostojic, L.; Gilic, B. The Impact of Scholastic Factors on Physical Activity Levels during the COVID-19 Lockdown: A Prospective Study on Adolescents from Bosnia and Herzegovina. *Children* **2021**, *8*, 877. [CrossRef]
27. Carvalho, J.C.; Declerck, D.; Jacquet, W.; Bottenberg, P. Dentist Related Factors Associated with Implementation of COVID-19 Protective Measures: A National Survey. *Int. J. Environ. Res. Public Health* **2021**, *18*, 8381. [CrossRef]
28. Cotrin, P.; Peloso, R.M.; Oliveira, R.C.; de Oliveira, R.C.G.; Pini, N.I.P.; Valarelli, F.P.; Freitas, K.M.S. Impact of coronavirus pandemic in appointments and anxiety/concerns of patients regarding orthodontic treatment. *Orthod. Craniofac. Res.* **2020**, *23*, 455–461. [CrossRef]
29. Xiong, X.; Wu, Y.; Fang, X.; Sun, W.; Ding, Q.; Yi, Y.; Huang, Y.; Gong, J.; Liu, J.; Wang, J. Mental distress in orthodontic patients during the coronavirus disease 2019 pandemic. *Am. J. Orthod. Dentofac. Orthop.* **2020**, *158*, 824–833.e1. [CrossRef]
30. Schmidt, J.; Waldova, E.; Balkova, S.; Suchanek, J.; Smucler, R. Impact of COVID-19 on Czech Dentistry: A Nationwide Cross-Sectional Preliminary Study among Dentists in the Czech Republic. *Int. J. Environ. Res. Public Health* **2021**, *18*, 9121. [CrossRef]
31. Habib, M.A.; Dayyab, F.M.; Iliyasu, G.; Habib, A.G. Knowledge, attitude and practice survey of COVID-19 pandemic in Northern Nigeria. *PLoS ONE* **2021**, *16*, e0245176. [CrossRef] [PubMed]
32. Vaida, L.; Corega, C.; Roşeanu, G. Letter to Editor. *J. Cogn. Behav. Psychother* **2009**, *9*, 131–133. [CrossRef]
33. Alansari, R.A. Youth Perception of Different Orthodontic Appliances. *Patient Prefer. Adherence* **2020**, *14*, 1011–1019. [CrossRef] [PubMed]
34. Alansari, R.A.; Faydhi, D.A.; Ashour, B.S.; Alsaggaf, D.H.; Shuman, M.T.; Ghoneim, S.H.; Linjawi, A.I.; Marghalani, H.Y.; Dause, R.R. Adult Perceptions of Different Orthodontic Appliances. *Patient Prefer. Adherence* **2019**, *13*, 2119–2128. [CrossRef] [PubMed]
35. Taylor, S.; Asmundson, G.J.G. Negative attitudes about facemasks during the COVID-19 pandemic: The dual importance of perceived ineffectiveness and psychological reactance. *PLoS ONE* **2021**, *16*, e0246317. [CrossRef]
36. Chen, X.; Chen, H. Differences in preventive behaviors of COVID-19 between urban and rural residents: Lessons learned from a cross-sectional study in China. *Int. J. Environ. Res. Public Health* **2020**, *17*, 4437. [CrossRef]
37. Zhang, B.; Li, Z.; Jiang, L. The Intentions to Wear Face Masks and the Differences in Preventive Behaviors between Urban and Rural Areas during COVID-19: An Analysis Based on the Technology Acceptance Model. *Int. J. Environ. Res. Public Health* **2021**, *18*, 9988. [CrossRef]
38. Stavridou, A.; Kapsali, E.; Panagouli, E.; Thirios, A.; Polychronis, K.; Bacopoulou, F.; Psaltopoulou, T.; Tsolia, M.; Sergentanis, T.N.; Tsitsika, A. Obesity in Children and Adolescents during COVID-19 Pandemic. *Children* **2021**, *8*, 135. [CrossRef]
39. Techasatian, L.; Lebsing, S.; Uppala, R.; Thaowandee, W.; Chaiyarit, J.; Supakunpinyo, C.; Panombualert, S.; Mairiang, D.; Saengnipanthkul, S.; Wichajarn, K.; et al. The Effects of the Face Mask on the Skin Underneath: A Prospective Survey During the COVID-19 Pandemic. *J. Prim. Care Community Health* **2020**, *11*, 2150132720966167. [CrossRef]
40. Howard, J.; Huang, A.; Li, Z.; Tufekci, Z.; Zdimal, V.; van der Westhuizen, H.M.; von Delft, A.; Price, A.; Fridman, L.; Tang, L.H.; et al. An evidence review of face masks against COVID-19. *Proc. Natl. Acad. Sci. USA* **2021**, *118*, e2014564118. [CrossRef]
41. Cheng, Y.; Ma, N.; Witt, C.; Rapp, S.; Wild, P.S.; Andreae, M.O.; Pöschl, U.; Su, H. Face masks effectively limit the probability of SARS-CoV-2 transmission. *Science* **2021**, eabg6296. [CrossRef] [PubMed]
42. Fischer, A. SARS-CoV-2 vaccines, where do we stand? *C. R. Biol.* **2021**, *344*, 43–55. [CrossRef] [PubMed]

43. Ashraf, O.; Virani, A.; Cheema, T. COVID-19: An Update on the Epidemiological, Clinical, Preventive, and Therapeutic Management of 2019 Novel Coronavirus Disease. *Crit. Care Nurs. Q.* **2021**, *44*, 128–137. [CrossRef] [PubMed]
44. Walsh, M.G.; Sawleshwarkar, S.; Hossain, S.; Mor, S.M. Whence the next pandemic? The intersecting global geography of the animal-human interface, poor health systems and air transit centrality reveals conduits for high-impact spillover. *One Health* **2020**, *11*, 100177. [CrossRef] [PubMed]

medicina

MDPI

Article

Relationship between Recovery from COVID-19-Induced Smell Loss and General and Oral Health Factors

Georgia Catton and Alexander Gardner *

Department of Restorative Dentistry, Dundee Dental Hospital and School, University of Dundee, Dundee DD1 4HR, UK; g.s.catton@dundee.ac.uk

* Correspondence: agardner001@dundee.ac.uk

Abstract: *Background and Objectives*: Loss of smell is one of the strongest predictors of coronavirus disease 2019 (COVID-19) and can persist long after other symptoms have resolved. "Long" cases (>28 days) of smell dysfunction present future challenges to medical and dental professionals, as there is a lack of evidence on the causes and any exacerbating or relieving factors. This study aimed to explore the persistence of COVID-19-induced smell loss and association with physical, lifestyle and oral health factors. *Materials and Methods*: This study was a cross-sectional survey of 235 participants. Recovery of smell was explored, comparing rapid recovery (≤28 days) with prolonged recovery (>28 days). Associative factors included age, sex, illness severity, diet, BMI, vitamin D supplementation, antidepressants, alcohol use, smoking, brushing frequency, flossing, missing teeth, appliances and number of dental restorations. *Results*: Smell loss showed 87% resolution within 30 days. Prolonged smell loss was significantly associated with older age (mean ± 95%, CI = 31.53 ± 1.36 years for rapid recovery vs. mean ± 95%, CI = 36.0 ± 3 years for prolonged recovery, $p = 0.003$) and increased self-reported illness severity (mean ± 95%, CI = 4.39 ± 0.27 for rapid recovery vs. 5.01 ± 0.54 for prolonged recovery, $p = 0.016$). Fisher's exact test revealed flossing was associated with rapid recovery, with flossers comprising 75% of the rapid-recovery group, compared to 56% in the prolonged-recovery group (odds ratio ± 95%, CI = 2.26 (1.23–4.15), $p = 0.01$). All other factors were not significantly associated ($p > 0.05$). *Conclusions*: Increased age and illness severity were associated with prolonged smell recovery. Use of floss was the only modifiable factor associated with rapid recovery of smell loss. As 87% of cases resolve within 30 days, future studies may benefit from targeted recruitment of individuals experiencing prolonged sense loss. This would increase statistical confidence when declaring no association with the other factors assessed, avoiding type II errors.

Keywords: COVID-19; anosmia; oral health; dental care

Citation: Catton, G.; Gardner, A. Relationship between Recovery from COVID-19-Induced Smell Loss and General and Oral Health Factors. *Medicina* **2022**, *58*, 283. https://doi.org/10.3390/medicina58020283

Academic Editor: Gaetano Isola

Received: 2 February 2022
Accepted: 9 February 2022
Published: 14 February 2022

1. Introduction

Alteration and loss of sense of taste and smell was widely observed in patients early in the severe acute respiratory syndrome coronavirus 2 (SARS-CoV-2) pandemic and quickly adopted by national and international bodies as a defining symptom of the disease, alongside fever and cough [1,2]. Indeed, sensory symptoms have been shown as one of the best predictors of the disease, short of the current gold-standard polymerase chain reaction (PCR) test [3,4]. A recent meta-analysis suggests sensory symptoms display comparable negative predictive value (0.78 vs. 0.80) and lower positive predictive value (0.78 vs. 0.98) when compared to PCR testing [3,5].

While there are relatively abundant reports of the prevalence of sensory symptoms in COVID-19, there are comparatively few studies on recovery from these symptoms [6,7]. In recent months, primary care dental services have been remobilising as the United Kingdom (UK) emerges from the worst of the pandemic, with the profession facing several challenges. Amongst these challenges, there is a likelihood of increased cases of patients reporting "long" COVID-19 symptoms, defined as symptoms persisting beyond 4 weeks [8]. Sensory complaints in particular have been shown to persist beyond other symptoms of the disease [9]. An exact mechanism for the sensory symptoms caused by COVID-19 infection has not yet been elucidated; however, inflammation is believed to play a key role, either peripherally at taste and smell receptors or centrally within the central nervous system (CNS) [10]. This process involves viral entry mediated by binding of viral surface protein via angiotensin-converting enzyme 2 (ACE-2) expressed on oral and nasal tissues. The virus may enter and destroy chemosensory cells directly or damage nerve cells involved in processing chemosensory signals [11]. Indirect damage may occur by locally or systemically raised inflammatory markers, such as interleukins and Tumour necrosis factor alpha (TNF-α). A further proposed mechanism is the presence of central hypoxia impairing sensory function, although there is less evidence for this hypothesis [12]. Interestingly, unlike with other respiratory viruses, smell loss appears to be independent of any nasal congestion [13].

The present study is a cross-sectional survey of individuals who have suffered COVID-19 and focuses on the recovery of smell in association with factors such as age; sex; smoking; alcohol use; and diet and dental factors, such as frequency of brushing, flossing, number of missing teeth, restorations and wearing appliances. The survey was hosted on the news-aggregator website reddit, in the community reddit.com/r/COVID19positive. Such an approach allows for crowdsourcing of responses, with over 170 studies relating to COVID-19 having been hosted at time of writing [14]. The rationale for selecting these variables stemmed from early observations from the medical community in the first few months of the pandemic of factors associated with COVID-19 infection. Many studies focused on outcomes such as hospitalisation, need for ventilation or mortality, with smell loss being considerably less studied. Other factors were chosen based on pre-existing associations with smell function, predating the COVID-19 pandemic. Age was observed as major risk factor for disease severity and mortality, and males were also observed to experience more severe disease early in the pandemic [15,16]. Diet and obesity are major risk factors for COVID-19 severity [17]; hence, fruit and vegetable intake and body mass index (BMI) were included in this study. Similarly, vitamin D deficiency was implicated in disease severity early in the pandemic, as well as in smell function [18,19]. Alcohol consumption was also recognised as an early risk factor for severe disease [20], as was smoking [21], which is a long recognised adverse health behaviour. Smoking is also known to diminish smell function in the absence of other disease [22].

Considerably less was known about the relation between oral health and COVID-19 in the early stages of the pandemic. The rationale for exploring oral hygiene, particularly flossing, was due to the observations that periodontal disease is associated with localised and systemic inflammation, which can impair immune function. Periodontal pockets may also harbour COVID-19 virions, representing a mechanism of entry via the oral cavity [11]. Furthermore, assessment of missing teeth not due to trauma or orthodontics is an indicator of past periodontal disease, and a recent study found 70% of COVID-19 patients had lost teeth due to severe periodontal disease [11]. The evaluation of dental restorations and oral appliances was related to the role of oral biofilms in modulating taste and smell function via retronasal olfaction [23,24]. Factors such as appliance wearing, tooth brushing habits and the restorative state of the dentition are recognised as modifying the oral microbiome, which, in turn, may alter oral function [25]. While less studied than the oral microbiome, the nasal microbiome may similarly have an impact of the process of olfaction [26], and its composition has been implicated in differentiating COVID-19 patients pre- and post-recovery [27].

The aim of this work was to investigate associations between self-reported smell loss in COVID-19 and biometric, lifestyle and oral health factors. The rationale for exploring these factors was to add to the literature base, particularly for medical and dental professionals who may encounter patients experiencing delayed smell recovery. Such cases are observed to occur with increasing frequency both in the authors' clinical practice and the wider literature [28]. Findings from this work are also intended to provide exploratory pilot data to serve as an indicator for future research directions related to smell loss in COVID-19, primarily by providing a baseline for sample size and split based on the distribution pattern of smell recovery.

2. Materials and Methods

2.1. Ethical Approval

This study was approved by the University of Dundee School of Health Sciences and Dentistry ethics committee (ref: UOD\SDEN\STAFF\2020\017, 25 June 2020).

2.2. Survey Design and Dissemination

A survey was designed using JISC Online Surveys (JISC, Bristol, UK) and hosted on https://www.reddit.com/r/COVID19positive (accessed on 10 March 2021), following written approval from the site administration team. The survey was open to individuals 18 years old or above who had suffered COVID-19 infection between March and August 2020, diagnosed by PCR test, a medical professional or self-diagnosis, where symptoms included acute changes to smell and/or taste. The survey was closed to respondents in October 2020. A breakdown of the variables explored is described below, and the full survey can be found in Supplementary Data S1.

2.3. Sample Size and Statistical Power

Based on a 95% confidence level, $p = 0.05$ and a precision of ±5%, a sample size of 400 was deemed necessary as a representation of the study population [29]. Preliminary exploration of early responders experiencing sensory loss suggested a cut-off of ~30 days would yield a sampling ratio of between 4:1 and 5:1 (recovery ≤ 28 days: recovery > 28 days). This distribution ratio was sufficient to detect effect sizes differing by 15–20% between groups with alpha = 0.05 and power = 0.8, based on a sample distribution of 234 (195:39) participants.

2.4. Data Gathering and Processing

Survey responses were manually processed and coded. Continuous variables were age, BMI, fruit and vegetable intake and duration of smell loss. Ordinal variables were severity of smell loss, severity of overall illness and severity of congestion, which were defined on an 11-point (0–10) scale, with 0 being no effect and 10 being total loss of sensation. Further ordinal variables were brushing frequency (daily, twice daily, >twice daily), alcohol consumption frequency (never, monthly, weekly, daily), smoking (never, former, current) and number of fillings (0, 1–5, 5–10, >10). Binary variables were biological sex, vitamin D supplementation, antidepressant use, use of floss/interproximal cleaning, missing teeth (not lost due to trauma, orthodontics or impaction) and appliance wearing. Low numbers of African and South Asian respondents prevented statistical analysis of ethnicity.

2.5. Statistical Analyses

Analyses and data visualisation were performed in Python3 (Centrum Wiskunde & Informatica, Amsterdam, The Netherlands) and SPSS 27 (IBM, Armonk, NY, USA). Variables were inspected and tested for normality (QQ plots and Shapiro–Wilk test). The relationship between disease severity and recovery times was explored by Spearman's rank correlation. A step plot for the duration of recovery for smell loss was created. Differences between rapid recovery (≤28 days) and prolonged recovery (>28 days) were then explored. Means were compared by two-tailed *t*-test or Mann–Whitney test where appropriate. Binary variables were compared using Fisher's exact test, and categorical variables were compared by Pearson's chi-squared test.

3. Results

3.1. Resolution of Smell Loss

A total of 421 participants reported some degree of smell, with 235 reporting either full recovery within 28 days or persisting symptoms beyond this time. A total of 207 participants reported full recovery at the time of completing the survey, allowing for the creation of a recovery curve (Figure 1). The recovery curve indicates that within 14 days, 64% of cases had resolved, and within 30 days, 87% had resolved, rising to 96% resolution within 90 days, whereas only two cases (<1%) persisted beyond 120 days.

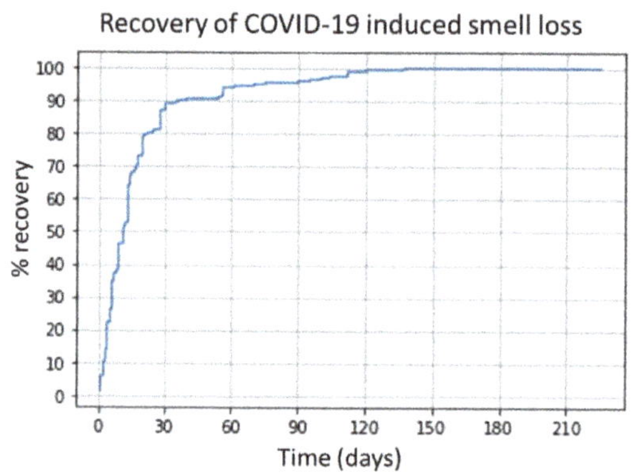

Figure 1. Recovery curve for smell loss, $n = 207$.

3.2. Differences between Rapid (≤28 Days) and Prolonged (>28 Days) Recovery

In total, 235 individuals were analysed with regards to smell loss, composed of 173 individuals who reported resolution in under 28 days and 28 individuals who reported smell loss persisting beyond 30 days. A full breakdown of the statistical analyses is presented in Table 1. The main significant findings were that individuals with prolonged recovery were, on average, older than individuals in the rapid-recovery group. Mean and 95% CI age for rapid smell recovery was 31.53 (30.17–32.88) years, compared to 36.0 (33.0–39.0) for prolonged recovery, $p = 0.003$. Data are presented graphically in Figure 2a.

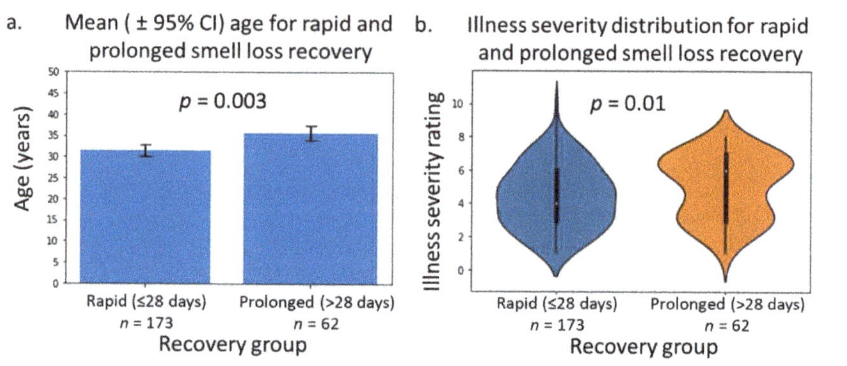

Figure 2. (**a**) Comparison of age between rapid and prolonged smell recovery; *p*-values are for two-tailed *t*-test. (**b**) Comparison of illness severity between rapid and prolonged smell recovery; *p*-values are for Mann–Whitney test.

Table 1. Comparison of short (≤28 days) and long (>28 days) smell loss.

Variable	Test	Short Smell Loss (≤28 Days) Mean ± 95% CI		Long Smell Loss (>28 Days) Mean ± 95% CI		Test Statistic	*p*-Value
Age	*t*-test	31.53 (30.17–32.88)		36.0 (33.0–39.0)		−3.04	0.003 **
BMI	*t*-test	26.81 (25.95–27.69)		25.92 (24.64–27.20)		1.077	0.28
Fruit/vegetable intake	*t*-test	2.91 (2.66–3.16)		3.07 (2.62–3.52)		−0.608	0.54
Illness severity	Mann–Whitney	4.39 (4.11–4.66)		5.01 (4.58–5.55)		−2.42	0.016 *
Smell-loss severity	Mann–Whitney	8.47 (8.12–8.83)		8.58 (7.93–9.24)		−0.77	0.44
Congestion	Mann–Whitney	3.08 (2.64–3.53)		2.72 (1.92–3.52)		−0.10	0.32
Sex	Fisher's exact	M	64 (65)	M	24 (23)	NA	0.88
		F	109 (108)	F	38 (39)		
Vitamin D	Fisher's exact	No	149 (151)	No	56 (54)	NA	0.27
		Yes	24 (22)	Yes	6 (8)		
Antidepressant	Fisher's exact	No	155 (155)	No	56 (56)	NA	0.54
		Yes	18 (18)	Yes	6 (6)		
Flossing	Fisher's exact	No	44 (52)	No	27 (19)	NA	0.01 **
		Yes	129 (121)	Yes	35 (43)		
Missing teeth	Fisher's exact	No	145 (145)	No	53 (53)	NA	0.83
		Yes	23 (23)	Yes	9 (9)		
Appliances	Fisher's exact	No	138 (140)	No	52 (50)	NA	0.57
		Yes	35 (33)	Yes	10 (12)		
Brushing freq.	Pearson's Chi^2	Daily	40 (34)	Daily	32 (38)	3.88	0.14
		2 × day	66 (69)	>2 × day	80 (77)		
		>2 × day	5 (8)	>2 × day	11 (8)		
Smoking	Pearson's Chi^2	Never	136 (135)	Never	47 (48)	0.21	0.90
		Former	12 (12)	Former	5 (5)		
		Current	25 (26)	Current	10 (9)		
Alcohol freq.	Pearson's Chi^2	Never	32 (37)	Never	18 (13)	4.61	0.20
		Monthly	43 (38)	Monthly	9 (14)		
		Weekly	63 (63)	Weekly	23 (23)		
		Daily	35 (35)	Daily	12 (12)		
No. fillings	Pearson's Chi^2	None	49 (50)	None	19 (18)	1.99	0.57
		<5	74 (71)	<5	23 (26)		
		5–10	36 (39)	5–10	17 (14)		
		>10	14 (13)	>10	3 (5)		

Fisher's exact test and Chi^2 test observed values are shown, followed by expected values in brackets. * = significant at $p < 0.05$, ** = significant at $p < 0.01$.

A further significant difference was found for severity of illness when comparing smell-loss recovery. Severity was 4.39 (4.11–4.66) in the rapid-recovery and 5.01 (4.58–5.55) in the prolonged-recovery group, $p = 0.016$. Data are presented in Figure 2b. Interestingly, severity of smell loss itself did not differ between the recovery groups. Smell loss severity was 8.47 (8.12–8.83) vs. 8.58 (7.93–9.24), $p = 0.44$, for rapid vs. prolonged smell recovery.

Of the lifestyle and oral-health parameters analysed, the only significant difference was for the use of floss. A higher proportion of flossers was found in the rapid-recovery groups compared to the prolonged-recovery group. The observed distribution was 129/173 (75%) in the rapid smell recovery compared to 35/62 (56%) in the prolonged smell recovery, odds ratio = 2.26 (1.23–4.15), $p = 0.01$. Flossing and age were found to be statistically independent when comparing mean age of flossers and non-flossers by t-test, $p = 0.68$. As shown in Table 1, distributions for the other analyses were generally very close to the expected values, with no significant differences between rapid and prolonged recovery.

4. Discussion

4.1. Pattern of Smell Recovery

The present study aimed to investigate factors that may be linked to the delayed recovery of smell due to COVID-19. We observed recovery of smell at 14 days to be 64%, which is slightly lower than some studies in Korean and Chinese populations, reporting 75% and 80% recovery at two weeks, respectively [30,31]. It has been reported, however, that East Asian populations experience reduced incidence of sensory dysfunction compared to Caucasian populations [32], although whether this also applies to recovery duration is unknown. In contrast, a study of Italian participants found recovery of both senses at two weeks to be as low as 50% [33]. We did observe 95% recovery of smell at two months, whereas others report recovery of 80–88% [1,34]. Furthermore, there are reports of chemosensory dysfunction at six months in 14% of individuals, a considerably higher proportion than was observed in our sample (<1%) [3].

4.2. Differences between Rapid and Prolonged Recovery

Our findings suggest that individuals reporting prolonged sensory recovery were significantly older and reported a more severe overall disease than those reporting rapid recovery. Such an association with age has been reported by others, with individuals >40 years reporting slower recovery of smell than those <40 years old [35]. Other work has found age is not a prognostic factor for smell recovery, and literature is sparse with respect to taste recovery [36,37]. Literature is similarly divided on the relationship between sensory recovery and severity of both disease and individual sensory loss. The present study found prolonged smell recovery was associated with significantly higher overall disease severity, although no difference was found for severity of smell loss. Other studies do not report a relationship between disease severity and recovery [31], whereas there are mixed reports associating severity of chemosensory loss with recovery time [1,34,38]. Interestingly, nasal congestion has been positively associated with smell recovery, a finding that the present study did not replicate [35].

To our knowledge, there are no reports to date investigating the relationship between oral-health behaviour and lifestyle and sensory recovery post-COVID-19. The only significant difference was found for flossing, which was more prevalent in the rapid-recovery group. The presence of periodontal disease has been previously associated with reduced COVID-19 outcomes, although sensory-dysfunction recovery was not specifically assessed [39,40]. Potential explanations for this include a baseline level of inflammation in periodontitis patients, with periodontally compromised COVID-19 patients having higher levels of C-reactive protein (CRP) [39]. Further evidence has linked CRP with adverse oral health and increased COVID-19 severity [41]. Other inflammatory markers, such as interleukin-6, have been shown to be raised in periodontal disease [41], and interleukin-6 has been shown to be inversely linked with sensory recovery [42]. The present study did not clinically examine periodontal disease, for example, by quantifying pocket depth and bleeding indices. Daily flossing has been shown to significantly reduce clinically measured gingival inflammation and thus bleeding [43,44], indicating daily flossing is associated with greater gingival health and reduced inflammation. Mechanistically, this observation ties in with previous hypotheses for local mechanisms of COVID-19 infection, such as viral infiltration of locally inflamed periodontal pockets [11] or increased systemic inflammatory markers due to prior periodontal infection [39]. Furthermore, many periodontal pathogens, such as *Porphyromonas Gingival* and *Treponema Denticola*, have been implicated in systemic inflammatory disease in organs such as the liver, heart and joints [45]. Increased periodontal pathogens have also been associated with neurological degeneration, particularly smell, in Parkinson's disease [46]. The management of periodontal pathogens via antiseptic mouthwashes is also a recognised clinical approach [47] and has been demonstrated to have efficacy for COVID-19 viral-load reduction [48]. The present work did not ask about mouthwash use, however, as alteration of taste perception can be induced by chlorhexidine itself [49].

4.3. Limitations

There are several limitations in the present study. The self-reporting nature of symptoms may result in under-recognition of the symptoms when compared to objective measures of smell loss [50]. Nevertheless, successful research of sensory loss has been conducted by similar means [51–53]. The demographics of our sample were imbalanced with regard to ethnicity, precluding statistical analysis. This was largely due to lower numbers of African and South Asian participants. As adverse COVID-19 outcomes have been reported for both groups, exploration of sensory symptoms in these groups is a key area for future research [54,55]. As most participants did not report prolonged sensory loss, statistical power in our sample distribution could only reliably detect relatively large effect sizes due to the imbalance between early and prolonged recovery. This is true of all datasets in this area of research. Thus, type II errors may be increased in our sample; however, based on our observed distributions for most variables, any statistically significant effect size would be unlikely to translate into clinical significance. A further limitation lies in the inclusion of cases diagnosed by a doctor or self-diagnosed based on symptoms. Further analyses of PCR tests confirmed cases do yield the same pattern of significant results at the $\alpha = 0.05$ level (Supplementary Table S1). Given the nature of inequitable access to testing at the stage of the pandemic when this survey was conducted, particularly in the USA, where most participants were from, the decision to include those unable to access a test was made [56]. Finally, we recommend cautious interpretation of the association of flossing and sensory recovery, which, of course, cannot be interpreted as causative. For example, flossing may be an inadvertent indicator of a generally more health-focused individual or perhaps someone more compliant and receptive to healthcare advice. Despite a statistically significant difference in flossers between smell-recovery groups (75% of rapid smell recovery vs. 58% of prolonged smell recovery) the clinical significance cannot be automatically assumed.

5. Conclusions

The present work found that smell was recovered following COVID-19 within 30 days in 87% of cases. Age and disease severity were positively associated, and use of floss was negatively associated with prolonged recovery (>28 days) of smell. Non-significant factors for sensory recovery included sex, diet, BMI, vitamin D, antidepressants, alcohol use, smoking, brushing frequency, missing teeth, appliances and number of restorations. Several previous studies have related periodontal disease with adverse COVID-19 outcomes, including ventilator use and mortality. The present work adds to the literature by suggesting recovery of smell loss may also be associated with flossing, supporting previous hypotheses of viral entry via inflamed gingival sulci. The other findings linking smell recovery with age and illness severity and the lack of association between the other factors studied adds to the collective understanding of COVID-19. Within the limitations of this study, further research and studies with higher participant numbers are needed to increase confidence in the lack of associations found to minimise the risk of type II errors. Future work will benefit from targeted recruitment of patients experiencing prolonged symptoms; our study suggests these comprise 13% of patients. Focus on these patients may also be highly useful in further elucidating the mechanism of COVID-19-induced smell dysfunction, for example, by exploring their oronasal tissue expression of ACE-2 or their oral and nasal microbiomes.

Supplementary Materials: The following are available online at https://www.mdpi.com/article/10.3390/medicina58020283/s1, Data S1: Information for participants and questionnaire, Table S1: Comparison of short ($\leq$28 days) and long (>28 days) smell and taste loss only in participants with confirmed PCR test (n = 118). For Fisher's exact test and Chi^2 test, observed values are shown, followed by expected values in brackets.

Author Contributions: Conceptualization, A.G. and G.C.; methodology, A.G.; software, A.G. and G.C.; validation, A.G. and G.C..; formal analysis, A.G.; investigation, A.G. and G.C.; resources, A.G. and G.C.; data curation, G.C.; writing—original draft preparation, A.G. and G.C.; writing—review and editing, A.G. and G.C.; visualization, A.G.; supervision, A.G.; project administration, A.G.; funding acquisition, G.C. All authors have read and agreed to the published version of the manuscript.

Funding: This research was funded by the Tattersall Foundation. The APC was funded by the University of Dundee Library and Learning Centre.

Institutional Review Board Statement: The study was conducted according to the guidelines of the Declaration of Helsinki and approved by the University of Dundee School of Health Sciences and Dentistry ethics committee (ref: UOD\SDEN\STAFF\2020\017, 25 June 2020).

Informed Consent Statement: Informed consent was obtained from all subjects involved in the study.

Data Availability Statement: The authors will make data available upon reasonable request.

Acknowledgments: The authors wish to thank the Tattersall Foundation for making this work possible.

Conflicts of Interest: The authors declare no conflict of interest.

References

1. Lechien, J.R.; Journe, F.; Hans, S.; Chiesa-Estomba, C.M.; Mustin, V.; Beckers, E.; Vaira, L.A.; De Riu, G.; Hopkins, C.; Saussez, S. Severity of anosmia as an early symptom of COVID-19 infection may predict lasting loss of smell. *Front. Med.* **2020**, *7*, 582802. [CrossRef] [PubMed]
2. Menni, C.; Valdes, A.M.; Freidin, M.B.; Sudre, C.H.; Nguyen, L.H.; Drew, D.A.; Ganesh, S.; Varavsky, T.; Cardoso, M.J.; El-Sayed Moustafa, J.S.; et al. Real-time tracking of self-reported symptoms to predict potential COVID-19. *Nat. Med.* **2020**, *26*, 1037–1040. [CrossRef] [PubMed]
3. Klein, H.; Asseo, K.; Karni, N.; Benjamini, Y.; Nir-Paz, R.; Muszkat, M.; Israel, S.; Niv, M.Y. Onset, duration and unresolved symptoms, including smell and taste changes, in mild COVID-19 infection: A cohort study in Israeli patients. *Clin. Microbiol. Infect.* **2020**, *27*, 769–774. [CrossRef] [PubMed]
4. Sudre, C.H.; Keshet, A.; Graham, M.S.; Joshi, A.D.; Shilo, S.; Rossman, H.; Murray, B.; Molteni, E.; Klaser, K.; Canas, L.D. Anosmia, ageusia, and other COVID-19-like symptoms in association with a positive SARS-CoV-2 test, across six national digital surveillance platforms: An observational study. *Lancet Digit. Health* **2021**, *3*, e577–e586. [CrossRef]
5. George, B.; McGee, J.; Giangrasso, E.; Finkelstein, S.; Wu, S.; Glatt, A.E. What Is the Predictive Value of a Single Nasopharyngeal SARS-CoV-2 PCR Swab Test in a Patient With COVID-Like Symptoms and/or Significant COVID-19 Exposure? *Open Forum Infect. Dis.* **2020**, *7*, ofaa399. [CrossRef]
6. Ibekwe, T.S.; Fasunla, A.J.; Orimadegun, A.E. Systematic review and meta-analysis of smell and taste disorders in COVID-19. *OTO Open* **2020**, *4*, 2473974X20957975. [CrossRef]
7. Agyeman, A.A.; Chin, K.L.; Landersdorfer, C.B.; Liew, D.; Ofori-Asenso, R. Smell and taste dysfunction in patients with COVID-19: A systematic review and meta-analysis. *Mayo Clin. Proc.* **2020**, *8*, 1621–1631. [CrossRef]
8. Gorna, R.; MacDermott, N.; Rayner, C.; O'Hara, M.; Evans, S.; Agyen, L.; Nutland, W.; Rogers, N.; Hastie, C. Long COVID guidelines need to reflect lived experience. *Lancet* **2021**, *397*, 455–457. [CrossRef]
9. Carvalho-Schneider, C.; Laurent, E.; Lemaignen, A.; Beaufils, E.; Bourbao-Tournois, C.; Laribi, S.; Flament, T.; Ferreira-Maldent, N.; Bruyère, F.; Stefic, K. Follow-up of adults with noncritical COVID-19 two months after symptom onset. *Clin. Microbio. Infect.* **2021**, *27*, 258–263. [CrossRef]
10. Eshraghi, A.A.; Mirsaeidi, M.; Davies, C.; Telischi, F.F.; Chaudhari, N.; Mittal, R. Potential mechanisms for COVID-19 induced anosmia and dysgeusia. *Front. Physiol.* **2020**, *11*, 1039. [CrossRef]

11. Sinjari, B.; D'Ardes, D.; Santilli, M.; Rexhepi, I.; D'Addazio, G.; Di Carlo, P.; Chiacchiaretta, P.; Caputi, S.; Cipollone, F. SARS-CoV-2 and Oral Manifestation: An Observational, Human Study. *J. Clin. Med.* **2020**, *9*, 3218. [CrossRef] [PubMed]
12. Gori, A.; Leone, F.; Loffredo, L.; Cinicola, B.L.; Brindisi, G.; De Castro, G.; Spalice, A.; Duse, M.; Zicari, A.M. COVID-19-Related Anosmia: The Olfactory Pathway Hypothesis and Early Intervention. *Front. Neurol.* **2020**, *11*, 956. [CrossRef] [PubMed]
13. Mercante, G.; Ferreli, F.; De Virgilio, A.; Gaino, F.; Di Bari, M.; Colombo, G.; Russo, E.; Costantino, A.; Pirola, F.; Cugini, G. Prevalence of taste and smell dysfunction in coronavirus disease 2019. *JAMA Otolaryngol. Head. Neck.* **2020**, *146*, 723–728. [CrossRef] [PubMed]
14. Shatz, I. Fast, free, and targeted: Reddit as a source for recruiting participants online. *Soc. Sci. Comput. Rev.* **2017**, *35*, 537–549. [CrossRef]
15. Lauc, G.; Sinclair, D. Biomarkers of biological age as predictors of COVID-19 disease severity. *Aging* **2020**, *12*, 6490. [CrossRef] [PubMed]
16. Pradhan, A.; Olsson, P.-E. Sex differences in severity and mortality from COVID-19: Are males more vulnerable? *Biol. Sex. Differ.* **2020**, *11*, 53. [CrossRef]
17. Popkin, B.M.; Du, S.; Green, W.D.; Beck, M.A.; Algaith, T.; Herbst, C.H.; Alsukait, R.F.; Alluhidan, M.; Alazemi, N.; Shekar, M. Individuals with obesity and COVID-19: A global perspective on the epidemiology and biological relationships. *Obes. Rev.* **2020**, *21*, e13128. [CrossRef]
18. Zabetakis, I.; Lordan, R.; Norton, C.; Tsoupras, A. COVID-19: The inflammation link and the role of nutrition in potential mitigation. *Nutrients* **2020**, *12*, 1466. [CrossRef]
19. Xu, Y.; Baylink, D.J.; Chen, C.-S.; Reeves, M.E.; Xiao, J.; Lacy, C.; Lau, E.; Cao, H. The importance of vitamin d metabolism as a potential prophylactic, immunoregulatory and neuroprotective treatment for COVID-19. *J. Transl. Med.* **2020**, *18*, 322. [CrossRef]
20. Saengow, U.; Assanangkornchai, S.; Casswell, S. Alcohol: A probable risk factor of COVID-19 severity. *Addiction* **2020**, *116*, 204–205. [CrossRef]
21. Patanavanich, R.; Glantz, S.A. Smoking is associated with COVID-19 progression: A meta-analysis. *Nicotine Tob. Res.* **2020**, *22*, 1653–1656. [CrossRef] [PubMed]
22. Vennemann, M.M.; Hummel, T.; Berger, K. The association between smoking and smell and taste impairment in the general population. *J. Neurol.* **2008**, *255*, 1121–1126. [CrossRef] [PubMed]
23. Neyraud, E.; Morzel, M. Biological films adhering to the oral soft tissues: Structure, composition, and potential impact on taste perception. *J. Texture Stud.* **2019**, *50*, 19–26. [CrossRef] [PubMed]
24. Schwartz, M.; Canon, F.; Feron, G.; Neiers, F.; Gamero, A. Impact of oral microbiota on flavor perception: From food processing to in-mouth metabolization. *Foods* **2021**, *10*, 2006. [CrossRef] [PubMed]
25. O'Donnell, L.E.; Robertson, D.; Nile, C.J.; Cross, L.J.; Riggio, M.; Sherriff, A.; Bradshaw, D.; Lambert, M.; Malcolm, J.; Buijs, M.J. The oral microbiome of denture wearers is influenced by levels of natural dentition. *PLoS ONE* **2015**, *10*, e0137717. [CrossRef]
26. Koskinen, K.; Reichert, J.L.; Hoier, S.; Schachenreiter, J.; Duller, S.; Moissl-Eichinger, C.; Schöpf, V. The nasal microbiome mirrors and potentially shapes olfactory function. *Sci. Rep.* **2018**, *8*, 1296. [CrossRef]
27. Feehan, A.K.; Rose, R.; Nolan, D.J.; Spitz, A.M.; Graubics, K.; Colwell, R.R.; Garcia-Diaz, J.; Lamers, S.L. Nasopharyngeal Microbiome Community Composition and Structure Is Associated with Severity of COVID-19 Disease and Breathing Treatment. *Appl. Microbiol.* **2021**, *1*, 177–188. [CrossRef]
28. Atukorallaya, D.S.; Ratnayake, R.K. Oral Mucosa, Saliva, and COVID-19 Infection in Oral Health Care. *Front. Med.* **2021**, *8*, 340. [CrossRef]
29. Islam, M.R. Sample size and its role in Central Limit Theorem (CLT). *J. Computat. Appl. Math.* **2018**, *4*, 1–7.
30. Lee, Y.; Min, P.; Lee, S.; Kim, S.-W. Prevalence and duration of acute loss of smell or taste in COVID-19 patients. *J. Korean Med. Sci.* **2020**, *35*, e174. [CrossRef]
31. Song, J.; Deng, Y.K.; Wang, H.; Wang, Z.C.; Liao, B.; Ma, J.; He, C.; Pan, L.; Liu, Y.; Alobid, I.; et al. Self-reported taste and smell disorders in patients with COVID-19: Distinct features in China. *Curr. Med. Sci.* **2021**, *41*, 14–23. [CrossRef] [PubMed]
32. Wong, D.K.C.; Gendeh, H.S.; Thong, H.K.; Lum, S.G.; Gendeh, B.S.; Saim, A.; Salina, H. A review of smell and taste dysfunction in COVID-19 patients. *Med. J. Malaysia* **2020**, *75*, 574–581. [PubMed]
33. Dell'Era, V.; Farri, F.; Garzaro, G.; Gatto, M.; Aluffi Valletti, P.; Garzaro, M. Smell and taste disorders during COVID-19 outbreak: Cross-sectional study on 355 patients. *Head Neck* **2020**, *42*, 1591–1596. [CrossRef] [PubMed]
34. Printza, A.; Katotomichelakis, M.; Valsamidis, K.; Metallidis, S.; Panagopoulos, P.; Panopoulou, M.; Petrakis, V.; Constantinidis, J. Smell and Taste Loss Recovery Time in COVID-19 Patients and Disease Severity. *J. Clin. Med.* **2021**, *10*, 966. [CrossRef] [PubMed]
35. Coelho, D.H.; Reiter, E.R.; Budd, S.G.; Shin, Y.; Kons, Z.A.; Costanzo, R.M. Predictors of smell recovery in a nationwide prospective cohort of patients with COVID-19. *Am. J. Otolaryngol.* **2022**, *43*, 103239. [CrossRef]
36. Schwab, J.; Jensen, C.D.; Fjaeldstad, A.W. Sustained Chemosensory Dysfunction during the COVID-19 Pandemic. *ORL* **2021**, *83*, 209–218. [CrossRef]
37. Chary, E.; Carsuzaa, F.; Trijolet, J.-P.; Capitaine, A.-L.; Roncato-Saberan, M.; Fouet, K.; Cazenave-Roblot, F.; Catroux, M.; Allix-Beguec, C.; Dufour, X. Prevalence and recovery from olfactory and gustatory dysfunctions in Covid-19 infection: A prospective multicenter study. *Am. J. Rhinol. Allergy* **2020**, *34*, 686–693. [CrossRef]

38. Chapurin, N.; Totten, D.J.; Chaballout, B.; Brennan, J.; Dennis, S.; Lubner, R.; Chowdhury, N.I.; Turner, J.H.; Trone, T.; Chandra, R.K. Differential olfactory outcomes in COVID-19: A large healthcare system population study. *Int. Forum Allergy Rhinol.* **2022**, *12*, 108–111. [CrossRef]
39. Marouf, N.; Cai, W.; Said, K.N.; Daas, H.; Diab, H.; Chinta, V.R.; Hssain, A.A.; Nicolau, B.; Sanz, M.; Tamimi, F. Association between periodontitis and severity of COVID-19 infection: A case–control study. *J. Clin Periodontol.* **2021**, *48*, 483–491. [CrossRef]
40. Gupta, S.; Mohindra, R.; Singla, M.; Khera, S.; Sahni, V.; Kanta, P.; Soni, R.K.; Kumar, A.; Gauba, K.; Goyal, K.; et al. The clinical association between Periodontitis and COVID-19. *Clin. Oral Investig.* **2021**, *126*, 1361–1374. [CrossRef]
41. Kamel, A.H.M.; Basuoni, A.; Salem, Z.A.; AbuBakr, N. The impact of oral health status on COVID-19 severity, recovery period and C-reactive protein values. *Br. Dent. J.* **2021**, *24*, 1–7. [CrossRef]
42. Cazzolla, A.P.; Lovero, R.; Lo Muzio, L.; Testa, N.F.; Schirinzi, A.; Palmieri, G.; Pozzessere, P.; Procacci, V.; Di Comite, M.; Ciavarella, D. Taste and smell disorders in COVID-19 patients: Role of interleukin-6. *ACS Chem. Neurosci.* **2020**, *11*, 2774–2781. [CrossRef] [PubMed]
43. Worthington, H.V.; MacDonald, L.; Pericic, T.P.; Sambunjak, D.; Johnson, T.M.; Imai, P.; Clarkson, J.E. Home use of interdental cleaning devices, in addition to toothbrushing, for preventing and controlling periodontal diseases and dental caries. *Cochrane Database Syst. Rev.* **2019**, *4*, 1–159. [CrossRef] [PubMed]
44. Graves, R.C.; Disney, J.A.; Stamm, J.W. Comparative effectiveness of flossing and brushing in reducing interproximal bleeding. *J. Periodontol.* **1989**, *60*, 243–247. [CrossRef] [PubMed]
45. Pitones-Rubio, V.; Chávez-Cortez, E.G.; Hurtado-Camarena, A.; González-Rascón, A.; Serafín-Higuera, N. Is periodontal disease a risk factor for severe COVID-19 illness? *Med. Hypotheses* **2020**, *144*, 109969. [CrossRef]
46. Shoemark, D.K.; Allen, S.J. The microbiome and disease: Reviewing the links between the oral microbiome, aging, and Alzheimer's disease. *J. Alzheimer's Dis.* **2015**, *43*, 725–738. [CrossRef]
47. D'Ercole, S.; D'Addazio, G.; Di Lodovico, S.; Traini, T.; Di Giulio, M.; Sinjari, B. Porphyromonas Gingivalis Load is Balanced by 0.20% Chlorhexidine Gel. A Randomized, Double-Blind, Controlled, Microbiological and Immunohistochemical Human Study. *J. Clin. Med.* **2020**, *9*, 284. [CrossRef]
48. Gandhi, G.; Thimmappa, L.; Upadhya, N.; Carnelio, S. Could mouth rinses be an adjuvant in the treatment of SARS-CoV-2 patients? An appraisal with a systematic review. *Int. J. Dent. Hyg.* **2021**, *20*, 136–144. [CrossRef]
49. Helms, J.A.; Della-Fera, M.A.; Mott, A.E.; Frank, M.E. Effects of chlorhexidine on human taste perception. *Arch. Oral Biol.* **1995**, *40*, 913–920. [CrossRef]
50. Hannum, M.E.; Ramirez, V.A.; Lipson, S.J.; Herriman, R.D.; Toskala, A.K.; Lin, C.; Joseph, P.V.; Reed, D.R. Objective Sensory Testing Methods Reveal a Higher Prevalence of Olfactory Loss in COVID-19–Positive Patients Compared to Subjective Methods: A Systematic Review and Meta-Analysis. *Chem. Senses* **2020**, *45*, 865–874. [CrossRef]
51. Printza, A.; Constantinidis, J. The role of self-reported smell and taste disorders in suspected COVID-19. *Eur. Arch. Oto-Rhino-L.* **2020**, *277*, 2625–2630. [CrossRef] [PubMed]
52. Hopkins, C.; Surda, P.; Vaira, L.A.; Lechien, J.R.; Safarian, M.; Saussez, S.; Kumar, N. Six month follow-up of self-reported loss of smell during the COVID-19 pandemic. *Rhinology* **2021**, *59*, 26–31. [CrossRef] [PubMed]
53. Borsetto, D.; Hopkins, C.; Philips, V.; Obholzer, R.; Tirelli, G.; Polesel, J.; Boscolo-Rizzo, P. Self-reported alteration of sense of smell or taste in patients with COVID-19: A systematic review and meta-analysis on 3563 patients. *Rhinology* **2020**, *58*, 430–436. [CrossRef] [PubMed]
54. Harrison, E.M.; Docherty, A.B.; Barr, B.; Buchan, I.; Carson, G.; Drake, T.M.; Dunning, J.; Fairfield, C.J.; Gamble, C.; Green, C.A. Ethnicity and outcomes from COVID-19: The ISARIC CCP-UK prospective observational cohort study of hospitalised patients. *Prepr. Lancet* **2020**, 1–41. [CrossRef]
55. Pan, D.; Sze, S.; Minhas, J.S.; Bangash, M.N.; Pareek, N.; Divall, P.; Williams, C.M.; Oggioni, M.R.; Squire, I.B.; Nellums, L.B. The impact of ethnicity on clinical outcomes in COVID-19: A systematic review. *EClinicalMedicine* **2020**, *23*, 100404. [CrossRef]
56. Hendricks, B.; Paul, R.; Smith, C.; Wen, S.; Kimble, W.; Amjad, A.; Atkins, A.; Hodder, S. Coronavirus testing disparities associated with community level deprivation, racial inequalities, and food insecurity in West Virginia. *Ann. Epidemiol.* **2021**, *59*, 44–49. [CrossRef]

medicina

MDPI

Article

Clinical Experience, Knowledge, Attitudes and Practice of Turkish Pediatric Dentists during the COVID-19 Pandemic

Yelda Koç [1], Serap Akyüz [2] and Damla Akşit-Bıçak [1,*]

1 Department of Pediatric Dentistry, Faculty of Dentistry, Near East University, Nicosia/TRNC, Mersin 10 99138, Turkey; kocyelda1994@gmail.com

2 Department of Pediatric Dentistry, Faculty of Dentistry, Marmara University, İstanbul 34854, Turkey; sakyuz@marmara.edu.tr

* Correspondence: damlaaksit@gmail.com

Abstract: *Background and Objectives*: "Coronavirus Disease 2019" (COVID-19) is a critical public health problem that has affected all fields, including dentistry. The dental management of children has become even more difficult during the COVID-19 pandemic. The purpose of this study was to evaluate the current knowledge, attitudes and practices of Turkish pediatric dentists who have been providing dental treatments to children during the COVID-19 pandemic. *Materials and Methods*: After receiving ethical approval, this cross-sectional study was conducted using the Google Forms online survey instrument. An online questionnaire link was sent to all the members of the Turkish Society of Paediatric Dentistry by e-mail and through social media. Statistical analyses were performed using descriptive statistics and Chi-square test; a *p*-value less than 0.05 was considered statistically significant. *Results:* A total of 200 pediatric dentists participated in this study and most of them (82%) only performed emergency dental treatments, whereas 18.5% performed both emergency and routine dental practices during the COVID-19 pandemic. The vast majority (72.5%) of pediatric dentists prescribed antibiotics and analgesics to their patients who were not cooperative with non-pharmacological behavior management techniques. The findings of the current study showed that the Turkish pediatric dentists had a good level of knowledge about COVID-19, satisfactorily conducted most of the infection control measures before and after the dental treatments, and attached importance to the use of PPEs; however, infection control measures during the dental treatments could be implemented better. *Conclusions:* Along with all precautions, the vaccination of healthcare workers and requesting a recent test result from patients showing a lack of COVID-19 disease before dental appointments could be used as effective infection control measures. Additionally, pediatric dentists should continue to follow local and universal guidelines, and education programmes should be frequently implemented in order to keep their COVID-19 management strategies up to date.

Keywords: anxiety; behavior management; children; coronavirus; COVID-19; infection control; oral health; pediatric dentistry; personal protective equipment; questionnaire

Citation: Koç, Y.; Akyüz, S.; Akşit-Bıçak, D. Clinical Experience, Knowledge, Attitudes and Practice of Turkish Pediatric Dentists during the COVID-19 Pandemic. *Medicina* **2021**, 57, 1140. https://doi.org/10.3390/medicina57111140

Academic Editors: Cesare D'Amico and Pier Paolo Poli

Received: 7 September 2021
Accepted: 15 October 2021
Published: 21 October 2021

1. Introduction

"Coronavirus Disease 2019" (COVID-19) became a critical public health problem after it was first detected in Wuhan, China towards the end of December 2019; the International Committee on Taxonomy of Viruses subsequently reported the name of the new coronavirus responsible for the disease to be SARS-CoV-2. From the beginning of the pandemic, despite all the measures taken to control viral spread, COVID-19 cases emerged worldwide, which indicates that the pandemic has yet to be effectively controlled [1,2]. The SARS-CoV-2 virus is known to be highly contagious, and the possible transmission routes include direct transmission with respiratory droplets through coughing and sneezing, contact with saliva, eye and blood, airborne transmission, indirect transmission via contact with fomites, and fecal–oral transmission [3]. In terms of the risk of COVID-19 exposure, healthcare workers who are constantly in physical contact with patients are among the risk groups. Dentists are recognized to be the highest-risk group among healthcare workers because the required distance for prevention is unobtainable during dental practices, and there is an increased risk of contamination with SARS-CoV-2 through the aerosols and droplets created while performing clinical procedures [1,4,5]. Thus, in order to control viral spread, daily dental practices were reduced/stopped in regions where COVID-19 was widespread, and only emergent/urgent cases were treated [2].

Although COVID-19 vaccinations have been started around the world, widespread immunization requires time and dental professionals are still at high risk of cross infection [5]. Furthermore, pre-symptomatic and asymptomatic patients are both primary sources of SARS-CoV-2 transmission, because at the time of contact, they display no warning signs or symptoms [6]. Pediatric dentists are at higher risk due to the fact that children present nonspecific/mild symptoms, or they could be asymptomatic. Therefore, all child patients and parents should be regarded as potential carriers of COVID- 19 unless confirmed otherwise [7]. Standard infection control procedures applied in daily clinical routines will not be as effective and sufficient for proper protection during the COVID-19 era. The World Health Organization (WHO), the American Dental Association (ADA) and The Centers for Disease Control and Prevention (CDC) recommend that dental practices and hospitals implement rigid and effective infection control protocols to ensure that dentists and dental staff prevent the spread of COVID-19. It is important to prevent the spread of the infectious disease with the precautions applied before the patient comes to the clinic, in the waiting room, during and after the treatment in line with the protocols that dental health personnel must adopt [8]. The WHO has defined this pandemic, of which countries will be at different stages at different times, as having six distinct phases. The planning and treatment options applied in the acute phase of the COVID-19 pandemic may change in the later stages. Therefore, it is difficult to give universal guidelines, which means that it is important to comply with local updated guidelines [7]. At the beginning of the COVID-19 pandemic, the Turkish Association of Paediatric dentistry responded quickly and published guidelines in the Turkish language in order to raise the knowledge and awareness of pediatric dentists in Turkey. Dental teams must follow the instructions and guidelines for better and safer practice during the COVID-19 pandemic [8–10].

According to all this information, the purpose of this study was to evaluate the current knowledge, attitudes and practices of Turkish pediatric dentists who have been providing dental treatments during the COVID-19 pandemic, and to compare and interpret the findings with other studies. The hypothesis of this study was that Turkish pediatric dentists have sufficient knowledge, attitudes and practices about COVID-19. It is predicted that the COVID-19 pandemic will ultimately end like the ones before, but the procedures applied/not applied and experiences evaluated will provide valuable learning for future possible epidemics. Additionally, this study aims to share and transfer the experiences, opinions and needs of Turkish pediatric dentists with other pediatric dentists during the pandemic period, and can therefore be considered as a guiding study in this field.

2. Materials and Methods

Ethical approval for this cross-sectional study was obtained from the Research Ethics Committee of Near East University (YDU/2020/79-1083). The study was conducted using the Google Forms (Google LLC, Menlo Park, CA, USA) online survey instrument. The sampling frame for this study comprised pediatric dentistry specialists and postgraduate students in pediatric dentistry who worked at a state university hospital, state clinic/center/hospital, private university hospital, or private practice/clinic/hospital in Turkey and the Turkish Republic of Northern Cyprus. The self-administered questionnaire prepared in Turkish was firstly piloted on 20 colleagues in order to ensure its clarity and feasibility. The English language version of the questionnaire can be found in Supplementary File S1 (See Supplementary Materials). After making minor changes, the questionnaire was deemed to be comprehensible and no other corrections were required. First of all, the online questionnaire link was sent to all the members of the Turkish Society of Paediatric

Dentistry by e-mail. In addition, pediatric dentists were invited to participate via the Facebook groups of Turkish pediatric dentists as well as WhatsApp. Attempts were made to reach all pediatric dentists working in all cities across the country. Participation in the study was voluntary and identification information was not collected from the participants. Information about the study was included in the form and the participants provided their consent to participate before observing the content of the questionnaire. Thus, participants participated voluntarily in the study. The data collection was performed from June 2020 to September 2020. The questionnaire consists of 40 questions divided into 5 parts in order to assess the knowledge, attitude and practice of Turkish pediatric dentists during the COVID-19 pandemic. The first part of the questionnaire consists of demographic data including the region, gender, age, years of practice, education status and institution of participants. In addition, this part includes questions related to the participants' working experience during the COVID-19 pandemic. The second part of the questionnaire includes questions aimed at assessing the knowledge of the pediatric dentists related to the COVID-19 pandemic. The third part includes the attitudes of participants when encountering a child patient or parent who had signs or symptoms of acute respiratory tract infection, and attitudes towards personal protective equipment (PPE) usage. The fourth part includes emergency situations encountered by participants during the COVID-19 pandemic. The final part includes infection control measures applied before/during/after dental treatments and participants' practice measures when treating non-cooperative children during the COVID-19 pandemic.

Statistical Analysis

In this study, IBM SPSS-21 software was used for statistical analysis. The mean, standard deviation, frequency and percentage distributions of the variables were found with descriptive statistics. With the Chi-square analysis applied to the categorical variables, we observed whether they had a statistically significant difference. As a result of categorical data analysis, those with a p-value less than 0.05 were considered statistically significant and are indicated in the tables.

3. Results

A total of 200 pediatric dentists participated in this study. The majority of the participants were from Turkey (96%), and the remainder were from the Turkish Republic of Northern Cyprus (4%). Additionally, most of the pediatric dentists were female (86%) and only 14% were male. In total, 47% of all pediatric dentists were between 20 and 30 years of age, 40% were 31–40 years of age, 11.5% were 41–50 years of age and only 3 pediatric dentists were 51 years of age or over. In total, 40% of participants were postgraduate students in pediatric dentistry, whereas 60% were pediatric dentistry specialists. Approximately 57% of all pediatric dentists worked in a state institution and 43.5% in a private institution. Among them, 64% of the study participants were academicians working in either state or private university hospitals (Table 1).

The vast majority of pediatric dentists (96%) reported that their working time decreased and 75% continued to live with their family during the COVID-19 lockdown period. None of the participants had a COVID-19 infection prior to participating in the study. Family members of three of the pediatric dentists had COVID-19 infection. Furthermore, 46 pediatric dentists' colleagues (healthcare workers in the same institution) also had COVID-19 infections. Only four female pediatric dentists worked in the filiation team and 55% of all participants had attended a webinar on COVID-19 (Table 2). The highest rate of participation in a webinar programmer was found at private university hospitals (77.4%) ($p < 0.05$).

Table 1. Participants' demographic data.

		n	%
Region	Turkish Republic of Northern Cyprus	8	4
	Turkey	192	96
Gender	Male	28	14
	Female	172	86
Age	20–30	94	47
	31–40	80	40
	41–50	23	11.5
	51–60	2	1
	≥60	1	0.5
Years of Practice In Pediatric Dentistry	0–5	92	46
	6–10	56	28
	11–20	46	23
	21–30	5	2.5
	≥31	1	0.5
Education Status	Pediatric Dentistry Specialist	120	60
	Postgraduate student in Pediatric Dentistry	80	40
Institution	State University Hospital	97	48.5
	State Clinic/Center/Hospital	16	8
	Private University Hospital	31	15.5
	Private Practice/Clinic/Hospital	56	28

Table 2. Participants' working experience during the COVID-19 pandemic period.

Questions	Yes (*n*/%)	No (*n*/%)
Did you continue to live with your family while working during the COVID-19 lockdown period?	150 (75)	50 (25)
Have you had COVID-19 infection?	0	200 (100)
Have any of your family members had a COVID-19 infection?	3 (1.5)	197 (98.5)
Have any dentists and healthcare personnel working in your institution had a COVID-19 infection?	46 (23)	154 (77)
Have you attended a webinar on COVID-19?	110 (55)	90 (45)
Have you worked in the filiation team?	4 (2)	196 (98)
Did your working time decrease during this period?	192 (96)	8 (4)

When pediatric dentists were asked about the symptoms of COVID-19, almost all of them knew the main symptoms, such as fever (99.5%), shortness of breath (98%) and dry cough (97%). Approximately 90% of all participants knew about asymptomatic infection joint or muscle pain (82.5%) and sore throat (79%). The least known symptoms were diarrhea (66.5%), sore eyes (51%), vomiting (46.5%), runny nose (37.5%) and skin rash (35%). Only 29.5% of all participants reported all of these as symptoms of COVID-19. Furthermore, pediatric dentists were asked about the transmission routes of COVID-19. All pediatric dentists knew about direct transmission via respiratory droplets through coughing and sneezing. Some participants listed contact with saliva (94%), indirect transmission through contact with fomites (89.5%), airborne transmission (87.5%) and contact with the eye (85%). The least known transmission routes were fecal–oral transmission (58%) and blood (53.5%) (Table 3).

Table 3. Knowledge of participants related to symptoms and transmission routes of COVID-19.

		n (%)
Symptoms	Fever	199 (99.5)
	Dry cough	194 (97.0)
	Shortness of breath	196 (98.0)
	Diarrhea	133 (66.5)
	Vomiting	93 (46.5)
	Runny nose	75 (37.5)
	Sore throat	158 (79.0)
	Sore eyes	102 (51.0)
	Skin Rash	70 (35.0)
	Joint or muscle pain	165 (82.5)
	Without Symptoms	181 (90.5)
	All of them	59 (29.5)
Transmission Routes	Direct transmission through: Coughing, sneezing	200 (100)
	Saliva	188 (94.0)
	Eye	170 (85)
	Blood	107 (53.5)
	Fecal–oral transmission	116 (58)
	Airborne transmission	175 (87.5)
	Indirect transmission through contact with fomites	179 (89.5)

All pediatric dentists stated that information such as "Dental Healthcare workers are at high risk of being infected with COVID-19 when compared with the general population," and "Aerosol and droplets formed during dental treatment, increase the risk of spread and transmission of COVID-19" were true. Regarding other statements, the vast majority of pediatric dentists said that the information was true, as shown in Table 4. However, 75% of participants said that the statement "Virus detection from saliva samples can be a diagnostic method" was true, and 57.5% of participants acknowledged that the statement "Protection with mask is not recommended for children under 2 years of age and children unable to remove mask without assistance" was true (Table 4).

Common infection control practices used in the participants' institutions before dental treatment included "establishing pre-control staff at the institution for screening the temperature with non-contact thermometer and checking appropriate use of face masks" (86.4%), "posting signs and posters at the entrance of the waiting room and in the areas visible to patients to provide instructions about social distance, hand hygiene and respiratory hygiene measures" (81.8%) and "in the waiting room, applying social distance rules, and asking some of the patients to wait outside the building if necessary" (81.3%) respectively. Approximately 70% of the participants obtained medical and dental anamnesis from pediatric patients and parents. Other infection control measures were used at rates varying between 70 and 80%. Approximately 57% of participants reported removing toys or reading materials that could be touched by other children in their institutions. All infection control measures used in the institutions of participants before dental treatment are shown in Table 5.

Table 4. Knowledge of participants related to the statements about COVID-19.

Statement	Answer		
	True	False	I Don't Know
Dental Healthcare workers are at high risk of being infected with COVID-19 when compared with the general population.	200 (100.0)	0 (0.0)	0 (0.0)
A single negative PCR test result does not exclude the possibility of COVID-19 infection among suspected patients.	195 (97.5)	3 (1.5)	2 (1.0)
Aerosol and droplets formed during dental treatment increase the risk of spread and transmission of COVID-19.	200 (100.0)	0 (0.0)	0 (0.0)
Pediatric patients present additional risks of transmission due to the use of appliances, difficulty in using personal protective equipment, and coming to the clinic with one or more parents.	197 (98.5)	3 (1.5)	0 (0.0)
Children can be asymptomatic or present mild, non-specific symptoms.	191 (95.5)	4 (2.0)	5 (2.5)
Asymptomatic patients and pre-symptomatic patients in the incubation period could be carriers of COVID-19.	198 (99.0)	0 (0.0)	2 (1.0)
All child patients and parents should be considered as potential carriers of COVID-19 unless proved otherwise.	194 (97.0)	5 (2.5)	1 (0.5)
Virus detection from saliva samples can be a diagnostic method.	150 (75.0)	11 (5.5)	39 (19.5)
Protection with mask is not recommended for children under 2 years of age and children unable to remove mask without assistance	115 (57.5)	27 (13.5)	58 (29.0)

Table 5. Infection control practices used in institutions of participants before dental treatment.

	n	(%)
Posting visual public notices for all visitors to the building entrances including signs and symptoms of COVID-19 and warning not to enter into the facility if they are exhibiting any of these symptoms.	156	78.8
Triaging dental patients by phone or online conferencing in order to decide the urgency of dental condition and COVID-19 risk status of patients.	120	60
Establishing pre-control staff at the institution for screening the temperature with a non-contact thermometer and checking appropriate use of face masks.	171	86.4
Questioning the travel history and presence of symptoms of everyone before entering the building.	143	72.2
Taking medical and dental anamnesis from pediatric patients and parents.	141	70.5
Placing hand sanitizer and asking children and parents to use it while entering the clinic.	145	73.2
Posting signs and posters at the entrance of the waiting room and in the areas visible to patients to provide instructions about social distancing, hand hygiene and respiratory hygiene measures.	162	81.8
Scheduling appointments of patients at times not close to each other in order to prevent crowding and establishment of the time required for disinfection and ventilation.	142	71.7
In the waiting room, applying social distance rules, and asking some of the patients to wait outside the building if necessary.	161	81.3
Ensuring that the pediatric patient comes to the clinic with a single accompanying person.	135	67.5
Removing toys or reading materials that could be touched by other children.	112	56.6

Forty-four pediatric dentists reported that they had encountered a child patient or parent who had signs and symptoms of acute respiratory infection. Among them, 14 (31.8%) pediatric dentists referred these patients to hospital after treating the patient, 28 (63.6%) referred the patients to the hospital with a medical mask without conducting the treatment and 2 (4.5%) refused to treat the patients and asked them to leave the clinic. On the other hand, 156 pediatric dentists reported that they had not encountered a child patient or parent who had signs and symptoms of acute respiratory infection. However, if they were faced with such a situation, 24 (15.4%) pediatric dentists said they would refer these patients to hospital after treating the patient, 110 (70.5%) said they would refer the patient to a hospital with a medical mask without conducting the treatment, and 22 (14.1%) would refuse to treat the patient and would ask them to leave the clinic (Table 6) ($p < 0.05$).

When the pediatric dentists were asked about the dental procedures they practiced during the COVID-19 pandemic, the vast majority (82%) said they only performed emergency dental treatments, whereas 37 (18.5%) performed both emergency and routine dental practices. The most common emergency situations were reported as severe pain caused by pulpal inflammation (94%), abscess or bacterial infection causing localized pain and extraoral swelling (86.5%), luxations, dental avulsions (41%), dental fractures causing pain or soft tissue injuries caused by trauma (35.5%), and the aerosol-free treatment of temporary restoration loss/fractures (27%), respectively. Other emergency situations are also presented in Table 7.

Table 6. Attitudes of participants when faced with a child patient or parent who had signs and symptoms of acute respiratory infection.

		What Would Your Attitude Be in Such a Situation?				
		I Refer Them to the Hospital after Treating the Patient (*n*/%)	**I Refer the Patient to the Hospital with Medical Mask without Conducting Treatment (*n*/%)**	**I Refuse to Treat the Patient and Ask Them to Leave the Clinic (*n*/%)**	**Total (*n*/%)**	***p***
Have you encountered a child patient or parent who had signs and symptoms of acute respiratory infection?	Yes	14 (31.8)	28 (63.6)	2 (4.5)	44 (100)	0.021
	No	24 (15.4)	110 (70.5)	22 (14.1)	156 (100)	

Pearson Chi-square test.

Table 7. Emergency situations encountered by participants during the COVID-19 pandemic period.

		n	%
Dental procedures performed during the COVID-19 lockdown period	Emergency dental treatments only	164	82
	Routine dental practices	6	3
	Both of them	37	18.5
Emergency dental treatment performed during the COVID-19 lockdown period	Severe pain caused by pulpal inflammation	188	94
	Pericoronitis, pain in the third molar region	0	0
	Abscess or bacterial infection causing localized pain and extraoral swelling	173	86.5
	Dental fractures causing pain or soft tissue injuries caused by trauma	71	35.5
	Luxations, dental avulsions	82	41
	Acute and painful lesions/ulcerations of the oral mucosa	39	19.5
	Dental treatments of oncology patients who are scheduled for organ transplantation	21	10.5
	Intraoral/extraoral infections that may compromise the patient's airway	19	9.5
	Dental treatments required before general medical procedures	18	8
	Aerosol-free treatment of temporary restoration loss/fractures	54	27
	Maxillofacial trauma	17	8.5
	Adjustment of the orthodontic apparatus if it has caused ulceration or pain on the oral mucosa	41	20.5
	Life-threatening or uncontrolled oral tissue bleeding	6	3
	Suture removal	6	3
	Breakage of space maintainer	1	0.5

When the pediatric dentists were asked about PPE usage, scrubs (87%), surgical masks (90%), face shields (83%), goggles (71%), disposable surgical gowns (70.5%), disposable gloves (92.5%), and disposable medical caps (83.5%) were found to be used widely in both aerosol-generating procedures (AGPs) and non-AGPs. N95 respirators were used only in AGPs by 21%, and used in both AGPs and non-AGPs by 51%. FFP2 respirators were used in only AGPs by 16%, and were used in both AGPs and non-AGPs by 43.5%. Some PPEs were reported to have never been used by participants, such as P100 respirators (85.5%), elastomeric half masks (79%), FFP3 respirators (64%), waterproof shoe covers (61.5%) and disposable protective coveralls (58.5%). All used PPEs are displayed in Table 8.

Table 8. Participants' attitudes towards personal protective equipment (PPE) usage.

	Only in Aerosol-Generating Procedures		Used in Both Aerosol Generating and Non-Aerosol Generating Procedures		Never Used	
	n	%	*n*	%	*n*	%
Scrubs	11	5.5	174	87	15	7.5
Surgical mask	14	7	180	90	6	3.0
N95 respirator	42	21	102	51	56	28
P100 respirator	10	5	19	9.5	171	85.5
FFP2 respirator	32	16	87	43.5	81	40.5
FFP3 respirator	18	9	54	27	128	64
Goggles	26	13	142	71	32	16
Face shield	29	14.5	166	83	5	2.5
Elastomeric half mask	9	4.5	33	16.5	158	79
Disposable surgical gown	25	12.5	141	70.5	34	17
Disposable protective coverall	35	17.5	48	24	7	58.5
Disposable gloves	14	7	185	92.5	1	0.5
Disposable medical cap	23	11.5	167	83.5	10	5
Waterproof shoe cover	13	6.5	64	32	123	61.5

One hundred and seventy-four (87%) pediatric dentists thought that their PPE increased the anxiety levels of children. In total, 110 (55%) participants explained their PPE to children by saying that they were wearing an astronaut suit, 52 (26%) said they had become a superhero, 119 (59.5%) explained the reason, and 43 (21.5%) said they did not give any explanation. One hundred and sixty-eight (84%) participants paid attention to the proper order for donning and doffing their PPE, but only 55% of the participants paid attention to removing their own and other dental healthcare workers' PPE in a separate isolation room. In total, 102/168 pediatric dentists who paid attention to the proper order for donning and doffing their PPE also paid attention to removing their own and other dental healthcare workers' PPE in a separate isolation room ($p < 0.05$). Approximately 80% of participants encountered burning, stinging, itching, dryness, etc. on their skin due to frequent hand cleaning and the long-term use of PPE. Furthermore, 141/168 (83.9%) pediatric dentists who paid attention to the proper order for donning and doffing their PPE also encountered a situation such as burning, stinging, itching or dryness on their skin due to frequent hand cleaning and the long-term use of PPE ($p < 0.05$) (Table 9).

Table 9. Participants' attitudes related to PPE.

		n	%
How did you explain your personal protective equipment to children?	I wore an astronaut suit	110	55
	I became a superhero	52	26
	I explained the reason	119	59.5
	Did not give any explanation	43	21.5
	Other	4	2
Do you think that personal protective equipment increases the anxiety levels of children?	Yes	174	87.0
	No	26	13.0
Have you paid attention to proper order for donning and doffing your personal protective equipment?	Yes	168	84.0
	No	32	16.0
Have you paid attention to removing your and other dental healthcare workers' protective equipment in a separate isolation room?	Yes	110	55.0
	No	90	45.0
Have you ever encountered a situation such as burning, stinging, itching, dryness on your skin due to frequent hand cleaning and long-term use of personal protective equipment?	Yes	161	80.5
	No	39	19.5

The infection control practices used by the participants during treatment are displayed in Table 10. In total, 62% of all participants used manual instrumentation, 59.5% continued to make patients' appointments via phone, WhatsApp and social networks, and 56.5% treated only one patient in a room. Furthermore, 39% of all participants did not let the parent into the treatment room, while 35.5% applied interim therapeutic restorations (ITR), 34.5% used high-volume saliva ejectors, 33.5% applied preprocedural oxidative or antimicrobial mouth rinse, 29.5% used four-handed dentistry, 29% used an aerosol box and 24.5% used slow-speed handpieces. Rarely used methods included dental extraoral suction systems (6.5%), rubber-dam (6%), chemomechanical caries removal systems (4.5%), two before three after hand hygiene (4.5%), and the use of a dental handpiece with anti-retraction function (2.5%). Only 23.5% of the participants reported that they used an air water syringe, and 19% used a high-speed handpiece and ultrasonic instruments (Table 10). When the pediatric dentists were asked about obtaining X-rays from child patients during the COVID-19 pandemic period, 59.5% stated that they obtained only panoramic radiographs, 24% obtained both panoramic and intraoral radiographs, 4% obtained only intraoral radiographs and 12.5% did not obtain any radiographs (Table 10). Approximately 65% of pediatric dentists reported that they had pediatric patients who were not cooperative with non-pharmacological behavior management techniques during the COVID-19 lockdown period (Table 10).

When pediatric dentists were asked about their treatment measures applied to children who were not cooperative with non-pharmacological behavior management techniques during the COVID-19 pandemic period, the vast majority (72.5%) reported that they prescribed antibiotics and analgesics to their pediatric patients. In total, 33% of participants said they conducted atraumatic restorative treatment (ART), 11.5% applied general anesthesia and 8% used physical restraining in order to control children's sudden movements during dental treatment. It was found that the Hall technique, chemomechanical caries removal, sedation applications, laser applications and silver diamine fluoride (SDF) applications were not widely used (Table 11).

Table 10. Infection control practices used by the participants during treatment.

		n	%
Which measures did you use while treating pediatric patients during the COVID-19 lockdown?	Not letting the parent into the treatment room	78	39.0
	Treatment of only one patient in a room	113	56.5
	Aerosol box	58	29.0
	Rubber dam	12	6.0
	High-speed handpiece and ultrasonic instruments	38	19.0
	Manual instruments, hand instrumentation	125	62.5
	Slow-speed handpieces	49	24.5
	Dental handpiece with anti-retraction function	5	2.5
	Chemomechanical caries removal	9	4.5
	Interim therapeutic restorations	71	35.5
	Four-handed technique	59	29.5
	Air water syringe	47	23.5
	Preprocedural oxidative or antimicrobial mouth-rinse	67	33.5
	High-volume saliva ejectors	69	34.5
	Dental extraoral suction system	13	6.5
	Providing two before three after hand hygiene	9	4.5
	Continuing patients' control appointments via phone, WhatsApp and social networks	119	59.5
Have you obtained X-rays from your pediatric patients during the COVID-19 lockdown?	Yes, both intraoral and panoramic radiographs	48	24
	Yes, intraoral radiographs only	8	4
	Yes, only panoramic radiographs	119	59.5
	No	25	12.5
During the COVID-19 lockdown, did you have a pediatric patient who was not cooperative with non-pharmacological behavior management techniques?	Yes	129	64.5
	No	71	35.5

Table 11. Participants' practice measures used with children who were not cooperative with non-pharmacological behavior management techniques during the COVID-19 pandemic period.

	n	(%)
Use of antibiotics and analgesics	145	72.5
Inhalation sedation	9	4.5
Enteral sedation	2	1.0
Parenteral sedation	2	1.0
General anesthesia	23	11.5
Physical restraining	16	8.0
Atraumatic restorative treatment	66	33.0
Hall technique	9	4.5
Chemomechanical caries removal	7	3.5
Laser applications	1	0.5
Silver diamine fluoride application	6	3.0
None of them	28	14.0

Infection control practices used by the participants after treatment are displayed in Table 12. The infection control measures used were stated as ventilation of the treatment room after each patient (85%), regular disinfection of common areas, door handles, chairs and tables with 0.1% sodium hypochlorite (72.5%), disinfection of reusable PPE with 70% alcohol after each usage (68%), disinfection of commonly used areas such as dental unit, dental light, dental X-ray machine after each patient with 70% ethanol, 0.1% sodium hypochlorite, or 0.5% hydrogen peroxide (66.5%), discharge of medical waste in accordance with the legislation (64.5%), cleaning and sterilization of the dental hand instruments immediately after usage (58.5%) and asking children and parents to use hand sanitizer when leaving the clinic (52.5%). Rarely used measures included fogging system for disinfection (35.5%), ventilation and air-purifying system (16%), ultraviolet radiation system (9%), and high-efficacy particulate air (HEPA) filtration system (7.0%).

Table 12. Infection control practices used by the participants/institutions after treatment.

	n	(%)
Asking children and parents to use hand sanitizer when leaving the clinic.	104	52.5
Disinfecting reusable personal protective equipment with 70% alcohol after each usage.	136	68
Disinfection of commonly used areas such as dental unit, dental light, dental X-ray machine after each patient with 70% ethanol, 0.1% sodium hypochlorite, or 0.5% hydrogen peroxide.	133	66.5
Cleaning and sterilization of the dental hand instruments immediately after usage.	117	58.5
Ventilation of the treatment room after each patient.	170	85.0
Regular disinfection of common areas, door handles, chairs and tables with 0.1% sodium hypochlorite.	145	72.5
Discharge of medical waste in accordance with the legislation.	129	64.5
Fogging system for disinfection.	71	35.5
High-efficacy particulate air (HEPA) filtration system.	14	7.0
Ventilation and air-purifying System.	32	16
Ultraviolet radiation system.	18	9

4. Discussion

This cross-sectional study, which assessed the knowledge, attitudes and practices of pediatric dentists during the COVID-19 lockdown period, is the first to be conducted among Turkish pediatric dentists and one of the first studies of its kind worldwide [11–14]. Additionally, this study revealed real-life evidence on the efficacy of the guidelines and protocols among Turkish pediatric dentists. In this study, most of the participating pediatric dentists were female (86%) and only 14% were male, which indicates that the number of female pediatric dentists is higher than males in Turkey. Similar results were also reported by other studies [11–14]. In addition, the vast majority of participating pediatric dentists (87%) were young, between the ages of 20 and 40. This might be because of the web-based nature of the study, and the rate of participation of young people in such studies could be higher because they spend more time on the internet. Moreover, 64% of the study participants were academicians working in either state or private university hospitals; thus, because of their interest in scientific studies, their participation rate might be higher than others.

Along with the closures that occurred in many parts of the world during the COVID-19 lockdown period, dental clinics were also affected, and many of them were closed [15]. The results of this study show that the vast majority of pediatric dentists' (96%) working time decreased during this period. Similarly, practice closures or reductions have been reported by previous studies [16–23]. Some reports in the literature have demonstrated that most dentists accepted that they were at high risk and were afraid of contracting/spreading the COVID-19 virus to their families [2,18,24,25]. Nevertheless, in this study, 75% of all pediatric dentists continued to live with their families during the COVID-19 lockdown period. Similar findings were presented by Duruk et al. [2] and Hua et al. [20]. The results of this study reveal that, at the time of our survey study, pediatric dentists and people in their surroundings had low rates of COVID-19 disease. Similar observations were also reported in previous studies [17,22–24,26]. The reason for this result might be the closure of clinics at the beginning of the pandemic and the disruption to interpersonal contact.

The present study showed that 55% of all participants attended a webinar on COVID-19. Previous studies [2,11,13,20,27–32] showed the various rates of attendance of dentists at an education program on COVID-19. Contrary to these results, some researchers reported insufficient training [12,14,33,34]. In this context, continuous training programs are necessary in order to acquire perfect infection management skills for the present and future possible pandemics.

In order to provide adequate protection, dentists and other healthcare personnel should be aware of the symptoms and transmission routes of COVID-19 disease. Clinical findings of COVID-19 infection in children involve runny nose, fever, shortness of breath, dry cough, muscle or joint pain and gastrointestinal symptoms such as vomiting and diarrhea [35]. Most of the pediatric dentists in this study knew the main symptoms, such as fever, shortness of breath, dry cough, joint or muscle pain, sore throat and diarrhea. However, it was detected that non-respiratory symptoms were not well known. Nearly half of the pediatric dentists knew about sore eyes and vomiting. The least known symptoms were runny nose and skin rash. Cai et al. [36] reported that some COVID-19-positive children did not present respiratory symptoms as the first manifestation. Therefore, pediatric dentists should have information about non-respiratory symptoms as well the main symptoms of COVID-19. Nevertheless, most of the pediatric dentists in this study were aware of the possible symptoms of COVID-19 that accompany an infection, in accordance with the previous studies [11,12,29–33,37–39]. Furthermore, most children can be asymptomatic, and do not show any warning signs to the practitioners; thus, asymptomatic and pre-symptomatic children significantly increase the transmission [6,40,41]. In this study, it was found that the vast majority of pediatric dentists (90%) knew that COVID-19 disease could be asymptomatic.

The potential COVID-19 transmission routes comprise direct transmission with respiratory droplets through coughing and sneezing, contact with saliva, eyes and blood, indirect transmission through contact with fomites, and fecal–oral and airborne transmissions [3]. The results of this study reveal that transmission routes are well-known among Turkish pediatric dentists, but the least known transmission routes were fecal–oral transmission and blood. The aerosols generated during dental treatment, including blood, saliva and organic particles, cause air and environmental pollution in the clinic. Thus, it is very important for dentists to know that the virus can be transmitted through blood. When dental treatments creating aerosols are conducted, the spread of viruses, bacteria and germs increases because of the presence of blood and saliva [32]. In the study of Bekes et al. [12], more than 80% of pediatric dentists specified all the factors related to close contact with the infection. In another study by Moheb et al. [13], most pediatric dentists knew the droplet (92.6%) and direct contact (65.8%) modes, but only 34.2% identified the indirect contact mode of infection. Maru et al. [11] reported that 66.7% of Indian pediatric dentists were informed about the transmission routes of COVID-19 infection. Most of the pediatric dentists in this study were knowledgeable about the possible COVID-19 transmission routes, which is in line with other studies [29–32,34,37–39,42,43] in the literature. On the contrary, Nasser et al. [33] reported poor knowledge among dentists in Lebanon related to transmission routes of the disease. Being conscious about the symptoms and transmission routes of COVID-19 is critical in order to not neglect the necessary measures during dental procedures.

The level of knowledge of participating pediatric dentists was also evaluated by asking about some important information related with COVID-19 besides the symptoms and transmission routes. Among these, all pediatric dentists accepted that dental healthcare workers are at high risk of being infected with COVID-19 when compared with the general population. Most of the dentists in other reports [12,17,26,31–33,44,45] expressed a similar opinion. Estrich et al. [26] declared that non-clinical activities in the dental office could be a reason for transmission. Banakar et al. [5] stated that dental settings contribute to the transmission of COVID-19 through AGPs. In the current study, all pediatric dentists stated that the statement "Aerosol and droplets formed during dental treatment, increase the risk of spread and transmission of COVID-19" was true. Similarly, in the study of Candeiro et al. [39], 98.5% of the participants affirmed that COVID-19 can be transmitted during dental procedures. Furthermore, in another study [31], nearly 74% of participants said that the dental treatments performed by using high-speed handpieces and ultrasonic scalers elevate the risk of virus transmission because of the creation of aerosol particles.

In this study, nearly all pediatric dentists knew that children can be asymptomatic or present mild, nonspecific symptoms, and accepted that asymptomatic/pre-symptomatic patients in the incubation period could be carriers of COVID-19. Similar observations were reported by Bekes et al. [12], Arora et al. [31], and Maru et al. [11]. On the contrary, in the study of Nasser et al. [33], 88.3% of Lebanese dentists agreed with the statement "Coronavirus does not infect children". Ahmed et al. [34] reported that most of the participants (78.7%) in their study knew that COVID-19 affects people from older age groups, but only 7.6% knew that infants could also be affected. In the study of Martina et al. [24], the majority of dentists accepted that adolescents and children had the same infection risk as adults. Asymptomatic carriers are the main cause of transmission and, if present, these mild symptoms can be easily confused with flu-like symptoms [31]. For this reason, dentists should consider each patient as COVID-19-positive and take the necessary precautions during dental treatments, as nearly all pediatric dentists confirmed this statement in our study. Furthermore, pediatric patients present additional risks of transmission due to the use of appliances, the difficulty in using PPE, and patients coming to the clinic with one or more parent [46]. The results of this study show that 98.5% of pediatric dentists accepted that this information was true.

It is important to have knowledge of the fact that wearing any type of mask is not recommended for children younger than 2 years of age and children unable to remove their mask without assistance. This is because of their small airways and the increased risk of suffocation [47]. Unfortunately, only 57.5% of participants knew this information in our study. Moreover, among the detection methods of COVID-19, nucleic acid-based detection has become reliable and rapid, although a negative result does not mean that the possibility of COVID-19 infection can be rejected, and it should not be considered as the only criteria for patient management or treatment determination [48]. In the current study, nearly all pediatric dentists knew that a single negative PCR test result does not exclude the possibility of COVID-19 infection among suspected patients. Together with this, saliva could be a fast, inexpensive and non-invasive method of detecting COVID-19 disease [49]. In this study, 75% of participants agreed that the statement "Virus detection from saliva samples can be a diagnostic method" was true.

Considering the present study, the vast majority of pediatric dentists had a good level of knowledge about COVID-19 disease. Although questions evaluating the knowledge level of dentists might be different among studies, previous studies have also found that dentists have a good knowledge level as well [11,12,28,30,34,50]. The results of this study showed that the knowledge level of dentists about COVID-19 is sufficient, but it is recommended that information should be continuously updated in the following periods according to the course of the disease, in order to optimize the management of COVID-19.

Many countries have restricted dental treatments and only permitted emergency treatments during the COVID-19 lockdown period; however, these arrangements were not long-sighted or economical. Thus, infection control regimens should be revised for the current pandemic and subsequently for the long-term endemic period [51]. There are important infection control measures and precautions that each institution should implement before conducting dental treatments [51–53]. Among these, "posting visual public notices for all visitors at the building entrances including signs and symptoms of COVID-19 and warning not to enter the facility if they are exhibiting any of these symptoms" was implemented by nearly 79% of pediatric dentists' institutions. In addition, posting signs and posters at the entrance of the waiting room and in the areas visible to patients to provide instructions about social distancing, hand hygiene and respiratory hygiene measures was conducted by 81.8% of participants. Similarly, Moheb et al. [13] reported that nearly 53% of dentists printed and placed patients' instructions for cough etiquette and social distancing. As another infection control measure, 60% of participants triaged dental patients by phone or online conferencing in order to obtain information on children's health and COVID-19 risk status, and to determine emergency dental problems in the current study. Furthermore, nearly the same percentage of pediatric dentists completed their patients' control appointments via phone, WhatsApp and social networks. Similarly, triaging dental patients was reported to have been conducted in previous studies [13,14,16,17,22,23,42,44,54,55].

Along with the infection control measures, employing pre-control staff at the institution for screening temperatures with a non-contact thermometer and checking the apropriate use of face masks was conducted by 86.4% of participants in the current study. This finding was found to be consistent with those of previous studies [14,18,21,26,27,54,56], but it contradicted the findings of Cagetti et al. [17], Consolo et al. [22] and Izzetti et al. [16], where taking the temperature of the patients before dental treatments was a practice that was implemented at a lower rate. Moreover, questioning the travel history and presence of symptoms of everyone before entering the building was conducted by 72.2% of participants in this study. Similarly, Ates et al. [54] reported that before the dental treatments, 73.4% asked if the patient had symptoms, shortness of breath, cough or fever. Contrarily, in the study of Duruk et al. [2], only 4% of participants conducted this procedure. In addition, nearly 70% of pediatric dentists obtained medical and dental anamnesis from children and parents. The dental management of children with special needs and medically compromised children requires careful consideration of their health condition as well during the COVID-19 pandemic era [40].

As another critical infection control measure, hand washing and/or using alcohol-based disinfectants before entering the operating room should be encouraged for all patients [32]. In our study, placing hand sanitizer and asking children and parents to use it when entering the clinic was conducted by 73.2% of participants. Moheb et al. [13] reported that nearly 93% of dentists offered alcohol hand sanitizers to patients and parents. In another study, asking patients to wash their hands was reported by nearly 78% of dentists in North Italy [17] and nearly 65% of dental hygienists in Italy [42]. According to Al-Khalifa et al. [56], 68% of participants reported patients' hand washing/sanitizing before going into the waiting area. However, in the study of Putrino et al. [32], the usage of alcohol disinfectant at the entrance for hand cleaning was reported by only 9.7% of participants. Additionally, scheduling the appointments of patients at times not close to each other in order to prevent crowding and the establishment of the time required for disinfection and ventilation was conducted by 71.7% of participants in our study. This finding is in accordance with the studies conducted by Bekes et al. [12], Cagetti et al. [17], Nasser et al. [33], and Consolo et al. [22]. Furthermore, applying social distancing rules in the waiting room, and asking some of the patients to wait outside the building if necessary, was conducted by 81.3% of participants. Similar procedures were also applied in previous studies [13,14,16,17,23,42,56].

Ensuring that the pediatric patient comes to the clinic with a single accompanying person was reported by 67.5% of participants in this study. Similarly, Moheb et al. [13] reported that nearly 97% of dentists instructed parents that only one accompanying person was allowed with the child. The results of the study conducted by Bekes et al. [12] showed that nearly 78% of dentists allowed children to come to their appointments with only one accompanying person. According to Allevi et al. [21], one of the most frequently used methods was limiting relatives' visits (96%). Izzetti et al. [16] also reported that 97.5% of participants discouraged the presence of accompanying people. Lastly, removing toys or reading materials that could be touched by other children was conducted by 56.6% of participants in this study. In line with our findings, dentists in other studies [13,14,16,17,42] removed reading materials and other materials that are not easily disinfected. According to this information, it is obvious that the vast majority of pediatric dentists in this study satisfactorily conducted most of the mentioned infection control measures before the dental treatments. However, procedures including removing all unnecessary materials in the dental office, triaging patients and only allowing one person to accompany the child could be better implemented.

CDC and ADA guidance reports that active COVID-19 patients and patients exposed to a person with confirmed/suspected COVID-19 infection, and patients who had been in countries under a travel ban, should not be treated in dental clinics. If emergency/urgent dental care is needed, patients should be assessed for COVID-19 symptoms. Patients who have/do not have fever together with signs and symptoms of acute respiratory infection need to go to the emergency department of a hospital for infection control and treatment measures. If patients do not have fever and signs and symptoms of acute respiratory infection, or only have fever, they can be treated at the dental clinic because the fever might because of a dental infection [6,52]. In the current study, among the pediatric dentists who encountered a child patient or parent who had signs and symptoms of acute respiratory infection, nearly 64% of them referred the patient to a hospital with a medical mask without conducting the treatment in accordance with the ADA and CDC guidelines, and 4.5% refused to treat the patient and asked them to leave the clinic. Among pediatric dentists who did not encounter a child patient or parent who had signs and symptoms of acute respiratory infection, nearly 70% reported that they referred the patient to a hospital with a medical mask without conducting the treatment, in line with the recommendations, and nearly 14% refused to treat the patient and asked them to leave the clinic. Moheb et al. [13] reported that nearly 55% of dentists prescribed medication if they faced a patient with fever and no other signs/symptoms of COVID-19 infection. Moreover, researchers also reported that 40% of dentists also chose to control the situation with medicines if they were faced with a patient who did not report any symptoms but the dentist observed signs of respiratory illness. Similarly, Nasser et al. [33] showed that more than 80% of the dentists were afraid to treat a patient suspected of or confirmed as having COVID-19. In another study by Khader et al. [38], nearly 44% of dentists declared that they would refer the patient to the hospital without conducting treatment, 4.6% declared that they would refuse to treat the patient and ask them to leave the clinic, and nearly half of the dentists would treat the patient and ask them to go to the hospital when they were faced with a patient coughing and sneezing in their dental clinic. Furthermore, in the study of De Stefani et al. [29], nearly 66% of dentists said they would have refused to treat a patient suffering from a runny nose and cough.

In our study, among the pediatric dentists who encountered a child patient or parent who had signs and symptoms of acute respiratory infection, nearly 32% of them referred these patients to a hospital after treating the patient. Among dentists who did not encounter a child patient or parent who had signs and symptoms of acute respiratory infection, nearly 15% reported that they referred these patients to a hospital after treating them. Similarly, in the study of Bekes et al. [12], 31% of pediatric dentists had self-confidence in the treatment of suspected COVID infections. Hua et al. [20] reported that nearly 64% of participants wanted to treat patients with suspected/confirmed COVID-19 infection. Maru et al. [11] reported that 57.5% of pediatric dentists had self-confidence in conducting treatment on children with suspected COVID-19; however, 10.80% of pediatric dentists exhibited no confidence. The results of the study conducted by Arora et al. [31] showed that nearly 42% of dentists displayed a positive attitude towards providing emergency dental treatment to COVID19-positive patients. In the study of Becker et al. [44], it was recommended that COVID-19-positive patients' dental treatments should be performed at dental university hospitals in isolated rooms. Thus, it was strongly recommended that emergent COVID-19 positive/suspected patients should be treated in the hospital's separate airborne infection isolation rooms (AIIR), which are kept under negative pressure with an HEPA filter. In addition, high-level protection with full usage of PPE is needed.

Furthermore, healthcare workers should follow donning and doffing procedures. It is important to know that COVID-19-positive/suspected patients should not be treated in a room that recirculates air within the hospital and without appropriate PPE usage [27,57]. Most of the pediatric dentists in this study referred or considered referring patients who had signs and symptoms of acute respiratory infection to a hospital with medical masks without conducting the treatment, or refused to treat the patient. If the necessary facilities such as AIIR including an HEPA filter are not available, this approach is more acceptable than conducting dental treatments of COVID-19-positive/suspected patients in the same environment with other patients.

When pediatric dentists were asked about the dental procedures they performed during the COVID-19 lockdown period, the vast majority (82%) said they only performed emergency dental treatments according to Turkish government recommendations. In line with the current report, the majority of previous studies [2,12,13,15,16,22,30,32,39,54,55,58,59] showed that dental practices were reduced to urgent/emergency procedures during the COVID-19 quarantine period. However, Nibali et al. [60] reported that most of the practitioners had completely ended all dental activities. Emergent dental situations include facial swellings, severe dental/facial pain that cannot be controlled with advised medications, traumatic dental injuries such as severe luxation injuries, complicated crown fractures, avulsions of permanent incisors, soft tissue infections, uncontrollable post-operative bleeding, conditions worsening systemic medical conditions, and suspected oral cancer [61]. Furthermore, in our study, the most common emergency situations were reported as severe pain caused by pulpal inflammation (94%), abscesses or bacterial infection causing localized pain and extraoral swelling (86.5%), luxations/dental avulsions (41%), dental fractures causing pain, or soft tissue injuries caused by trauma (35.5%). Ilyas et al. [61] reported irreversible pulpitis, Moheb et al. [13] reported severe pain, infection and trauma, Üstün et al. [62] reported severe dental pain because of pulpal inflammation and swelling, Faccini et al. [58] reported toothache (71.4%), broken restorations (40.4%) and dental trauma (37.3%), Alsaleh et al. [14] reported abscesses (51.8%) and cellulitis (44.6%) in Jordan and abscesses (44.6%) and pulpitis (35.5%) in India, Izzetti et al. [16] reported pulpitis, prosthesis de-cementation and abscesses, and Sinjari et al. [55] reported severe dental pain, swelling and dental trauma as the most common emergency situations managed. Thus, the findings of this study were found to be in accordance with those others [13,14,16,55,58,61,62]. However, differently from our findings, Limbu et al. [63] reported exfoliating mobility (23.3%), acute pulpitis (5.8%) and dental abscesses (22.1%), and Martinho and Griffin [18] reported trauma (82.1%) followed by swelling (81.9%) and pain (76.1%) as dental emergencies.

In order to achieve efficient infection control, dentists and all healthcare workers in the dental clinic should pay attention to appropriate PPE usage while working in the dental clinic, especially during the COVID-19 era [33]. PPE includes disposable scrubs, shoe covers, hair covers, goggles, gloves, gown, masks and face shields. While conducting non-AGPs, work clothes, usage of goggles/face shields, fluid-resistant surgical masks, disposable gloves, disposable aprons and hair covers are recommended. In addition to all these protections, the usage of particulate respirators, disposable gowns, medical protective clothing and shoe covers are required during AGPs. The most effective/protective masks are N99/N100/FFP2/FFP3/N95 masks [64,65]. Scrubs (87%) and surgical masks (90%) were found to be widely used in both AGPs and non-AGPs in the current study. Similarly, Duruk et al. [2], Estrich et al. [26], and Izzetti et al. [16] also reported nearly 86%, 99% and 98% mask usage, respectively. Disposable gloves (92.5%) were found to be used widely in both AGPs and non-AGPs in line with previous studies [2,14,17]. Face shield (83%) usage was found to be similar to that reported by Sinjari et al. [55]. In line with our findings, in studies by Alsaleh et al. [14] and Duruk et al. [2], face shield usage was shown to have high percentages. Furthermore, goggles (71%), disposable surgical gowns (70.5%), and disposable medical caps (83.5%) were found to be used widely in both AGP and non-AGPs in this study. Alsaleh et al. [14] reported a similar rate of goggle usage in India (75.2%). Duruk et al. [2], Izzetti et al. [16] and Sinjari et al. [55] reported that nearly 46%, 80% and

82% of participating dentists used disposable aprons/gowns. Martinho and Griffin [18] showed that 36.8% of participants used protective suits; however, 24% of pediatric dentists used protective coveralls in this study. Moreover, disposable medical caps (83.5%) were found to be widely used in both AGPs and non-AGPs. Similarly, Izzetti et al. [16], and Duruk et al. [2] reported medical cap usage rates of 84.4% and 56%, respectively.

When we consider the usage of particulate respirators, Alsaleh et al. [14] reported N95 respirator usage rates of 80.4% in Jordan and 87.6% in India. Ammar et al. [37] reported N95/FFP2 usage of 91.7%. Martinho and Griffin [18] reported that the usage rate of N95 respirators was 83.1%. N95 respirator usage was found to be lower in our study, where 21% of pediatric dentists only used AGPs and 51% used both AGPs and non-AGPs. However, lower percentages than in this study were also reported by Duruk et al. [2] (12.36%) and Ahmed et al. [34] (11.6%). In addition, FFP2 respirators were used only in AGPs by 16%, and were used in both AGPs and non-AGPs by 43.5%. Cagetti et al. [17] and Izzetti et al. [16] reported rates of usage of FFP2/FFP3 masks of 54.84% and 15.4%, respectively. Sinjari et al. [55] reported FFP2 usage of nearly 62% and Bekes et al. [12] reported rates of nearly 45% for FFP2 and 60% for FFP3e. Estrich et al. [26] also showed that dental practitioners wore surgical masks over particulate respirators, and replaced the surgical masks more often. Considering PPE usage, it was detected in our study that pediatric dentists attach importance to the use of PPEs. Scrubs, surgical masks, disposable gloves, goggles, face shields, disposable surgical gowns, and disposable medical caps were found to be widely used in both AGPs and non-AGPs. However, the usage of particulate respirators such as N95, FFP2/FFP3 and overshoes should be increased. The reasons for this result could be that the dentists thought that a surgical mask combined with a face shield could offer sufficient protection, the fact that wearing a respirator for long time is not easy, and the high costs of respirators [13]. Furthermore, difficulty in accessing PPE supplies could be another reason [16].

Knowing the correct sequence for donning and doffing PPE is also important, besides using the required PPE, among dental practitioners in order to reduce contamination [57,66]. Furthermore, after the dental treatment, patients and the dental team should leave the clinic from separate exits, and all clinical personnel should pay attention to doffing their PPE in the buffer zone [67]. In our study, most of the pediatric dentists (84%) reported that they paid attention to the proper order of donning and doffing their PPEs; however, only 55% paid attention to removing their and other dental healthcare workers' PPEs in a separate isolation room. Bekes et al. [12] reported that nearly 52% of the dentists knew the correct sequence of donning PPE (gown, mask, eye protection, gloves). Maru et al. [11] showed that 66.5% and 64.8% of Indian pediatric dentists knew the correct sequence of donning (gown, mask, eye protector, gloves) and doffing PPE (gloves, eye protector, gown, mask), respectively.

The parents should prepare their children mentally prior to dental appointments because the dental team behind the PPE may frighten the child [68]. Successful behavior management is crucial for pediatric dentists because uncooperative, crying children spread more aerosols than calm ones. Thus, in order to reduce the anxiety of children related to the dental team's PPEs, including face mask, it is recommended that they put them on in front of the children and explain the necessity of this equipment [40]. In our study, most of the pediatric dentists thought that their PPE increased the anxiety levels of children. Furthermore, more than half of participants explained their PPE to their pediatric patients as them wearing an astronaut suit, 26% said they had become a superhero, 59.5% explained the reason of usage and 21.5% did not give any explanation. In another study, nearly 28% of dentists reported that children did not react differently, nearly 32% reported children were interested, nearly 30% reported children were distressed and worried, but nearly 10% of dentists reported that they did not use advanced PPE while treating children [13]. Additionally, extra PPE covers facial expressions and complicates behavior management in children. Thus, PPE could be modified in order to make it more child friendly [14]. Before dental treatment, meeting with the pediatric patient via video call without wearing

PPE and introducing PPE with the tell–show–do technique, using colorful/painted gowns, and placing stickers or the dentist's picture on the PPE were suggested modifications for pediatric dental clinic practices [14].

When we evaluated the infection control measures used during dental treatments, using hand instrumentation, avoiding high-speed handpiece/ultrasonic instruments/air water syringe usage, and the treatment of only one patient in a room were conducted by most of the pediatric dentists. Moheb et al. [13] reported that nearly 85% of dentists used hand instruments as much as possible to avoid aerosols, and nearly 84% minimized the use of a three in one syringe. Additionally, in another study, most of the dentists (88.5%) made the effort to reduce aerosol formation [16]. Ates et al. [54] reported that half of the participants used slow-speed handpieces without water to minimize contamination risk. However, in this study, only 49 pediatric dentists used this approach. The use of a dental handpiece with an anti-retraction function was reported as a preventive measure [42], but only five pediatric dentists reported using those instruments. Among the infection control measures, only 39% of pediatric dentist said they did not allow parents into the treatment room. The reason for this result might be due to the fact young children in particular do not want to be separated from their families during dental treatments. If the child does not want to enter the treatment room alone, a maximum of one parent should be accepted, and other accompanying people should be prevented from entering the treatment room. In addition, chemomechanical caries removal was only conducted by nine pediatric dentists in our study. This might be related to the preference for conventional treatments among pediatric dentists before the COVID-19 pandemic period and the lack of essential dental materials. Furthermore, ITR were conducted by nearly 34% of pediatric dentists, and this result might be because of the delay of routine dental practices and the treatment of emergency dental treatments, mainly abscesses or bacterial infection causing localized pain and extraoral swelling (86.5%). However, since it is not possible to carry out only emergency treatments, approaches that prevent aerosol formation, such as chemomechanical caries removal, ART, ITR and SDF, should be preferred for routine dental treatments after the quarantine period in order to reduce aerosol formation and to prevent contamination with SARS-COV2 during long-term pandemic conditions. Rubber dam usage also reduces the risk of aerosols during the COVID-19 pandemic period. However, in our study, rubber dam usage was found to be unsatisfactory and lower than in other studies conducted by Moheb et al. [13], Izzetti et al. [16], and Sinjari et al. [55]. The findings of Duruk et al. [2] (13.84%) and Ataş and Yıldırım [69] (15.9%) also revealed that rubber dam usage was infrequent. Moheb et al. [13] declared that it is not always feasible to excavate caries only using hand instruments; the application of a rubber dam is not possible for some children, and an air water syringe might be required. Even in such cases, dentists have to do their best to reduce aerosol formation.

Among the infection control methods used during dental treatments, the four-handed technique was used by nearly 30% of participants in this study. Similarly, 37.8% of dentists used this technique in the study of Izzetti et al. [16]. Preprocedural oxidative or antimicrobial mouth-rinse usage was reported by nearly 34% of pediatric dentists in this study. Moheb et al. [13] reported that nearly 56% and Al-Khalifa et al. [56] reported that 47% of dentists preferred patients using antiseptic mouth rinse before dental treatments. Furthermore, high-volume saliva ejector usage was reported by nearly 35% of participants; however, Moheb et al. [13], Duruk et al. [2], and Ataş and Yıldırım [69] reported strong saliva absorber usage rates of 87.2%, 63.79% and 42.4%, respectively. In the study of Martinho and Griffin [18], nearly 17% of participants reported usage of an oral aerosol vacuum. In another study by Estrich et al. [26], 17% of participants said they used an extraoral suction device. Al- Khalifa et al. [56] reported that 59% of participating dentists did not use extraoral suction systems. Unfortunately, in the current study, only 6.5% of participants used a dental extraoral suction system. Lastly, in order to prevent the spread of infections, ensuring good hand hygiene is one of the most efficient methods. A two before (before conducting examination and before performing dental treatment) and three after

(after touching the patient, after touching the undisinfected surroundings/equipment, and after touching blood/wound/oral mucosa/damaged skin) hand hygiene system should be conducted by the dental team to strengthen hand hygiene [10]. The results of this study show that nearly 80% of the pediatric dentists encountered a situation such as burning, stinging, itching or dryness on the skin due to frequent hand cleaning and the long-term use of PPEs. However, it was detected that the recommended two before three after hand hygiene protocol was not well known among pediatric dentists in our study. According to our findings, it is obvious that pediatric dentists wash their hands before and after the procedures, and struggle to achieve sufficient disinfection; however, increased hand hygiene following the two before three after hand hygiene protocol should definitely be performed to increase protection against the COVID-19 disease. Therefore, dentists should be familiar with the concept of two before three after hand hygiene. To conclude, in our study, the most crucial control measures, such as the treatment of one patient in a room, not using high-speed handpieces and ultrasonic instruments, not using air water syringes, and preference for hand instrumentation, were found to be more widely used by pediatric dentists than other precautions. However, the lack of implementation of rubber dams, four-handed dentistry, dental extraoral suction systems, high-volume saliva ejectors and two before three after hand hygiene should be increased via education programs.

Another important point that needs to be considered is the radiographic evaluation of patients during the COVID-19 pandemic period. If radiographs are required from patients, extraoral radiographs should be preferred instead of intraoral radiographs in order not to stimulate the secretion of saliva and coughing [70]. In line with the recommendations, most of the pediatric dentists obtained panoramic radiographs in this study. Similarly, Moheb et al. [13] also reported that nearly 62% of dentist shifted from intraoral to extraoral radiographs, if available. In another study, Ammar et al. [37] reported that nearly 60% of dental academics used extraoral radiographs rather than intraoral radiographs.

The dental management of uncooperative patients during the COVID-19 lockdown period is also an issue that needs to be carefully evaluated. Similar to our study, Moheb et al. [13] reported that the majority of dentists (73%) did not use sedation or general anesthesia during the pandemic period. Additionally, they reported that nearly 70% of pediatric dentists refused to use physical restraining. A similar finding was observed in our study, as only 8% of pediatric dentists used physical restraining in order to control children's sudden movements. Alsaleh et al. [14] reported that most dentists (71.1% in India and 80.4% in Jordan) did not use N2O sedation for their pediatric patients. For less aerosol production, in India ART (52.1%) and SDF (28.9%), and in Jordan the Hall technique (26.8%) and ART (25.0%), were performed. In the current study, ART (33%) was the most preferred treatment in accordance with Alsaleh et al. [14]; however, SDF and the Hall technique were used less than in the study by Alsaleh et al. [14]. As previously mentioned, minimally invasive treatment approaches were not widely used since most of the pediatric dentists in our study only performed emergency treatments during the lockdown period. However, lockdown periods are not permanent and they are rotative; thus, in order to reduce the risk of transmission, treatments that reduce aerosol formation should be used widely in dental practice.

Among the infection control measures performed after dental treatments, the disinfection of commonly used areas, such as dental units, dental lights and dental X-ray machines, after each patient was conducted by 66.5% of pediatric dentists in this study. Similarly, in the studies of Bontà et al. [42] and Cagetti et al. [17], 74.13% and 80.49% of participants reported that they removed and disinfected disposable protective devices, respectively. In another study, nearly 68% of healthcare professionals said they applied universal precautions for infection control [34]. Khader et al. [38] reported that nearly 94% of participants routinely cleaned and disinfected surfaces that had been in contact with known or suspected patients. On the other hand, the regular disinfection of common areas, door handles, chairs and tables was also deemed to be important and conducted by 72.5% of pediatric dentists in this study. Similarly, in the study of Estrich et al. [26], almost all practicing dentists reported that they disinfected commonly touched equipment and surfaces. Similar observations were reported in previous studies [17,32,33,42,71]. Furthermore, the ventilation of the treatment room after each patient was conducted by 85% of pediatric dentists in our study. In accordance with our findings, in the studies of Bontà et al. [42] and Izzetti et al. [16], nearly 71% and 98% of participants provided room ventilation after dental treatments, respectively. However, Putrino et al. [32] reported that less (14.9%) participants ventilated the treatment room between patients. Air-purifying systems were found to be used by only 16% of pediatric dentists in this study. Martinho and Griffin [18] indicated that 42.3% of endodontists could implement an air-purifying unit. In another study by Huntley et al. [27], 42.5% of the participants reported that they had no access to an air-purifying unit. Among the infection control measures mentioned, the least conducted measures were a fogging system for disinfection (35.5%) and a HEPA filtration system (7%). Similarly, Alsaleh et al. [14] reported that the least conducted measure was the use of HEPA filters in India (41.3%) and in Jordan (8.9%).

Infection control measures after dental treatments are mandatory, and in our study, those precautions were found to be satisfactory applied, such as ventilation of the treatment room after each patient, regular disinfection of common areas in the dental clinic and treatment room, disinfection of reusable PPEs, discharge of medical waste, cleaning and sterilization of the dental hand instruments immediately after usage, and making children and parents use hand sanitizer when leaving the clinic. However, the rarely used measures were fogging systems for disinfection, ventilation and air conditioning systems, ultraviolet radiation systems, and HEPA filtration systems.

5. Conclusions

The findings of the current study show that Turkish pediatric dentists had a good level of knowledge about COVID-19, sufficient to perform dental treatments safely and not neglect the necessary precautions during dental procedures. Turkish pediatric dentists satisfactorily conducted most of the infection control measures before and after the dental treatments, and they attached importance to the use of PPEs; however, infection control measures during the dental treatments could be better implemented. At the beginning of the pandemic, most pediatric dentists only performed emergency treatments; however, lockdown periods are not long-lasting and they are rotative. Thus, in order to reduce the risk of transmission, minimally invasive approaches should be used widely in routine dental practices. Along with all precautions, the vaccination of healthcare workers and requesting a recent test result from patients that shows the absence of COVID-19 before dental appointments can be added to the effective infection control measures. Additionally, pediatric dentists should continue to follow local and universal guidelines, and education programs should be implemented frequently in order to keep COVID-19 management strategies up to date.

Supplementary Materials: The following are available online at https://www.mdpi.com/article/10.3390/medicina57111140/s1. Supplementary File S1: Survey Questionnaire.

Author Contributions: Conceptualization, Y.K., D.A.-B., S.A.; methodology, Y.K., D.A.-B., S.A.; formal analysis, Y.K., D.A.-B.; investigation, Y.K., D.A.-B., S.A.; resources, Y.K., D.A.-B., S.A.; data curation, Y.K., D.A.-B., S.A.; writing—original draft preparation, D.A.-B., Y.K.; writing—review and editing, Y.K., D.A.-B., S.A.; visualization, Y.K., D.A.-B., S.A.; supervision, D.A.-B., S.A. All authors have read and agreed to the published version of the manuscript.

Funding: This research received no external funding.

Institutional Review Board Statement: The study was conducted according to the guidelines of the Declaration of Helsinki, and approved by the Institutional Review Board (or Ethics Committee) of Near East University (protocol code: YDU/2020/79-1083; 28 May 2020).

Informed Consent Statement: Informed consent was obtained from all participants involved in the study.

Data Availability Statement: The data that support the findings of this study are available on request from the corresponding author.

Acknowledgments: We would like to thank the Turkish Association of Paediatric Dentistry and all pediatric dentists for their contributions to this study.

Conflicts of Interest: The authors declare no conflict of interest.

References

1. Lai, C.C.; Shih, T.P.; Ko, W.C.; Tang, H.J.; Hsueh, P.R. Severe acute respiratory syndrome coronavirus 2 (SARS-CoV-2) and coronavirus disease-2019 (COVID-19): The epidemic and the challenges. *Int. J. Antimicrob. Agents* **2020**, *55*, 105924. [CrossRef] [PubMed]
2. Duruk, G.; Gümüşboğa, Z.Ş.; Çolak, C. Investigation of Turkish dentists' clinical attitudes and behaviors towards the COVID-19 pandemic: A survey study. *Braz. Oral Res.* **2020**, *34*, 1–12. [CrossRef] [PubMed]
3. Ferrazzano, G.F.; Ingenito, A.; Cantile, T. COVID-19 disease in children: What dentists should know and do to prevent viral spread. The Italian point of view. *Int. J. Environ. Res. Public Health* **2020**, *17*, 3642. [CrossRef]
4. Meng, L.; Hua, F.; Bian, Z. Coronavirus disease 2019 (COVID-19): Emerging and future challenges for dental and oral medicine. *J. Dent. Res.* **2020**, *99*, 481–487. [CrossRef] [PubMed]
5. Banakar, M.; Lankarani, K.B.; Jafarpour, D.; Moayedi, S.; Banakar, M.H.; MohammadSadeghi, A. COVID-19 transmission risk and protective protocols in dentistry: A systematic review. *BMC Oral Health* **2020**, *20*, 1–12. [CrossRef]
6. Ren, Y.F.; Rasubala, L.; Malmstrom, H.; Eliav, E. Dental care and oral health under the clouds of COVID-19. *JDR Clin. Transl. Res.* **2020**, *5*, 202–210. [CrossRef]
7. Mallineni, S.K.; Innes, N.P.; Raggio, D.P.; Araujo, M.P.; Robertson, M.D.; Jayaraman, J. Coronavirus disease (COVID-19): Characteristics in children and considerations for dentists providing their care. *Int. J. Paediatr. Dent.* **2020**, *30*, 245–250. [CrossRef]
8. Available online: https://turkpedo.org/covid-19-2/ (accessed on 27 August 2021).
9. Ayyed, A.B. Dental Practice Infection Control Measurements: Coronavirus Disease (COVID-19) Outbreaks. *Int. J. Clin. Pediatr. Dent.* **2020**, *13*, 279. [CrossRef]
10. Bhanushali, P.; Katge, F.; Deshpande, S.; Chimata, V.K.; Shetty, S.; Pradhan, D. COVID-19: Changing trends and its impact on future of dentistry. *Int. J. Dent.* **2020**, *2020*, 8817424. [CrossRef]
11. Maru, V.; Padawe, D.; Singh, A.; Takate, V.; Dighe, K.; Singh, S. Awareness, Perception, Attitude Regarding CoViD-19 and Infection Control among Indian Pediatric Dentists: A Cross Sectional Study. *J. Clin. Pediatr. Dent.* **2020**, *44*, 211–220. [CrossRef]
12. Bekes, K.; Ritschl, V.; Stamm, T. COVID-19 pandemic and its impact on pediatric dentistry in Austria: Knowledge, perception and attitude among pediatric dentists in a cross-sectional survey. *J. Multidiscip. Healthc.* **2021**, *14*, 161. [CrossRef] [PubMed]
13. Moheb, D.; Nasr, R.A.; Azab, M.M. Pediatric Dentists in the Time of COVID-19 Pandemic; the Challenges and Burden. *Egypt. Dent. J.* **2021**, *67*, 85–99. [CrossRef]
14. Alsaleh, M.M.; Sabbarini, J.M.; Al-Batayneh, O.B.; Khader, Y.S. Changes in behavior management and treatment modalities in pediatric dentistry during covid-19 pandemic. *Int. J. Clin. Pediatr. Dent.* **2020**, *13*, S125. [CrossRef]
15. Isiekwe, I.G.; Adeyemi, T.E.; Aikins, E.A.; Umeh, O.D. Perceived impact of the COVID-19 pandemic on orthodontic practice by orthodontists and orthodontic residents in Nigeria. *J. World Fed. Orthod.* **2020**, *9*, 123–128. [CrossRef]
16. Izzetti, R.; Gennai, S.; Nisi, M.; Barone, A.; Giuca, M.R.; Gabriele, M.; Graziani, F. A perspective on dental activity during COVID-19: The Italian survey. *Oral Dis.* **2021**, *27*, 694–702. [CrossRef]
17. Cagetti, M.G.; Cairoli, J.L.; Senna, A.; Campus, G. COVID-19 outbreak in North Italy: An overview on dentistry. A questionnaire survey. *Int. J. Environ. Res. Public Health* **2020**, *17*, 3835. [CrossRef]
18. Martinho, F.C.; Griffin, I.L. A cross-sectional survey on the impact of Coronavirus disease 2019 on the clinical practice of endodontists across the United States. *J. Endod.* **2021**, *47*, 28–38. [CrossRef]
19. Maffia, F.; Fontanari, M.; Vellone, V.; Cascone, P.; Mercuri, L.G. Impact of COVID-19 on maxillofacial surgery practice: A worldwide survey. *Int. J. Oral Maxillofac. Surg.* **2020**, *49*, 827–835. [CrossRef]
20. Hua, F.; Qin, D.; Yan, J.; Zhao, T.; He, H. COVID-19 related experience, knowledge, attitude, and behaviors among 2669 orthodontists, orthodontic residents, and nurses in China: A cross-sectional survey. *Front. Med.* **2020**, *7*, 481. [CrossRef]
21. Allevi, F.; Dionisio, A.; Baciliero, U.; Balercia, P.; Beltramini, G.A.; Bertossi, D.; Bozzetti, A.; Califano, L.; Cascone, P.; Colombo, L. Impact of COVID-19 epidemic on maxillofacial surgery in Italy. *Br. J. Oral Maxillofac. Surg.* **2020**, *58*, 692–697. [CrossRef] [PubMed]
22. Consolo, U.; Bellini, P.; Bencivenni, D.; Iani, C.; Checchi, V. Epidemiological aspects and psychological reactions to COVID-19 of dental practitioners in the Northern Italy Districts of Modena and Reggio Emilia. *Int. J. Environ. Res. Public Health* **2020**, *17*, 3459. [CrossRef]
23. Bellini, P.; Checchi, V.; Iani, C.; Bencivenni, D.; Consolo, U. Psychological reactions to COVID-19 and epidemiological aspects of dental practitioners during lockdown in Italy. *Minerva Dent. Oral Sci.* **2021**, *70*, 32–43. [CrossRef]
24. Martina, S.; Amato, A.; Rongo, R.; Caggiano, M.; Amato, M. The perception of COVID-19 among Italian dentists: An orthodontic point of view. *Int. J. Environ. Res. Public Health* **2020**, *17*, 4384. [CrossRef] [PubMed]

25. Key, T.; Mathai, N.J.; Venkatesan, A.S.; Farnell, D.; Mohanty, K. Personal protective equipment during the COVID-19 crisis: A snapshot and recommendations from the frontline of a university teaching hospital. *Bone Jt. Open* **2020**, *1*, 131–136. [CrossRef]
26. Estrich, C.G.; Mikkelsen, M.; Morrissey, R.; Geisinger, M.L.; Ioannidou, E.; Vujicic, M.; Araujo, M.W. Estimating COVID-19 prevalence and infection control practices among US dentists. *J. Am. Dent. Assoc.* **2020**, *151*, 815–824. [CrossRef]
27. Huntley, R.E.; Ludwig, D.C.; Dillon, J.K. Early effects of COVID-19 on oral and maxillofacial surgery residency training—Results from a national survey. *J. Oral Maxillofac. Surg.* **2020**, *78*, 1257–1267. [CrossRef] [PubMed]
28. Sah, M.K.; Singh, A.; Sangroula, R.K. Knowledge of novel coronavirus disease (COVID-19) among dental surgeons of Nepal: A nationwide study. *BMC Infect. Dis.* **2020**, *20*, 871. [CrossRef] [PubMed]
29. De Stefani, A.; Bruno, G.; Mutinelli, S.; Gracco, A. COVID-19 outbreak perception in Italian dentists. *Int. J. Environ. Res. Public Health* **2020**, *17*, 3867. [CrossRef] [PubMed]
30. Sezgin, G.P.; Şirinoğlu Çapan, B. Assessment of dentists' awareness and knowledge levels on the Novel Coronavirus (COVID-19). *Braz. Oral Res.* **2020**, *34*. [CrossRef] [PubMed]
31. Arora, S.; Saquib, S.A.; Attar, N.; Pimpale, S.; Zafar, K.S.; Saluja, P.; Abdulla, A.M.; Shamsuddin, S. Evaluation of knowledge and preparedness among indian dentists during the current COVID-19 pandemic: A cross-sectional study. *J. Multidiscip. Healthc.* **2020**, *13*, 841. [CrossRef]
32. Putrino, A.; Raso, M.; Magazzino, C.; Galluccio, G. Coronavirus (COVID-19) in Italy: Knowledge, management of patients and clinical experience of Italian dentists during the spread of contagion. *BMC Oral Health* **2020**, *20*, 200. [CrossRef]
33. Nasser, Z.; Fares, Y.; Daoud, R.; Abou-Abbas, L. Assessment of knowledge and practice of dentists towards Coronavirus Disease (COVID-19): A cross-sectional survey from Lebanon. *BMC Oral Health* **2020**, *20*, 281. [CrossRef]
34. Ahmed, N.; Shakoor, M.; Vohra, F.; Abduljabbar, T.; Mariam, Q.; Rehman, M.A. Knowledge, awareness and practice of health care professionals amid SARS-CoV-2, corona virus disease outbreak. *Pak. J. Med Sci.* **2020**, *36*, S49. [CrossRef]
35. Bahramian, H.; Gharib, B.; Baghalian, A. COVID-19 considerations in pediatric dentistry. *JDR Clin. Transl. Res.* **2020**, *5*, 307–311. [CrossRef]
36. Cai, X.; Ma, Y.; Li, S.; Chen, Y.; Rong, Z.; Li, W. Clinical characteristics of 5 COVID-19 cases with non-respiratory symptoms as the first manifestation in children. *Front. Pediatr.* **2020**, *8*, 258. [CrossRef]
37. Ammar, N.; Aly, N.M.; Folayan, M.O.; Mohebbi, S.Z.; Attia, S.; Howaldt, H.P.; Boettger, S.; Khader, Y.; Maharani, D.A.; Rahardjo, A. Knowledge of dental academics about the COVID-19 pandemic: A multi-country online survey. *BMC Med. Educ.* **2020**, *20*, 399. [CrossRef]
38. Khader, Y.; Al Nsour, M.; Al-Batayneh, O.B.; Saadeh, R.; Bashier, H.; Alfaqih, M.; Al-Azzam, S. Dentists' awareness, perception, and attitude regarding COVID-19 and infection control: Cross-sectional study among Jordanian dentists. *JMIR Public Health Surveill.* **2020**, *6*, e18798. [CrossRef] [PubMed]
39. Candeiro, G.T.D.M.; Gavini, G.; Vivan, R.R.; Carvalho, B.M.D.F.; Duarte, M.A.H.; FeijÃo, C.P. Knowledge about Coronavirus disease 19 (COVID-19) and its professional repercussions among Brazilian endodontists. *Braz. Oral Res.* **2020**, *34*. [CrossRef]
40. Al-Halabi, M.; Salami, A.; Alnuaimi, E.; Kowash, M.; Hussein, I. Assessment of paediatric dental guidelines and caries management alternatives in the post COVID-19 period. A critical review and clinical recommendations. *Eur. Arch. Paediatr. Dent.* **2020**, *21*, 543–556. [CrossRef] [PubMed]
41. Dong, Y.; Mo, X.; Hu, Y.; Qi, X.; Jiang, F.; Jiang, Z.; Tong, S. Epidemiology of COVID-19 among children in China. *Pediatrics* **2020**, *145*, e20200702. [CrossRef] [PubMed]
42. Bontà, G.; Campus, G.; Cagetti, M.G. COVID-19 pandemic and dental hygienists in Italy: A questionnaire survey. *BMC Health Serv. Res.* **2020**, *20*, 994. [CrossRef] [PubMed]
43. Alduraywish, A.A.; Srivastava, K.C.; Shrivastava, D.; Sghaireen, M.G.; Alsharari, A.F.; Al-Johani, K.; Alam, M.K. A countrywide survey in Saudi Arabia regarding the knowledge and attitude of health care professionals about coronavirus disease (COVID-19). *Int. J. Environ. Res. Public Health* **2020**, *17*, 7415. [CrossRef]
44. Becker, K.; Brunello, G.; Gurzawska-Comis, K.; Becker, J.; Sivolella, S.; Schwarz, F.; Klinge, B. Dental care during COVID-19 pandemic: Survey of experts' opinion. *Clin. Oral Implant. Res.* **2020**, *31*, 1253–1260. [CrossRef] [PubMed]
45. Hakim, M.; Khattak, F.A.; Muhammad, S.; Ismail, M.; Ullah, N.; Atiq Orakzai, M.; Ulislam, S.; Ul-Haq, Z. Access and Use Experience of Personal Protective Equipment Among Frontline Healthcare Workers in Pakistan During the COVID-19 Emergency: A Cross-Sectional Study. *Health Secur.* **2021**, *19*, 140–149. [CrossRef] [PubMed]
46. Luzzi, V.; Ierardo, G.; Bossù, M.; Polimeni, A. Paediatric Oral Health during and after the COVID-19 Pandemic. *Int. J. Paediatr. Dent.* **2021**, *31*, 20–26. [CrossRef] [PubMed]
47. Esposito, S.; Principi, N. To mask or not to mask children to overcome COVID-19. *Eur. J. Pediatr.* **2020**, *179*, 1267–1270. [CrossRef]
48. Tahamtan, A.; Ardebili, A. Real-time RT-PCR in COVID-19 detection: Issues affecting the results. *Expert Rev. Mol. Diagn.* **2020**, *20*, 453–454. [CrossRef]
49. Sabino-Silva, R.; Jardim, A.C.G.; Siqueira, W.L. Coronavirus COVID-19 impacts to dentistry and potential salivary diagnosis. *Clin. Oral Investig.* **2020**, *24*, 1619–1621. [CrossRef]
50. Quadri, M.F.; Jafer, M.A.; Alqahtani, A.S.; Odabi, N.I.; Daghriri, A.A.; Tadakamadla, S.K. Novel corona virus disease (COVID-19) awareness among the dental interns, dental auxiliaries and dental specialists in Saudi Arabia: A nationwide study. *J. Infect. Public Health* **2020**, *13*, 856–864. [CrossRef]
51. Patel, M. Infection control in dentistry during COVID-19 pandemic: What has changed? *Heliyon* **2020**, *6*, e05402. [CrossRef]

52. Melo Neto, C.L.M.; Bannwart, L.C.; de Melo Moreno, A.L.; Goiato, M.C. SARS-CoV-2 and Dentistry-Review. *Eur. J. Dent.* **2020**, *14*, S130–S139. [CrossRef] [PubMed]
53. Ather, A.; Patel, B.; Ruparel, N.B.; Diogenes, A.; Hargreaves, K.M. Coronavirus disease 19 (COVID-19): Implications for clinical dental care. *J. Endod.* **2020**, *46*, 584–595. [CrossRef]
54. Ates, A.A.; Alomari, T.; Bhardwaj, A.; Tabnjh, A.; Gambarini, G. Differences in endodontic emergency management by endodontists and general dental practitioners in COVID-19 times. *Braz. Oral Res.* **2020**, *34*. [CrossRef]
55. Sinjari, B.; Rexhepi, I.; Santilli, M.; Chiacchiaretta, P.; Di Carlo, P.; Caputi, S. The impact of COVID-19 related lockdown on dental practice in Central Italy—outcomes of a survey. *Int. J. Environ. Res. Public Health* **2020**, *17*, 5780. [CrossRef] [PubMed]
56. Al-Khalifa, K.S.; AlSheikh, R.; Al-Swuailem, A.S.; Alkhalifa, M.S.; Al-Johani, M.H.; Al-Moumen, S.A.; Almomen, Z.I. Pandemic preparedness of dentists against coronavirus disease: A Saudi Arabian experience. *PLoS ONE* **2020**, *15*, e0237630. [CrossRef] [PubMed]
57. Modi, P.D.; Nair, G.; Uppe, A.; Modi, J.; Tuppekar, B.; Gharpure, A.S.; Langade, D. COVID-19 awareness among healthcare students and professionals in Mumbai metropolitan region: A questionnaire-based survey. *Cureus* **2020**, *12*, e7514. [CrossRef]
58. Faccini, M.; Ferruzzi, F.; Mori, A.A.; Santin, G.C.; Oliveira, R.C.; de Oliveira, R.C.G.; Queiroz, P.M.; Salmeron, S.; Pini, N.I.P.; Sundfeld, D.; et al. Dental care during COVID-19 outbreak: A web-based survey. *Eur. J. Dent.* **2020**, *14*, S14–S19. [CrossRef]
59. Cotrin, P.; Peloso, R.M.; Pini, N.I.P.; Oliveira, R.C.; de Oliveira, R.C.G.; Valarelli, F.P.; Freitas, K.M.S. Urgencies and emergencies in orthodontics during the coronavirus disease 2019 pandemic: Brazilian orthodontists' experience. *Am. J. Orthod. Dentofac. Orthop.* **2020**, *158*, 661–667. [CrossRef]
60. Nibali, L.; Ide, M.; Ng, D.; Buontempo, Z.; Clayton, Y.; Asimakopoulou, K. The perceived impact of Covid-19 on periodontal practice in the United Kingdom: A questionnaire study. *J. Dent.* **2020**, *102*, 103481. [CrossRef]
61. Ilyas, N.; Agel, M.; Mitchell, J.; Sood, S. COVID-19 pandemic: The first wave-an audit and guidance for paediatric dentistry. *Br. Dent. J.* **2020**, *228*, 927–931. [CrossRef]
62. Üstün, N.; Akgöl, B.B.; Bayram, M. Influence of COVID-19 pandemic on paediatric dental attendance. *Clin. Oral Investig.* **2021**, 1–7. [CrossRef]
63. Limbu, S.; Dikshit, P.; Malla, M.; Verma, L.; Khapung, A. Pediatric Dental Emergency Pattern and Dental Care Provided during COVID-19 Pandemic Lockdown at a Tertiary Care Center in Kathmandu, Nepal. *J. Nepal Assoc. Pediatr Dent.* **2021**, *2*, 3–11.
64. Kumar, G.; Ramos-Gomez, F.; Dhillon, J.K.; Singh, N.; Rehman, F. Pediatric Dental Management in COVID-19 Era: A Contemporary Outlook. *J. South. Asian Assoc. Pediatr. Dent.* **2021**, *4*, 34.
65. Chen, X.C.; Ding, J.F.; Xu, D.H.; Cai, Z.G.; Li, X.E.; Shi, Z.D.; Guo, C.B.; Zhou, Y.S. Preventive and control measures for the coronavirus pandemic in clinical dentistry. *Chin. J. Dent. Res.* **2020**, *23*, 99–104. [CrossRef]
66. Gallagher, J.E.; Johnson, I.; Verbeek, J.H.; Clarkson, J.E.; Innes, N. Relevance and paucity of evidence: A dental perspective on personal protective equipment during the COVID-19 pandemic. *Br. Dent. J.* **2020**, *229*, 121–124. [CrossRef]
67. Sa, Y.; Lin, W.S.; Morton, D.; Huang, C. Coronavirus disease 2019 (COVID-19): Experiences and protocols from the Department of Prosthodontics at the Wuhan University. *J. Prosthet. Dent.* **2021**, *126*, 41–50. [CrossRef] [PubMed]
68. Acharya, S.; Singh, B.; Godhi, B.; Pandey, S. How to deal and learn from the threat of COVID-19 in paediatric dentistry. *Eur. J. Paediatr. Dent.* **2020**, *21*, 173–175. [CrossRef] [PubMed]
69. Ataş, O.; Yildirim, T.T. Evaluation of knowledge, attitudes, and clinical education of dental students about COVID-19 pandemic. *PeerJ* **2020**, *8*, e9575. [CrossRef] [PubMed]
70. Falahchai, M.; Babaee Hemmati, Y.; Hasanzade, M. Dental care management during the COVID-19 outbreak. *Spec. Care Dent.* **2020**, *40*, 539–548. [CrossRef]
71. Sarfaraz, S.; Shabbir, J.; Mudasser, M.A.; Khurshid, Z.; Al-Quraini, A.A.A.; Abbasi, M.S.; Ratnayake, J.; Zafar, M.S. Knowledge and attitude of dental practitioners related to disinfection during the COVID-19 pandemic. *Healthcare* **2020**, *8*, 232. [CrossRef]

medicina

MDPI

Article

Effects of COVID-19 Pandemic on Working Conditions of Dentists in Poland and Turkey

Sarkis Sozkes [1,*] and Iwona Olszewska-Czyż [2]

[1] Biomedical Engineering Biomaterials Department, Tekirdag Namik Kemal University, Tekirdag 59860, Turkey
[2] Periodontology and Clinical Oral Pathology Department, Jagiellonian University Medical College, 31155 Krakow, Poland; iwona.olszewska-czyz@uj.edu.pl
* Correspondence: ssozkes@nku.edu.tr; Tel.: +90-282-2502-347; Fax: +90-282-2509-924

Abstract: *Background and Objectives*: Due to the specific working conditions dental professionals represent a group of high risk of infection and COVID-19 pandemic in many ways have influenced their working environment. The aim of this study was to evaluate effects of COVID-19 pandemic on working conditions of dentists in Poland and Turkey. *Materials and Methods*: The study was an anonymous online questionnaire conducted among thedentists in two countries: Poland and Turkey. The survey consisted of general questions, COVID-19 pandemic infection and working history as well as working conditions before and during pandemic. Chi-square test, Fisher's Exact test, Fisher Freeman Halton test and Continuity (Yates) Correction were used to compare qualitative data. *Results*: The study was conducted with a total of 400 participants, 162 (40.5%) men and 238 (59.5%) women, aged between 23 and 67. The mean age of the participants was 42.39 ± 9.99 years. Positive COVID-19 test results among dentists in Poland were found to be significantly higher than in Turkey. Time of dental procedures during the COVID-19 pandemic in Poland and Turkey was significantly increased. The usage of N95/FFP2 or N99/FFP3 masks and surgical gowns during COVID-19 pandemic compared to pre-COVID-19 periods was clearly higher ($p < 0.05$). Reusable full-face and half-face elastomeric respirators are increasingly used in Turkey. During the COVID-19 pandemic a 25% decrease in dentists' income in Poland (81%) was significantly high than in Turkey (47.5%). *Conclusions*: COVID-19 pandemic has influenced working conditions of dentists. Many dentists got infected during the pandemic, dental procedures' time has increased, and protective equipment usage has become higher. Further studies analyzing the working conditions of dentists during COVID-19 pandemic should be conducted for better planning of future decisions taken by governments and authorities.

Keywords: COVID-19; dentists; SARS-CoV-2; PPE personal protective equipment; occupational medicine; working conditions

Citation: Sozkes, S.; Olszewska-Czyż, I. Effects of COVID-19 Pandemic on Working Conditions of Dentists in Poland and Turkey. *Medicina* **2021**, *57*, 1082. https://doi.org/10.3390/medicina57101082

Academic Editors: Cesare D Amico and Pier Paolo Poli

Received: 10 September 2021
Accepted: 8 October 2021
Published: 11 October 2021

1. Introduction

The World Health Organization (WHO) declared the novel coronavirus disease 2019 (COVID-19) a pandemic on March 11, 2020 [1]. Globally, as of 14 July 2021, more than 186 million confirmed cases of COVID-19 and unfortunately more than 4 million deaths were reported by WHO. It was reported that more than 3.4 billion COVID-19 vaccine doses have been administered [2]. The year 2020 and first quarter of 2021 has passed under the influence of the COVID-19 pandemic, and there have been measures and restrictions affecting social life in many countries. Health services have focused on canceling or delaying many non-urgent treatments to give priority to individuals affected by the pandemic [3].

Oral and dental health treatments have an important place among health services [4]. The necessity of providing uninterrupted emergency dental treatment to patients is a reality accepted by everyone and primarily all non-urgent dental treatments were postponed. As a result of the prolongation of the pandemic process, dental problems that were not very urgent, but likely to cause permanent damage in case of delay, have to be followed now and cannot be postponed anymore. The most frequent dental emergency cases are: tooth fractures, pulpal infections, periodontal abscesses, fractures of prosthetic restorations and urgent extractions, however there are many other conditions within the oral cavity which, even though not urgent, may result in serious oral and also general health issues [5].

Due to the nature of their working conditions, dentists communicate very closely with virus carrier patients, are exposed to saliva, blood and other body fluids, and therefore face the risk of 2019-nCoV infection. During the COVID-19 pandemic, many authorities have published guidelines on the precautions to be taken against COVID-19 during the implementation of oral and dental health services and the provision of treatment services. Infection control measures are necessary to prevent further spread of the virus and to help control the pandemic situation. Dental treatments should be carried out in protective and preventive environment. Dentists should protect themselves by using personal equipment and also protect their patients from contamination by taking pandemic measures [6–9]. These pandemic measures require a higher usage of protective equipment what not only increase the expenses but also consume more chair time for dental procedures. During pandemic governments also ruled lockdowns and limitations of public mobility. Apart from all those factors, dentists were also afraid to work because of the fear of being infected.

Considering all above aspects, a hypothesis of influence of COVID-19 pandemic on working conditions of dentists has been raised parallel to possible differences between countries and other factors related to dental environment nowadays.

1.1. *Objectives*

The aim of the study was to evaluate effects of COVID-19 pandemic on working conditions of Polish and Turkish dentists and to investigate any differentiating factors relevantly. The main research objective was to investigate if the COVID-19 pandemic changed the working conditions of the dentists and analyze eventual differences between nationalities and different aspects affecting the dentists during pandemic.

1.2. *Trial Design*

The study was an anonymous online questionnaire based trial conducted among dentists in two countries: Poland and Turkey. It was performed in accordance with Public Opinion Research Guidelines and based on the Computer Assisted Web Interview methodology. Ethical approval for this study was obtained.

2. Materials and Methods

2.1. *Participants*

The study was conducted among 400 dentists: 200 in Poland and 200 in Turkey. Only the dentists working in Poland or in Turkey were enrolled in the study. Participation was voluntary and participants were allowed to terminate the survey at any time. Confidentiality and privacy was protected according to General Data Protection Regulation.

2.2. *Data Collection*

Online social media Facebook and Twitter were employed for sampling. The survey was posted in the form of a link to be filled in directly by a person willing to participate. The questionnaire was placed in professional social media groups (in which members are subject to prior verification confirming the dental license) and only to groups which allow posting content of this type.

2.3. *Questionnaire*

The authors followed Study Protocol for an Online Questionnaire Survey to build up and develop the questionnaire [10]. The survey consisted of two parts. First part comprised of demographic data, including age, gender, country of origin, COVID -19 infection history (being tested for COVID-19, test results, hospitalization, symptoms), place of work (private, public, mixed), lockdown history, working status during pandemic (changes in treatment time and income) and opinion about the risk of COVID-19 infection. The dentists were also asked to self-assess their perception of having enough knowledge about Covid-19. Second part of the survey consisted of questions related to the usage of protective equipment and prophylactic procedures. The dentists were asked to mark what they have used before pandemic and what they are using during it out from: masks (surgical, N95, N99/FFP2, FFP3), reusable full-face respirators, reusable half-face respirators, gowns (sterile disposable, disposable), glasses(protection), gloves (sterile, non-sterile), anti-retraction system valve rotaries, triage and disinfection procedures. A pre-testing of the questionnaire was carried out with 20 dentists. Then Interclass Correlation Coefficients for Reliability was controlled and discussed to create the final structure of the questionnaire [11,12]. To evaluate the study parameters age, gender, country of residence and working status questions were included in the questionnaire.

2.4. Statistical Methods

IBM SPSS Statistics 22 (IBM SPSS, Istanbul, Turkey) program was used for statistical analysis. The conformity of the parameters to the normal distribution was evaluated with the Shapiro Wilks test. Student's *t* test was used for the comparison of normally distributed parameters (quantitative data) between two groups in addition to descriptive statistical methods (mean, standard deviation, frequency). Chi-square test, Fisher's Exact test, Fisher Freeman Halton test and Continuity (Yates) Correction were used to compare qualitative data. Significance was evaluated at the $p < 0.05$ level.

2.5. Ethics

The study was performed in accordance with the Helsinki Declaration and official approval from the Jagiellonian University Ethics Committee was obtained (No.1072.6120.157.2021).

3. Results

The study was conducted among 400 participants, 162 (40.5%) men and 238 (59.5%) women, aged between 23 and 67, between 9–12 July 2021. The mean age of the participants was 42.39 ± 9.99 years. The study was conducted in 2 countries: 200 (50%) Poland and 200 (50%) Turkey.

Evaluation of study parameters across countries are listed in Table 1. Employment in the private sector in Poland was found to be statistically significantly lower than in Turkey. The rate of positive COVID-19 test results in Poland (51%) was found to be higher than Turkey (16%), and the hospitalization rate due to COVID-19 in Poland (6%) was found to be higher than in Turkey (2%). The symptoms development rate (52%) in Poland due to COVID-19 was found to be statistically significantly higher than in Turkey (15%).

Working history of participants during COVID-19 showed that one-fourth of dentists (23%) mostly from Turkey has continued to work as usual, whereas approximately two-thirds of dentists (63.7%): 162 Polish and 93 Turkish dentists have had a break (lock down) to their practice for some period. Even though there were significant differences in percentage of dentists who kept working as usual and the ones having breaks in dental services by stopping all activities for some periods (due to lockdowns, quarantines, COVID-19 infection etc.), the emergencies were treated in both countries by similar number of dentists, usually the ones who limited their service to urgent procedures.

Treatment time for dental procedures during the COVID-19 pandemic in Poland was found to be 25% longer and significantly higher than in Turkey, whereas decrease in income among Polish dentists (81%) was found to be statistically higher than among Turkish dentists (47.5%).

Polish dentists self assessed their perception of having enough knowledge about COVID-19 significantly lower than dentists in Turkey. Meanwhile the rate of Polish dentists marking that COVID-19 is most likely a risk for infection for them; being unsure of ability to prevent the transmission of COVID-19 during business activities and apprehension of infection transmission's risk in the dental practice was found to be higher than in Turkey.

The participants, who have mentioned that they had COVID-19 positive test results, were also asked to give the details about their symptoms (Table 2).

Table 1. Evaluation of study parameters across countries.

		Country		Total	p
		Poland	Turkey		
		M ± SD	M ± SD	M ± SD	
Age		41.32 ± 8.88	43.46 ± 10.91	42.39 ± 9.99	0.032 [1,*]
		n (%)	n (%)	n (%)	
Gender	Male	74 (37%)	88 (44%)	162 (40.5%)	0.154 [2]
	Female	126 (63%)	112 (56%)	238 (59.5%)	
Working status	Private	83 (41.5%)	127 (63.5%)	210 (52.5%)	0.000 [2,*]
	Public	51 (25.5%)	38 (19%)	89 (22.3%)	
	Mixed	66 (33%)	35 (17.5%)	101 (25.3%)	
Positive COVID-19 test result	Yes	108 (54%)	32 (16%)	140 (35%)	0.000 [2,*]
	No	10 (5%)	168 (84%)	178 (44.5%)	
	No test	82 (41%)	0 (0%)	82 (20.5%)	
Hospitalization rate due to COVID-19	Yes	12 (6%)	4 (2%)	16 (4%)	0.000 [2,*]
	No	98 (49%)	28 (14%)	126 (31.5%)	
	NA	90 (45%)	168 (84%)	258 (64.5%)	
Symptoms development rate	Yes	104 (52%)	30 (15%)	134 (33.5%)	0.000 [3,*]
	No	4 (2%)	2 (1%)	6 (1.5%)	
	NA	92 (46%)	168 (84%)	260 (65%)	
Currently working	Yes	200 (100%)	181 (90.5%)	381 (95.3%)	0.000 [4,*]
	No	0 (0%)	19 (9.5%)	19 (4.8%)	
COVID-19 working history	As Usual	14 (7%)	78 (39%)	92 (23%)	0.000 [2,*]
	Emergencies	24 (12%)	29 (14.5%)	53 (13.3%)	
	Break	162 (81%)	93 (46.5%)	255 (63.7%)	
Treatment time for dental procedures	<25%	0 (0%)	16 (8%)	16 (4%)	0.000 [2,*]
	>25%	200 (100%)	120 (60%)	320 (80%)	
	No change	0 (0%)	64 (32%)	64 (16%)	
Income of dentists	D < 25%	162 (81%)	95 (47.5%)	257 (64.3%)	0.000 [2,*]
	D > 25%	24 (12%)	36 (18%)	60 (15%)	
	No change	14 (7%)	69 (34.5%)	83 (20.8%)	
COVID-19 self-assessed perception of knowledge	Yes	0 (0%)	145 (72.5%)	145 (36.3%)	0.000 [4,*]
	No	200 (100%)	55 (27.5%)	255 (63.7%)	
Risk of infection for the dentist	Very likely	200 (100%)	141 (70.5%)	341 (85.3%)	0.000 [2,*]
	Likely	0 (0%)	49 (24.5%)	49 (12.3%)	
	Unlikely	0 (0%)	10 (5%)	10 (2.5%)	
Infection avoidance at clinic	NC	200 (100%)	44 (22%)	244 (61%)	0.000 [2,*]
	AC	0 (0%)	56 (28%)	56 (14%)	
	C	0 (0%)	100 (50%)	100 (25%)	
Rate of apprehension of infection transmission's risk	Higher	200 (100%)	87 (43.5%)	287 (71.8%)	0.000 [2,*]
	Lower	0 (0%)	76 (38%)	76 (19%)	
	Same	0 (0%)	37 (18.5%)	37 (9.3%)	

[1] Student t Test. [2] Ki-Kare Test. [3] Fisher Freeman Halton Test. [4] Continuity (Yates) Correction. * $p < 0.05$. Notes: NA: Not applicable, NC: No confident, AC: Abit confident, C: Confident, M ± SD: Mean ± Standart deviation.

Table 2. Evaluation of COVID-19 symptoms across countries.

You Had One/More Symptoms/Signs		Country		Total	p
		Poland	Turkey		
		n (%)	n (%)	n (%)	
Fever	Yes	86 (43%)	14 (7%)	100 (25%)	0.000 [1,*]
	No	22 (11%)	18 (9%)	40 (10%)	
	NA	92 (46%)	168 (84%)	260 (65%)	
Cough	Yes	68 (34%)	9 (4.5%)	77 (19.3%)	0.000 [1,*]
	No	40 (20%)	23 (11.5%)	63 (15.8%)	
	NA	92 (46%)	168 (84)%	260 (65%)	
Fattigue	Yes	86 (43%)	25 (12.5%)	111 (27.8%)	0.000 [1,*]
	No	22 (11%)	7 (3.5%)	29 (7.2%)	
	NA	92 (46%)	168 (84%)	260 (65%)	
Pain	Yes	86 (43%)	9 (4.5%)	95 (23.8%)	0.000 [1,*]
	No	22 (11%)	23 (11.5%)	45 (11.3%)	
	NA	92 (46%)	168 (84%)	260 (65%)	
Headache	Yes	81 (40.5%)	16 (8%)	97 (24.3%)	0.000 [1,*]
	No	27 (13.5%)	16 (8%)	43 (10.8%)	
	NA	92 (46%)	168 (84%)	260 (65%)	

[1] Ki-Kare Test. * $p < 0.05$. Note: NA: Not applicable.

The rate of symptoms such as fever, cough, fatigue, pain and headache was significantly higher in Poland than in Turkey. This correlates with higher number of positive COVID-19 test results and symptoms development rate among Polish dentists in comparison to Turkish ones.

Evaluation of equipment used in dental clinics before COVID-19 between countries Poland and Turkey mostly gave similar results before COVID-19 (Table 3).

Table 3. Evaluation of equipment used before COVID-19 in both countries.

Which of the Following Protective Equipment Did You Wear/Use before COVID-19 Pandemic?		Country		Total	p
		Poland	Turkey		
		n (%)	n (%)	n (%)	
Masks (Surgical)	Yes	200 (100%)	187 (93.5%)	387 (96.8%)	0.001 [1,*]
	No	0 (0%)	13 (6.5%)	13 (3.3%)	
Masks (N95,N99/FFP2,FFP3)	Yes	0 (0%)	38 (19%)	38 (9.5%)	0.000 [1,*]
	No	200 (100%)	162 (81%)	362 (90.5%)	
Reusable Full-face Respirators	Yes	0 (0%)	11 (5.5%)	11 (2.8%)	0.002 [1,*]
	No	200 (100%)	189 (94.5%)	389 (97.3%)	
Reusable Half-face Respirators	Yes	0 (0%)	12 (6%)	12 (3%)	0.001 [1,*]
	No	200 (100%)	188 (94%)	388 (97%)	
Gown (Sterile disposable)	Yes	0 (0%)	29 (14.5%)	29 (7.2%)	0.000 [1,*]
	No	200 (100%)	171 (85.5%)	371 (92.8%)	
Gown (Disposable)	Yes	0 (0%)	96 (48%)	96 (24%)	0.000 [1,*]
	No	200 (100%)	104 (52%)	304 (76%)	
Glasses(protection)	Yes	200 (100%)	120 (60%)	320 (80%)	0.000 [1,*]
	No	0 (0%)	80 (40%)	80 (20%)	
Gloves Sterile	Yes	200 (100%)	91 (45.5%)	291 (72.8%)	0.000 [1,*]
	No	0 (0%)	109 (54.5%)	109 (27.3%)	
Gloves Non-sterile	Yes	200 (100%)	172 (86%)	372 (93%)	0.000 [1,*]
	No	0 (0%)	28 (14%)	28 (7%)	
Anti-retraction system valve rotaries	Yes	200 (100%)	0 (0%)	200 (50%)	0.000 [1,*]
	No	0 (0%)	200 (100%)	200 (50%)	

[1] Continuity (Yates) Correction. * $p < 0.05$.

Evaluation of equipment used during COVID-19 in Poland and Turkey mostly gave similar results (Table 4). The rates of usage of surgical masks and N95/FFP2 or N99/FFP3 masks in Poland and Turkey were significantly high. Reusable full face mask and half face mask usage rate was significantly higher in Turkey (23%; 16.5%). All survey participants in Poland prefer to use disposable gowns (100%) during the COVID-19 pandemic, whereas in Turkey even though most of participants prefer to use disposable gowns (65%) many other also use sterile disposable gowns (32.5%).

Table 4. Evaluation of equipment used during the COVID-19 pandemic in both countries.

Which of the Following Protective Equipment Did You Wear/Use during COVID-19 Pandemic?		Country		Total	*p*
		Poland	Turkey		
		n (%)	*n* (%)	*n* (%)	
Masks (Surgical)	Yes	200 (100%)	162 (81%)	362 (90.5%)	0.000 *
	No	0 (0%)	38 (19%)	38 (9.5%)	
Masks (N95,N99/FFP2,FFP3)	Yes	200 (100%)	183 (91.5%)	383 (95.8%)	0.000 *
	No	0 (0%)	17 (8.5%)	17 (4.3%)	
Reusable Full-face Respirators	Yes	0 (0%)	33 (16.5%)	33 (8.3%)	0.000 *
	No	200 (100%)	167 (83.5%)	367 (91.8%)	
Reusable Half-face Respirators	Yes	0 (0%)	46 (23%)	46 (11.5%)	0.000 *
	No	200 (100%)	154 (77%)	354 (88.5%)	
Gown (Sterile disposable)	Yes	0 (0%)	65 (32.5%)	65 (16.3%)	0.000 *
	No	200 (100%)	135 (67.5%)	335 (83.8%)	
Gown (Disposable)	Yes	200 (100%)	130 (65%)	330 (82.5%)	0.000 *
	No	0 (0%)	70 (35%)	70 (17.5%)	
Glasses(protection)	Yes	200 (100%)	161 (80.5%)	361 (90.3%)	0.000 *
	No	0 (0%)	39 (19.5%)	39 (9.8%)	
Gloves Sterile	Yes	200 (100%)	91 (45.5%)	291 (72.8%)	0.000 *
	No	0 (0%)	109 (54.5%)	109 (27.3%)	
Gloves Non-sterile	Yes	200 (100%)	172 (86%)	372 (93%)	0.000 *
	No	0 (0%)	28 (14%)	28 (7%)	
Anti-retraction system valve rotaries	Yes	200 (100%)	27 (13.5%)	227 (56.8%)	0.000 *
	No	0 (0%)	173 (86.5%)	173 (43.3%)	

Continuity (Yates) Correction. * $p < 0.05$.

4. Discussion

There are not many researches in the subject of the working environment and conditions of dentists during the COVID-19 pandemic. Most of the existing research have been carried out in the form of online surveys due to the pandemic restrictions in many countries. In the cross-sectional study performed in Switzerland and Liechtenstein, the economic effects of the protective measures taken by the governments were examined [8]. The authors pointed out that the strategies for additional protective measures should be better defined and that political decision makers should consider the serious economic implications when creating new rules. It has been reported that drastic measures such as "isolation", which can lead to closures and unemployment, should be taken into account labor and economic losses.

Another published article evaluated COVID-19 preventive measures: awareness and perception among Italian dentists in Lombardy [9]. In this survey study, symptoms were collected in regions where the prevalence of the disease was different. Although this survey reported that dentists in the region where COVID-19 was most prevalent, had more symptoms than the rest of the sample, those who adopted a few precautionary measures were more confident in avoiding infection.

In our study the number of positive COVID-19 test results among dentists in Poland was found to be significantly higher than in Turkey, what consequently might explain the three times higher hospitalization rate in investigated group in Poland. The symptoms development rate in Poland due to COVID-19 was found to be statistically significantly higher than in Turkey, and the symptoms were: fever, cough, fatigue, pain and headache as also reported by Cagetti et al. [9].

Dental-related aspects on COVID-19 pandemic were also studied by another recent survey conducted on 440 participants from Central Italy [13]. Results of this research revealed that most professionals respected the advices given by authorities, showing parallel results with our study. In Central Italy mainly only emergency procedures were performed during the lockdown and the dental pulp inflammation treatment was one of the most frequent procedures. Authors concluded with very important recommendations stating that procedures such as telemedicine and triage are useful tools to assess patients conditions before the dental visit [13].

The oral manifestation of SARS-CoV-2 and the importance of the professional figure of the dentist in the diagnosis of COVID-19 should be discussed as well. In an observational human study on 20 patients hospitalized in Chieti, Italy, such oral manifestation as xerostomia and low salivary flow rate has been followed, even though according to the evidence, it was hard to conclude that those clinical conditions were due to SARS-CoV-2 infection [14]. Furthermore, the dysgeusia symptom was reported as a warning signal for the patients. The decrease of the proper oral hygiene level among hospitalized patients was also noticed. Authors emphasized the importance of the dentists in following the infected patients and suggested to have a team specialized in dentistry within hospitals treating the COVID-19 patients [14].

Treatment time of dental procedures during the COVID-19 pandemic in Poland and Turkey was found to be increased. This has to be carefully evaluated considering the workforce of dentistry. As also mentioned in article published by Wolf et al. the lockdowns have important effect on income of dentists [8]. In our survey we found that Polish dentists had more decrease in their income, which may be explained by lockdowns. In Turkey decrease in income may have been felt less than in Poland. Dentists in public service were directed to COVID-19 testing and vaccination activities by Ministry of Health, what nearly caused the public dental clinics stopping dental services and parallel more patients were treated in private clinics.

Evaluation of the changes in equipment usage before and during COVID-19 pandemic in Poland reveals the increase in the usage of N95/FFP2 or N99/FFP3 masks during pandemic compared to pre-COVID-19 periods. Also the usage of surgical gown was statistically significant. It may be very easily explained by the working protection guidelines for Polish dentists created by authorities for the pandemic period. The decrease in normal surgical masks' usage in Turkey may be caused by high increase in the use of more protective masks such as N95/FFP2 or N99/FFP3 during pandemic compared to pre-COVID-19 time [6]. Reusable full-face and half-face elastomeric respirators were also increasingly used in Turkey during COVID-19.

Lack of uniform blueprints and guidelines for working conditions of dentists during the pandemic such as the COVID-19 was also mentioned by Wiesmüller et al. [13]. The high risk of infection in the dental working conditions in Austria, Germany and Switzerland was acknowledged in this study as well as the need of evaluation of the number of infections among dentists in other European countries was mentioned. Also previously mentioned studies suggest more researches on the influence of pandemic on dental working environment should be carried out [8,9,15]. Thus our study reports data from two countries in Europe and allows making primary conclusions on how the working conditions of the dentists were affected by COVID-19.

5. Conclusions

The increase in the dental treatment procedures' time, higher usage of personal protective equipment, bigger risk of infection at work and decrease in income during COVID-19 pandemic were expected results of our study. Even though all efforts were given to reach as many dentists as possible, the study investigates random group of 400 dentists, but despite this limitation of this research, there were enough data for primary analysis. Regardless the fact that the evaluation was addressed to dentists from two countries and pandemic situation may vary from country to country in terms of infection rate, legislation etc., when the specific dental working conditions and evidence is taken into account, the overall conclusions may be addressed in a wider perspective. Many different aspects of the evaluated dental working conditions were affected by COVID-19 pandemic in both countries. The study results reveal the increase in the dental treatment procedures' time compared to pre-pandemic situation in Turkey and Poland. Also the usage of protective equipment was higher, what can be considered as an additional cost for dentists. At the same time there was a decrease of income reported in as well as many dentists got infected at work in Turkey and Poland.

Governments, national bodies and all those who influence the workplaces of dentists have to introduce minimum standards for facilities and working conditions for dentists during pandemic. Countries should also significantly increase their investments in the healthcare sector in order to improve the working conditions and occupational safety of dentists. Further studies in more countries or multi-centered international researches analyzing the working conditions of dentists during COVID-19 pandemic would be a very important source for regulating institutions to prepare guidelines for similar future pandemic situations.

Author Contributions: Conceptualization, I.O.-C. and S.S.; methodology, I.O.-C. and S.S.; software, S.S.; validation, I.O.-C. and S.S.; formal analysis, I.O.-C. and S.S.; investigation, I.O.-C. and S.S., resources, I.O.-C.; data curation, I.O.-C. and S.S.; writing—original draft preparation, S.S.; writing—review and editing, I.O.-C.; visualization, I.O.-C. and S.S.; supervision, I.O.-C. and S.S.; project administration, I.O.-C. All authors have read and agreed to the published version of the manuscript.

Funding: This research received no external funding.

Institutional Review Board Statement: The study was conducted according to the guidelines of the Declaration of Helsinki, and approved by the Ethics Committee of Jagiellonian University (protocol No. 1072.6120.157.2021 and approval date 16 June 2021).

Informed Consent Statement: Informed consent was obtained from all participants in the study.

Data Availability Statement: The data presented in this study are available on request from the corresponding author. The data are not publicly available due to ethical restrictions.

Conflicts of Interest: The authors declare no conflict of interest.

References

1. Khajuria, A.; Tomaszewski, W.; Liu, Z.; Chen, J.-H.; Mehdian, R.; Fleming, S.; Vig, S.; Crawford, M.J. Workplace factors associated with mental health of healthcare workers during the COVID-19 pandemic: An international cross-sectional study. *BMC Health Serv. Res.* **2021**, *21*, 262. [CrossRef] [PubMed]
2. World Health Organization. Corona Virus Situation Reports. Available online: https://www.who.int/docs/default-source/coronaviruse/situation-reports/20210709_weekly_epi_update_48_draft.pdf?sfvrsn=a0036c11_26&download=true (accessed on 14 July 2021).
3. Rothe, C.; Schunk, M.; Sothmann, P.; Bretzel, G.; Froeschl, G.; Wallrauch, C.; Zimmer, T.; Thiel, V.; Janke, C.; Guggemos, W.; et al. Transmission of 2019-nCoV Infection from an Asymptomatic Contact in Germany. *N. Engl. J. Med.* **2020**, *382*, 970–971. [CrossRef] [PubMed]
4. Daly, J. Editorial: The impact of COVID-19 on population oral health. *Community Dent. Health* **2020**, *37*, 236–239. [PubMed]
5. Peng, X.; Xu, X.; Li, Y.; Cheng, L.; Zhou, X.; Ren, B. Transmission routes of 2019-nCoV and controls in dental practice. *Int. J. Oral Sci.* **2020**, *12*, 9. [CrossRef] [PubMed]
6. Sozkes, S.; Sozkes, S. COVID-19 and respiratory protection for healthcare providers. *Int. J. Occup. Med. Environ. Health* **2021**, *34*, 307–318. [CrossRef] [PubMed]

7. Radonovich, L.J.; Simberkoff, M.S.; Bessesen, M.T.; Brown, A.C.; Cummings, D.A.T.; Gaydos, C.A.; Los, J.G.; Krosche, A.E.; Gibert, C.L.; Gorse, G.J.; et al. N95 Respirators vs. Medical Masks for Preventing Influenza Among Health Care Personnel. *JAMA* **2019**, *322*, 824–833. [CrossRef] [PubMed]
8. Wolf, T.G.; Zeyer, O. Guglielmo Campus COVID-19 in Switzerland and Liechtenstein: A Cross-Sectional Survey among Dentists' Awareness, Protective Measures and Economic Effects. *Int. J. Environ. Res. Public Health* **2020**, *17*, 9051. [CrossRef] [PubMed]
9. Cagetti, M.G.; Cairoli, J.L.; Senna, A. Guglielmo Campus COVID-19 Outbreak in North Italy: An Overview on Dentistry. A Questionnaire Survey. *Int. J. Environ. Res. Public Health* **2020**, *17*, 3835. [CrossRef] [PubMed]
10. Campus, G.; Diaz-Betancourt, M.; Cagetti, M.; Carvalho, J.; Carvalho, T.; Cortés-Martinicorena, J.; Deschner, J.; Douglas, G.; Giacaman, R.; Machiulskiene, V.; et al. Study Protocol for an Online Questionnaire Survey on Symptoms/Signs, Protective Measures, Level of Awareness and Perception Regarding COVID-19 Outbreak among Dentists. A Global Survey. *Int. J. Environ. Res. Public Health* **2020**, *17*, 5598. [CrossRef] [PubMed]
11. Koo, T.K.; Li, M.Y. A Guideline of Selecting and Reporting Intraclass Correlation Coefficients for Reliability Research. *J. Chiropr. Med.* **2016**, *15*, 155–163. [CrossRef] [PubMed]
12. Karataban, P.K. Anxiety of Dental Professionals during Covid-19 Pandemic. In *Anxiety, Uncertainty, and Resilience during the Pandemic Period-Anthropological and Psychological Perspectives*; IntechOpen: London, UK, 2021. [CrossRef]
13. Sinjari, B.; Rexhepi, I.; Santilli, M.; D'addazio, G.; Chiacchiaretta, P.; Di Carlo, P.; Caputi, S. The Impact of COVID-19 Related Lockdown on Dental Practice in Central Italy—Outcomes of A Survey. *Int. J. Environ. Res. Public Health* **2020**, *17*, 5780. [CrossRef] [PubMed]
14. Sinjari, B.; D'Ardes, D.; Santilli, M.; Rexhepi, I.; D'Addazio, G.; Di Carlo, P.; Chiacchiaretta, P.; Caputi, S.; Cipollone, F. SARS-CoV-2 and Oral Manifestation: An Observational, Human Study. *J. Clin. Med.* **2020**, *9*, 3218. [CrossRef] [PubMed]
15. Wiesmüller, V.; Bruckmoser, E.; Kapferer-Seebacher, I.; Fink, K.; Neururer, S.; Schnabl, D.; Laimer, J. Dentists' Working Conditions during the First COVID-19 Pandemic Lockdown: An Online Survey. *Healthcare* **2021**, *9*, 364. [CrossRef] [PubMed]

medicina

MDPI

Review

COVID-19 and Its Repercussions on Oral Health: A Review

Laura-Cristina Rusu [1], Lavinia Cosmina Ardelean [2,*], Codruta Victoria Tigmeanu [2], Anamaria Matichescu [3,*], Iulia Sauciur [1] and Emanuel Adrian Bratu [4]

1 Department of Oral Pathology, Multidisciplinary Center for Research, Evaluation, Diagnosis and Therapies in Oral Medicine, "Victor Babeș" University of Medicine and Pharmacy Timisoara, 2 Eftimie Murgu Sq., 300041 Timisoara, Romania; laura.rusu@umft.ro (L.-C.R.); sauciuriulia@yahoo.com (I.S.)
2 Department of Technology of Materials and Devices in Dental Medicine, Multidisciplinary Center for Research, Evaluation, Diagnosis and Therapies in Oral Medicine, "Victor Babeș" University of Medicine and Pharmacy Timisoara, 2 Eftimie Murgu Sq., 300041 Timisoara, Romania; tigmeanu.codruta@umft.ro
3 Department of Preventive Dentistry, Community and Oral Health, Translational and Experimental Clinical Research Center in Oral Health, "Victor Babeș" University of Medicine and Pharmacy Timisoara, 2 Eftimie Murgu Sq., 300041 Timisoara, Romania
4 Department of Implant Supported Restorations, "Victor Babeș" University of Medicine and Pharmacy Timisoara, 2 Eftimie Murgu Sq., 300041 Timisoara, Romania; ebratu@umft.ro
* Correspondence: lavinia_ardelean@umft.ro (L.C.A.); matichescu.anamaria@umft.ro (A.M.)

Abstract: In 2019, a new type of coronavirus, SARS-CoV-2, the causing agent of COVID-19, was first detected in Wuhan, China. On 11 March 2020, the World Health Organization declared a pandemic. The manifestations of COVID-19 are mostly age-dependent and potentially more severe in cases with involved co-morbidities. The gravity of the symptoms depends on the clinical stage of the infection. The most common symptoms include runny nose and nasal congestion, anosmia, dysgeusia or hypogeusia, diarrhea, nausea/vomiting, respiratory distress, fatigue, ocular symptoms, diarrhea, vomiting, and abdominal pain. These systemic conditions are often accompanied by skin and mucosal lesions. Oral lesions reported in patients with COVID-19 include: herpex simplex, candidiasis, geographic tongue, aphthous-like ulcers, hemorrhagic ulcerations, necrotic ulcerations, white hairy tongue, reddish macules, erythematous surfaces, petechiae, and pustular enanthema. It is still unclear if these manifestations are a direct result of the viral infection, a consequence of systemic deterioration, or adverse reactions to treatments. Poor oral hygiene in hospitalized or quarantined COVID-19 patients should also be considered as an aggravating condition. This narrative review is focused on presenting the most relevant data from the literature regarding oral manifestations related to SARS-CoV-2, as well as the challenges faced by the dental system during this pandemic. A routine intraoral examination is recommended in COVID-19 patients, either suspected or confirmed, as, in certain cases, oral manifestations represent a sign of severe infection or even of a life-threatening condition. It is our belief that extensive knowledge of all possible manifestations, including oral lesions, in cases of COVID-19 is of great importance in the present uncertain context, including new, currently emerging viral variants with unknown future impact.

Keywords: COVID-19; SARS-CoV-2; pandemic; oral lesions; oral manifestations; periodontal disease; temporomandibular disorders; dental medicine

Citation: Rusu, L.-C.; Ardelean, L.C.; Tigmeanu, C.V.; Matichescu, A.; Sauciur, I.; Bratu, E.A. COVID-19 and Its Repercussions on Oral Health: A Review. *Medicina* **2021**, *57*, 1189. https://doi.org/10.3390/medicina57111189

Academic Editors: Cesare D'Amico and Pier Paolo Poli

Received: 6 October 2021
Accepted: 28 October 2021
Published: 1 November 2021

1. The Essentials about CoVs

Coronaviruses (CoVs) are members of the Coronaviridae family. These enveloped viruses possess a non-segmented, single-stranded, positive-sense RNA, with a unique replication strategy [1].

CoVs are known to affect different animal species and cause mild to severe respiratory infections in humans. In 2002 and 2012, two highly pathogenic coronaviruses of zoonotic origin, causing the severe acute respiratory coronavirus syndrome (SARS-CoV-1) and the Middle East respiratory coronavirus syndrome (MERS-CoV), respectively, affected humans, resulting in fatal respiratory diseases [2,3], and turning coronaviruses into a 21st century public health problem. The virus has been identified in various non-human hosts [4–7]. Extremely pathogenic CoVs belong to the genus Beta-coronavirus, group 2, which causes severe disease [8].

In 2019, a new type of coronavirus, SARS-CoV-2, a Beta-coronavirus causing the COVID-19 disease, was first detected in Wuhan, China [9]. SARS-CoV-2 is composed of 16 non-structural proteins with specific roles in replication [10]. COVID-19 has spread rapidly around the world and, on 11 March 2020, the World Health Organization declared it a pandemic [11].

The SARS-CoV-2 genome sequence shares ~80% sequence identity with SARS-CoV-1 and ~50% with MERS-CoV [12]. The structural spike protein (S), which mediates SARS-CoV's entry into host cells, is highly variable in the case of SARS-CoV-2. Its receptor-binding domain enables direct contact with the cell receptor angiotensin-converting enzyme II (ACE2) [5,13].

ACE2, and thus any cells that express ACE2, may be target cells and therefore susceptible to COVID-19 infection [12]. Zou et al. [14] explored the expression of the ACE2 receptor on different cells from human body tissues and classified the infectious risk potential. Lung, heart, esophagus, kidney, bladder, and ileum have been considered organs at risk [14]. A high ACE2 expression was found in the oral mucosa and the epithelial cells of the tongue [15]. After entering the cell, the virus delays the immune system response, allowing the infection to progress, and it becomes much harder to fight [16].

2. Main Characteristics of COVID-19

2.1. General Characteristics

The host's response represents an important factor in the disease process and tissue damage. In most cases of SARS-CoV-2 infection, the primary immune response leads to viral elimination. In certain patients, the secondary immune response may be exaggerated and lead to inflammation-induced lung damage, pneumonia, acute respiratory distress syndrome, respiratory failure, shock, organ failure, and possible death [17].

Severe COVID-19 is also characterized by hypercoagulopathy and neurological and/or gastrointestinal tract damage, the fatal outcome in severe cases being due to the macrophage activation syndrome, which causes a "cytokine storm" [18].

Age, acute cardiac injury, heart failure, skeletal muscle injury, and lymphopenia have been associated with mortality in COVID-19 cases [19,20].

The most common symptoms (Figure 1) include fever, cough, runny nose and nasal congestion, anosmia, dysgeusia/hypogeusia, diarrhea, and nausea/vomiting [21,22]. Other clinical manifestations include: fatigue, ocular symptoms (conjunctival secretion), and arrhythmias. Gastrointestinal symptoms or abdominal pain can occur in the absence of respiratory symptoms. Acute cholestasis and pancreatitis have also been reported in children and adolescents [23,24].

The gravity of the symptoms depends on the clinical stage of the infection [25,26]. Moderate infection has been reported as pneumonia, without obvious hypoxemia or difficulty in breathing. Clinical signs and symptoms, as well as the thoracic CT, suggest subclinical lung lesions. In cases of severe infection, oxygen saturation is less than 92%, with manifestations of hypoxia [24]. Critical infection is characterized by respiratory failure, shock, encephalopathy, myocardial injury or heart failure, coagulation dysfunction and acute kidney damage, and multiple organ dysfunction [23].

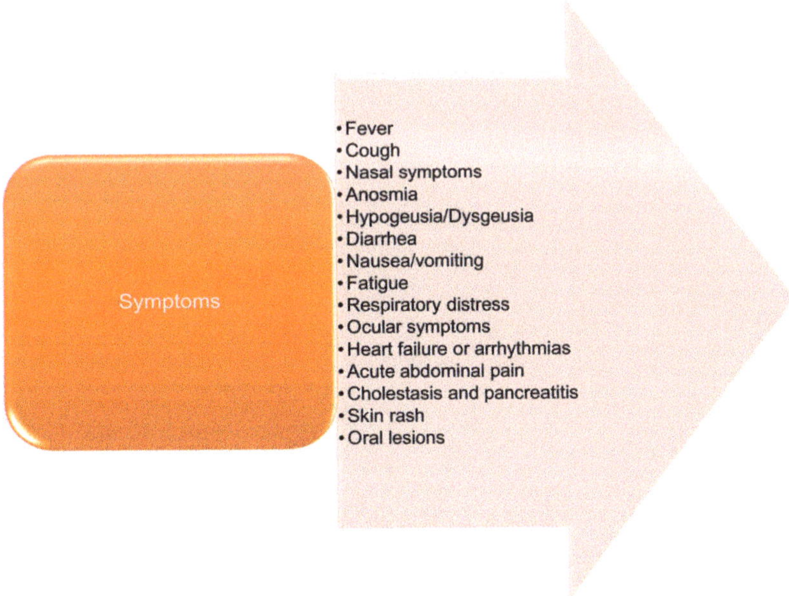

Figure 1. Main symptoms of COVID-19.

2.2. Severity by Age

The manifestations of COVID-19 are mostly age-dependent and potentially more severe in cases with involved co-morbidities. The severity of the disease was found to correlate with increasing age [27]. Patients over 65 years of age have a high risk for COVID-19 infection, develop more severe forms, and show increased mortality [19,28,29] due to low immune response [30]. In addition, other factors, such as underlying cardiovascular disease (CVD), may negatively influence the clinical outcome and explain the higher mortality rate, as CVD prevalence increases with age [20]. Older patients show higher incidences of skeletal muscle injury and acute kidney injury [19].

In the early stages of the pandemic, young patients had better clinical outcomes compared to adults, and death rates were lower. In most cases, children diagnosed with COVID-19 developed asymptomatic, mild, or moderate illnesses and recovered one or two weeks after the onset of the disease [23], the clinical symptoms being milder then in adults [26]. Children, even if asymptomatic, can transmit the disease very easily, nasal and fecal secretions being a further challenge for infection control [31].

No differences were identified between young patients and elderly patients in terms of the degree of lung damage [32] but, in elderly patients, the involvement of multiple lobes was higher [29].

As older age groups are vaccinated, children and unvaccinated populations are becoming at higher risk of contracting COVID-19, and developing severe illness. Furthermore, the more contagious Delta strain, which is dominant at present, seems to be impacting younger age groups more than previous variants, despite the fact that does not specifically target children [33].

2.3. Skin Involvement

The systemic conditions may be accompanied by skin lesions in which the innate immune system is involved [34,35]. Associated immune-mediated skin diseases, such as psoriasis, atopic dermatitis, and suppurative hidradenitis, have been reported [36,37].

The skin lesions most often associated with COVID-19 are morbilliform, pernio-like, urticarial, macular erythematous, vesicular, and papulosquamous lesions, as well as retiform purpura and chilblains [38–45]. Skin lesions such as maculopapular lesions and urticarial and vesicular eruptions, as well as transient livedo reticularis and acral peeling, are also frequently mentioned. In children and young adults, red-purple nodules have also been described on distal figures (sometimes called "COVID toes"), similar in appearance to perblio (chilblains) [46].

Skin manifestations are often accompanied by mucosal damage. Extensive skin lesions over the fleshy portion of the buttocks and on the mucosa of the nostrils, tongue, lips, and urethra were reported in hospitalized COVID-19 patients, despite the minimal exposure to pressure. Their extent suggests an inflammatory vascular process beyond pressure-related skin damage [47].

3. Oral Lesions Related to COVID-19

This narrative review is focused on presenting the most relevant data from the literature regarding oral manifestations related to SARS-CoV-2, as well as the challenges faced by the dental system during this pandemic.

An electronic search was conducted in PubMed, Scopus, and Web of Science for studies published up to April 2021, with the following keywords used: "oral lesions", "mucosal lesions", "COVID-19", OR "SARS-CoV-2". The full-text articles were evaluated, and the references cited by the relevant studies were further manually searched. Given the available data limited, only literature reviews were excluded. Articles for which the full text was not accessible or not available in English were also excluded.

Reports of different oral manifestations related to COVID-19 cases were described in the literature. Oral lesions reported in patients with COVID-19 were quite heterogeneous (Table 1), varying in the kind of lesion and location. In most cases, the pathogenesis of these manifestations was not clearly defined, being categorized as a direct result of the viral infection, a consequence of immune misbalance, or an adverse reaction to treatment [47–49]. Poor oral hygiene in hospitalized or quarantined COVID-19 patients should also be considered as an aggravating condition [50].

Amorim dos Santos et al. [51] described the case of multiple oral lesions in a 67-year-old man diagnosed with COVID-19. After 20 days of hospitalization, a persistent white plaque on the tongue dorsum was detected and diagnosed as fungus infection. This lesion was treated with intravenous fluconazole and oral nystatin, without any result. Multiple yellowish pinpoint ulcers, diagnosed as recurrent oral herpes, were also present on the tongue dorsum. A fibroma, about 1 cm in diameter, in the lower lip, related to previous conditions, was also observed. The tongue scraping culture presented Saccharomyces cerevisiae. These conditions were accompanied by extremely viscous saliva. As treatment, antifungals were administered and chlorhexidine digluconate (0.12%) non-alcoholic mouthwashes and daily applications of 1% hydrogen peroxide were performed. After 2 weeks, the lesions showed an almost complete remission, but severe, asymptomatic geographical tongue was observed, according to the severity index [52]. Ten days after removing the patient from hospital, the geographical tongue was still present, but it was reclassified as moderate according to the severity index. [52] The authors suggested that the oral lesions, coinfections, and secondary manifestations may have been due to systemic condition of the patient.

Ansari et al. [53] presented two cases, a 75-year-old male and a 56-year-old female, involving several painful ulcers with irregular margins and varying sizes, with red and non-hemorrhagic backgrounds, located on the hard palate and anterior region of the tongue, respectively. In case 1, the lesions appeared five days after the onset of the symptoms and, in case 2, one week after hospitalization. The diagnostic was of diffuse edema with desquamation, granulation, and ulceration under the mucosa and with invasion of mononuclear and neutrophilic cells, indicating a secondary bacterial infection. The serologic tests for herpes simplex virus (HSV-1 and HSV-2) were negative. The treatment consisted of diphenhydramine, dexamethasone, tetracycline, and lidocaine, and complete recovery was obtained after approximately 7 days. The authors suggested that the oral lesions were due to COVID-19.

Bezerra et al. [54] reported a case of a 33-year-old male patient, treated with ivermectin and azithromycin for suspicion of COVID-19, who developed a painful mouth ulceration in the floor of mouth. After 10 days of topical application of corticosteroids, the lesion showed full remission. After twenty days, ageusia was still present, and two other crateriform ulcers with a necrotic background and no erythematous halo were detected in the left retromolar region and lip mucosa. The patient did not report any history of recurrent aphthous ulceration. After 7 days of topical treatment with triamcinolone acetonide and 0.12% chlorhexidine digluconate mouthwash, the oral ulcerations showed total remission.

Brandao et al. [55] presented eight cases of different oral manifestations in patients with COVID-19.

Case 1. A case of an 81-year-old male, presenting multiple painful, shallow aphthous-like ulcers with irregular margins covered with mucopurulent membrane in the mucosa of the upper and lower lips, as well as in the anterior tongue dorsum, was reported. HSV-1 was identified by saliva testing. Treatment with intravenous acyclovir three times a day for 10 days showed no clinical improvement. To relieve the pain caused by oral ulcers, photobiomodular (PBMT) therapy was performed for 10 days. The symptoms improved after 2 days and after 11 days they were completely resolved.

Case 2. A 71-year-old female presented small hemorrhagic ulcerations on the upper and lower lips. Focal areas of superficial necrosis on the anterior tongue dorsum, developed at the time of hospitalization, were also observed. Following the PCR saliva test, HSV-1 was identified. Intravenous acyclovir was administrated three times a day for 7 days, without any results. Pain was treated with PBMT and regression was observed after 10 days of light therapy, but the lip ulcers did not heal even after 15 days of therapy.

Case 3. In the case of an 83-year-old female, the oral examination revealed an ulcer of 1.5×1.5 cm^2 on the right lateral edge of the tongue, accompanied by a petechiae and a superficial necrotic area in the anterior hard palate. These lesions were painful. Following the PCR test, a negative result was obtained for the HSV-1. After 5 days of PBMT treatment, the pain started to diminish, with remission after 10 days.

Case 4. The case of a 72-year-old male with small hemorrhagic ulcerations affecting the upper and lower lips and a painful necrotic ulceration on the mucosa of the lower right lip, detected a few days after hospitalization, was described. The HSV-1 was detected following the PCR test. The patient received intravenous acyclovir treatment for 7 days, but no improvement was observed. The painful oral necrotic ulcers were treated with PBMT, and regression was observed after 7 days of light therapy.

Case 5. A 32-year-old female, isolated at home with a mild form of COVID-19, showed multiple ulcers on the tip and lateral edges of the tongue, after 10 days of treatment. A teleconsultation was performed by a dentist, following which small superficial and circular lesions with a whitish center and surrounded by an erythematous halo were observed. The patient had no history of recurrent oral ulcers, oral inflammatory diseases, or allergies. After 14 days, the patient recovered from COVID-19 and 8 days later the oral lesions showed remission.

Case 6. Another case was that of a 35-year-old male, quarantined at home, who presented ageusia 6 days later and an oral ulcer on the tonsillar pillar, which caused mild odynophagia. Following the teleconsultation, the following information was obtained: this was the patient's first episode of oral ulcers and he had no history of recurrent aphthous stomatitis or any other ulcerative disease of the mouth. The lesion was superficial and circular, covered by a fibrinopurulent membrane and surrounded by an erythematous halo. After 14 days of isolation the patient recovered completely.

Case 7. A 29-year-old male, isolated at home, presented ageusia on the sixth day of isolation. At teleconsultation, a superficial, painful ulcer, with a diameter of 1 cm and a whitish pseudomembrane, surrounded by an erythematous halo, was detected on the ventral portion of the tongue. After 6 days the patient recovered.

Case 8. Another 28-year-old male was placed in isolation at home; after 2 days of isolation, ageusia developed and, after 8 days, aphthous-like ulcers in the upper and lower labial mucosae were observed. After 2 days, another ulcer was observed on the right side of the tongue. The recommended treatment was 0.12% non-alcoholic chlorhexidine mouthwash. The oral lesions healed completely after 9 days.

The authors' opinion was that the oral manifestations were directly associated with COVID-19 infection and/or the severely compromised state of the patients.

Cebeci Kahraman and Caskurlu [56] described a case of a 51-year-old male patient, treated with clarithromycin 500 mg b.i.d., who reported worsened sore throat symptoms 10 days after the onset. The oral examination revealed a largely erythematous surface in the oropharynx, a few petechiae on the hard palate, and numerous pustular enanthema, 1–3 mm in diameter, near the soft palate border, more prominent on the left side. The lesions resolved after a few days of antibiotherapy. The authors suggested that oral mucosa may be involved in COVID-19 symptoms.

Chaux-Bodard et al. [48] described the case of a 45-year-old female patient who presented an irregular asymptomatic ulcer on the tongue dorsum following a painful inflammation of a tongue papilla, which evolved in an erythematous macula. After 10 days, the ulcer showed complete remission. Three days after the debut of the oral lesion, a painful erythematous plane lesion also appeared on the big toe, which became asymptomatic after 2 days. The authors suggested that the macular erythematous lesion could be explained by vasculitis, an inflammatory reaction to COVID-19. Thus, the irregular oral ulcer could be considered as an inaugural symptom of COVID-19.

Ciccarese et al. [57] described the case of a previously healthy 19-year-old female, without comorbidities, who had started taking oral cefixime 3 days prior to admission. She reported asymptomatic cutaneous and oropharyngeal lesions that started 2 days before admission. Upon examination, the following lesions were detected: erythematous macules, papules and petechiae on the lower extremities, erosions, ulcerations, and blood crusts on the inner surface of the lips and palatal and gingival petechiae. The oral lesions were painless, heterogeneous in morphology, and associated with severe thrombocytopenia. Intravenous immune globulins and methylprednisolone were administered for 5 days, while antibiotic therapy was stopped. On day 10, the skin and mucosal lesions disappeared. The authors' opinion was that the severe thrombocytopenia was probably of great importance in triggering the cutaneous and mucosal petechiae, while the oral erosions probable cause was direct viral vascular and mucosal damage.

Corchuelo and Ulloa [58] reported a case of a 40-year-old female, diagnosed positive for COVID-19 three weeks before the dental teleconsultation and treated with azithromycin. She presented painless reddish plaques on the lower lip and dark brown pigmentation of the gingiva. A whitish area was detected on the tongue dorsum, apparently accompanied by bacterial plaque. A well-defined brown band was observed in the attached gingiva, which did not transgress the mucogingival junction and partially affected the interpapillary gingiva. A painful aphthous ulcerative lesion on the attached lower left gingiva at the level of the first premolar was also detected. Petechiae were present on the upper part of the face. As treatment, nystatin oral suspension was prescribed, as well as rinses with chlorhexidine gluconate 0.12% and more frequent brush changes. Another dental teleconsultation was performed after 20 days: the recovery of the lesions of the lips was observed, no aphthous ulcers were present, and the whitish color of the tongue was significantly reduced. The melanin pigmentation in the attached gingiva of the anterior teeth was explained by the proliferation of melanocytes in that part of the body, as an inflammatory process induced by SARS-CoV-2.

Cruz Tapia et al. [59] reported a series of four cases with different oral manifestations.

Case 1. A 41-year-old female in home isolation, who had tested positive for SARS-CoV-2 and was treated with acetaminophen and fexofenadine, described discomfort in the palate. The clinical examination revealed an erythematous, asymptomatic, 6-mm-diameter, soft-consistency, nonbleeding bulla on the hard palate, diagnosed as an angina bullosa hemorrhagic-like lesion. The authors' opinion was that the lesions were probably associated with COVID-19 and self-control measures were recommended.

Case 2. A hospitalized 51-year-old female presented diffuse vascular-like purple macule, 12 mm in size, on the left palatal mucosa and papule plaque of 8 mm on the right palatal mucosa. Dexamethasone, azithromycin, and indomethacin were administrated. The lesions, non-bleeding and asymptomatic, were considered a vascular disorder, probably associated with COVID-19.

Case 3. A 55-year-old female, isolated at home and treated with acetaminophen, noticed an enlargement of the tongue. Clinical examination revealed an asymptomatic purple bulla, 8 mm in diameter and of soft consistency, on the right side of the tongue, diagnosed as an angina bullosa hemorrhagic-like lesion, probably associated with COVID-19. The lesion presented a complete remission after 5 days.

Case 4. A 42-year-old male, confirmed positive for SARS-CoV-2, described associated burning-mouth symptoms. The oral examination showed multiple and irregular reddish macules, of 3–4 mm in diameter and indurated consistency, on the hard palate, and a nonspecific mucositis was considered. The patient received acetaminophen for 5 days, and clorhexidine 0.12% mouthwash was recommended. As the oral lesions persisted, after 14 days, an incisional biopsy was performed, leading to the diagnosis of mucosal, nonspecific, localized vasculitis and thrombosis associated with COVID-19. Topical mometasone furoate 0.1% and clorhexidine 0.12% mouthwash were prescribed, and after 7 days of treatment complete remission was observed.

Diaz Rodriguez et al. [60] reported three cases of oral manifestations in patients with confirmed COVID-19.

Case 1. A 43-year-old female was quarantined for 56 days. In the last 2 weeks, she reported aphthous-like lesions, a burning sensation, and tongue depapillation. Rinses with a triamcinolone acetonide 0.05% solution, three times a day for a 10-day period, were prescribed. After treatment, lingual depapillation persisted, but the ulcers and burning sensation disappeared.

Case 2. A 53-year-old man, a few days after being discharged from hospital, described a burning-mouth sensation and unilateral commissural fissures. Complaints of dysgeusia were also recorded. Lesions were diagnosed as commissural cheilitis and treated with an ointment containing neomycin, nystatin, and triamcinolone acetonide three times a day. Between ointment applications, use of a gauze with chlorhexidine for local hygiene was also described. Commissural lesions disappeared completely after treatment but dysgeusia persisted.

Case 3. A hospitalized 78-year-old woman reported a very intense sensation of dry mouth. Dental consultation revealed lesions on the tongue, palate, and commissure, compatible with pseudomembranous candidiasis and angular cheilitis. Solutions and gels to improve salivary dryness and nystatin solution rinses four times a day for 15 days were prescribed. Angular cheilitis was treated using ointment containing neomycin, nystatin, and triamcinolone acetonide. After treatment, the pseudomembranous lesions and commissural fissures healed and salivary flow and dry mouth sensation improved.

The authors noted that the cases were related to a certain state of immunosuppression and that stress might have played an important role in the appearance of these oral conditions. The authors' opinion was that a cause–effect relationship between COVID-19 and the oral manifestations could not be established.

Dominguez-Santos et al. [61] presented four cases of young COVID-19 patients who developed minor aphthae during the course of the disease. The patients developed a low number of aphthae (ranging from one to more than five), measuring less than 1 cm, with a creamy-white fibrin surface and an erythematous peripheral ring, mostly affecting the non-keratinized mucosa. Only one patient had a history of recurrent aphthous stomatitis. Tests to exclude secondary causes of aphthosis were performed and PCR testing for HSV was negative. The authors stated that a causal association of oral aphthous ulcers with COVID-19 infection could not be demonstrated.

Glavina et al. [62] presented the oral manifestations related to COVID-19 in a 40-year-old female with no comorbidities and a history of frequent eruptions of recurrent herpes labialis. Dysgeusia was described as the initial symptom, followed by pain and burning sensation in the oral cavity 7 days after the patient was confirmed positive for SARS-CoV-2. The telemedical consultation revealed recurrent HSV of the hard palate, a white, hairy tongue, and non specific white lesions of the ventral side of the tongue. Systemic acyclovir therapy was administrated five times a day for 5 days and local therapy (antiseptic, nystatin, panthenol, local anesthetic) for 2 weeks, until complete recovery. The authors' opinion was that the recurrent HSV lesions were not caused, but triggered, by SARS-CoV-2 infection, as recurrent oral HSV infection is stress-induced and indicates a compromised immune system.

Jimenez-Cauhe et al. [63] reported cases of three patients who returned to the emergency department because of skin rashes 6, 7, and 4 days after being discharged, respectively. The oral cavity examination revealed palatal macules and petechiae. Following treatment with systemic corticosteroids, the erythema multiforme-like eruption showed progressive resolution after 2–3 weeks. The authors suspected an infectious cause rather than a drug reaction but could not positively exclude the involvement of the various drugs administered.

Kitakawa et al. [64] described the case of a female patient, 20 years old, who tested positive for COVID-19 and was treated with azithromycin and dipyrone. She showed lesions in the median lower lip semimucosa and severe pruritus, with a clinical course of 14 days. These lesions were treated with nebacetin ointment for 2 days, showing a good resolution. After a photographic examination, a differential diagnosis of recurrent herpes was established. The authors' opinion was that it could have been a coincidence; however, the patient did not show any episodes of herpes infection in her history.

Labe et al. [65] described the cases of two children in which the cutaneous manifestations were at the forefront of the clinical picture.

Case 1. A 6-year-old male was hospitalized for painful cheilitis, which developed a week before admission and was followed by a rash of the extremities, and conjunctivitis. Oral examination revealed severe erosive cheilitis with diffuse gingival erosions and thick haemorrhagic crusts. The HSV test was negative. The diagnosis of erythema multiforme was established. As the child's condition improved, he was discharged after 2 weeks.

Case 2. A 3-year-old male, hospitalized, showed cheilitis, stomatitis, and glossitis, accompanied by skin manifestations. After the diagnosis of COVID-19-associated Kawasaki disease was established, an initial dose of intravenous gamma globulin was administrated. Kawasaki disease is a systemic vasculitis with unknown etiology, associated with either viruses or bacteria. The authors stated that this case strongly suggests that SARS-CoV-2 is a trigger for Kawasaki disease and supports previous studies focused on possible associations between HCoV and Kawasaki disease [66,67].

Table 1. Main aspects of the included studies.

Study	Number of Cases	Patient Data	Oral Lesion	Localization
Amorim dos Santos et al. [51]	1	M, 67, confirmed	White plaque Yellowish pinpoint ulcers Geographical tongue	Tongue dorsum
Ansari et al. [53]	2	1. M, 75, confirmed 2. F, 56, confirmed	Several painful ulcers, with irregular margins and varying sizes against red and nonhemorrhagic backgrounds	1. Hard palate 2. Anterior region of the tongue

Table 1. *Cont.*

Study	Number of Cases	Patient Data	Oral Lesion	Localization
Bezerra et al. [54]	1	M, 33, suspicion	Painful mouth ulceration Two crateriform ulcers with a necrotic background and no erythematous halo	The floor of the mouth Left retromolar region and lip mucosa
Brandao et al. [55]	8	1. M, 81, confirmed 2. F, 71, confirmed 3. F, 83, confirmed 4. M, 72, confirmed 5. F, 32, confirmed 6. M, 35, confirmed 7. M, 29, confirmed 8. M, 28, confirmed	1. Multiple painful, shallow aphthous-like ulcers covered with mucopurulent membrane HSV-1 identified 2. Small hemorrhagic ulcerations Areas of superficial necrosis HSV-1 identified 3. Ulcer of 1.5 × 1.5 cm^2 Discrete area affected by petechiae and a superficial necrotic area 4. Small hemorrhagic ulcerations Painful necrotic ulceration HSV-1 identified 5. Multiple ulcers, superficial and circular lesions with a whitish center and surrounded by an erythematous halo 6. Superficial, circular ulcer, covered by a fibrinopurulent membrane and surrounded by an erythematous halo of 0.5 cm Mild odynophagia. 7. Superficial, painful ulcer, with a diameter of 1 cm and a whitish pseudomembrane surrounded by an erythematous halo 8. Aphthous-like ulcers	1. The mucosa of the upper and lower lips Anterior tongue dorsum 2. Upper and lower lip Anterior tongue dorsum 3. Right lateral edge of the tongue Anterior hard palate 4. Upper and lower lip Lower right lip 5. Tip and lateral edges of the tongue 6. Tonsillar pillar 7. Ventral portion of the tongue 8. Upper and lower labial mucosae, right side of the tongue Oropharynx
Cebeci Kahraman and Caskurlu [56]	1	M, 51, confirmed	Large erythematous surface A few petechiae Numerous pustular enanthemata	Hard palate midline Left side of soft palate border
Chaux-Bodard et al. [48]	1	F, 45, confirmed	Painful inflammation of tongue papilla, followed by an erythematous macula and an asymptomatic irregular ulcer	Tongue dorsum
Ciccarese et al. [57]	1	F, 19, confirmed	Erosions, ulcerations, and blood crust Petechiae	The inner surface of the lips Palate and gingiva

Table 1. *Cont.*

Study	Number of Cases	Patient Data	Oral Lesion	Localization
Corchuelo and Ulloa [58]	1	F, 40, confirmed	Reddish plaques Dark brown pigmentation Aphtous-like ulcer White area, probably candida	Lower lip Gingiva Attached lower left gingiva Tongue dorsum
Cruz Tapia et al. [59]	4	1. F, 41, confirmed 2. F, 42, confirmed 3. F, 55, confirmed 4. M, 41, confirmed	1. Bulla 2. Macule 3. Bulla 4. Small macule	1. Hard palate 2. Hard palate (left side) 3. Tongue 4. Hard palate
Diaz Rodriguez et al. [60]	3	1. F, 43, confirmed 2. M, 53, confirmed 3. F, 78, confirmed	1. Aphthous-like lesions, burning sensation, and tongue depapillation 2. Burning-mouth sensation and unilateral angular cheilitis 3. Pseudomembranous candidiasis and angular cheilitis	1. N/A 2. Lips 3. Tongue, palate
Dominguez-Santos et al. [61]	4	1. F, 43, confirmed 2. M, 33, confirmed 3. M, 37, confirmed 4. M, 19, confirmed	1. Single ulcer, with peripheral erythematous rim 2. Single aphtous ulcer 3. Seven aphtae 4. Four clustered aphtae	1. Right buccal mucosa 2. Superior mucogingival junction 3. Ventral right side of the tongue 4. Right side of the inferior labial mucosa
Glavina et al. [62]	1	F, 40, confirmed	Pain and burning in the oral cavity Recurent HSV White, hairy tongue	Hard palate Tongue
Jimenez Cauhe et al. [63]	3	F, 77, confirmed F, 58, confirmed F, 69, confirmed	Macules and petechiae	Palate
Kitakawa et al. [64]	1	F, 20, confirmed	Herpetic lesions, pruritus	Median lower lip semimucosa
Labe et al. [65]	2	1. M, 6, confirmed 2. M, 3, suspicion	1. Painful cheilitis 2. Cheilitis, stomatitis, glossitis	N/A N/A
Martin Carreras-Presas et al. [68]	3	1. M, 56, suspicion 2. M, 58, suspicion 3. F, 65, confimed	1. Painful lesions resembling a herpetic recurrent stomatitis 2. Multiple small, painful yellowish ulcers with erythematous halo 3. Pain Blisters Desquamative gingivitis	1. Palate 2. Palate 3. Tongue Internal lip mucosa Gingiva
Nuno-Gonzalez et al. [69]	78	Adults, average age of 55.7 years, confirmed/suspicion	Lingual papillitis, glossitis, aphthous stomatitis, mucositis, and burning sensation	N/A
Patel et al. [70]	1	F, 35, suspicion	Erithematous and edematous gingiva and necrotic interdental papillae	Gingiva and interdental papillae

Table 1. *Cont.*

Study	Number of Cases	Patient Data	Oral Lesion	Localization
Putra et al. [71]	1	M, 29, confirmed	Aphthous stomatitis	N/A
Riad et al. [72]	17	12 F, 5 M; average age of 39.94, confirmed	Angular cheilitis	Lips
Riad et al. [73]	26	9 M, 17 F; average age of 36.81, confirmed	Tongue ulcers	Tongue
Sakaida et al. [74]	1	F, 52, confirmed	Erythematous and erosive lesions	Lips and oral mucosa
Soares et al. [75]	1	M, 42, confirmed	Painful ulceration Multiple reddish macules of different sizes	Buccal mucosa Hard palate, tongue, and lips

Martin Carreras-Presas et al. [68] presented three cases of oral manifestations associated with COVID-19. In all cases, video consultations were performed.

Case 1. A healthy 56-year-old male patient, suspected of having COVID-19, presented dysgeusia, pain in his palate, and sore throat. Lesions resembling recurrent herpetic stomatitis were detected; however, the patient denied any HSV history. The prescribed treatment was valaciclovir for 10 days, and topical antiseptics with chlorhexidine and hyaluronic acid. After 10 days, the oral lesions showed full recovery.

Case 2. A 58-year-old male patient, suspected of having COVID-19, also reported pain in his palate. Multiple small, yellowish ulcers with an erythematous halo were detected on his palate. The patient did not have any previous history of herpetic infection. After 1 week of using topical antiseptic mouthwash, the painful lesions healed completely.

Case 3. A 65-year-old female patient, hospitalized and treated with antibiotics, corticosteroids, and antiviral drugs, developed a rash after being discharged. She described pain in her tongue from the beginning of the disease but had not been given an intraoral examination. After one week of antifungal administration, blisters in the internal lip mucosa, as well as desquamative gingivitis, could be observed. Hyaluronic acid and chlorhexidine mouthwash were prescribed, as well as prednisolone. The oral lesions improved within 3 days. In the authors' opinion, it can be assumed that SARS-CoV-2 can provoke exanthematic lesions similar to other viral processes usually diagnosed in the dental clinic.

Nuno-Gonzalez et al. [69] provided the results of a cross-sectional study that aimed to evaluate cutaneous findings in 666 COVID-19 patients with mild-to-moderate pneumonia and a mean age of 55.7 years. A total of 304 of them presented one or more mucocutaneous manifestations. Oral manifestations, such as transient lingual papillitis, glossitis with lateral indentations or patchy depapillation, aphthous stomatitis, and mucositis, were also found in 78 cases. A burning sensation was also reported, and dysgeusia was commonly associated. The authors stated that, due to the frequency of the oral lesions, a specific examination was in order to avoid contagion risk.

The case of a 35-year-old female patient, who attended the dental emergency department describing fever, halitosis, intense gingival pain, and bleeding, was described by Patel [70]. Bilateral submandibular lymphadenopathy, severe halitosis, generalized erythematous and edematous gingivae, and necrotic interdental papillae in both the maxillary and mandibular labial sextants were accompanied by unprovoked bleeding from the gingival sulcus. A clinical diagnosis of necrotizing gingivitis was made and treatment with metronidazole three times daily for 5 days and 0.12% chlorhexidine mouthwash twice daily for 10 days was prescribed. Five days later, complete resolution of oral symptoms and fever was observed. Despite the fact that the patient was not tested and only a suspicion of COVID-19 infection could be stated, the authors emphasized the role of bacterial co-infections in COVID-19 severity.

Putra et al. [71] described a case of a 29-year-old male who presented cutaneous manifestations and was treated with azithromycin, hydroxychloroquine, oseltamivir, vitamin C3, and vitamin D1. Stomatitis aphthous, noticed on day seven, with no other treatment besides typical hygiene oral care, showed complete remission on day ten. The diagnosis of hand, foot, and mouth disease was supported by the appearance of stomatitis aphthous.

Riad et al. [72,73] presented two series of cases involving oral manifestations in patients confirmed to be infected with COVID-19.

The first series [72] consisted of 17 confirmed COVID-19 patients with angular cheilitis. The patients had a mean age 39.94 and 12 of them were female. The authors' opinion was that angular cheilitis in COVID-19 patients can be attributed to numerous local irritants, including hypersalivation.

The second case series [73] included 26 confirmed COVID-19 patients with painful tongue ulcers. Their average age was 36.81, there were 9 males and 17 females, and they were treated with oral paracetamol and chlorhexidine mouthwash. The ulcers disappeared after 1–2 weeks. The authors' opinion was that tongue ulcers can be a direct manifestation of SARS-CoV-2 infection or a co-infection due to the immune dysregulation.

Sakaida et al. [74] presented a case of a 52-year-old woman with itchy erythematous lesions on her limbs after being treated for 3 days with antibiotics and a non-steroid anti-inflammatory drug for previous dental problems. After 2 days of treatment, erosions on her lips and buccal mucosa appeared. The skin lesions were clinically diagnosed as a drug eruption. Oral prednisolone was administrated to treat oral lesions, which gradually improved. Five days after decreasing the prednisolone, symptoms of SARS-CoV-2 appeared and the patient tested positive. The authors' opinion was that the drug eruption during the latency period might have been related to a COVID-19-induced cytokine storm.

Soares et al. [75] reported a case of a 42-year-old male patient, confirmed positive for SARS-CoV-2, who developed reddish oral lesions and a painful ulceration in the buccal mucosa, associated with petechia-like skin and small vesicobullous lesions of unknown etiology. The multiple reddish macules of different sizes were scattered along the hard palate, tongue, and lips. A treatment with dexamethasone and dipyrone was established for 1 week, and after 3 weeks the lesions presented complete remission. The authors suggested that SARS-CoV-2 can cause oral lesions and therefore that all positive patients should have a full mouth check-up.

The general aspects of the abovementioned studies are summarized in Table 1.

According to the reviewed data, the most frequent types of oral lesions found in COVID-19 patients are: ulcers (42 cases, 25.92%), aphthous stomatitis/aphtae (29 cases, 17.90%), angular cheilitis/cheilitis (21 cases, 12.96%), glossitis/lingual papillitis (21 cases, 12.96%), petechiae (8 cases, 4.93%), macules (7 cases, 4.32%), erythematous and erosive lesions (6 cases, 3.70%), herpetic lesions (6 cases, 3.70%), candidiasis (4 cases, 2.46%), and bulla (2 cases, 1.23%).

4. The Association between Periodontal Disease and COVID-19

Periodontal disease, a severe inflammatory gum disease, mainly affects the supporting structures of the teeth, gingiva, and alveolar bone, and it is frequently associated with poor oral hygiene and age. As the human organism normally responds to bacterial infection through inflammation, this process can result in a "cytokine storm", where proteins are released and associated with an exuberant inflammatory response that destroy tissues in other parts of the body [76].

The inflammatory products can enter the bloodstream through periodontal pockets and reach other organs, causing tissue damage [77]. Pro-inflammatory cytokines and oxidative stress, involved in the development of periodontal disease and other metabolic diseases, are highly elevated among COVID-19 patients [78]. Bacteria in the gums spread the IL-6 inflammatory protein. High levels of IL-6 in the body are a predictor of respiratory failure, with a 22 times higher risk for respiratory complications being reported, thus highlighting the importance of reducing the amount of oral bacteria and subsequent systemic inflammation [79].

On the other hand, the high prevalence of periodontal disease among patients experiencing metabolic diseases, such as obesity and diabetes, and cardiovascular diseases is well-documented. These types of comorbidities, which affect systemic health, are also known to increase the risk for severe COVID-19 [80–82]. The association between periodontal disease and severe COVID-19 could help identify risk groups and establish pertinent recommendations [83].

A study on 568 patients, showed a clear association between periodontitis and increased levels of biomarkers associated with severe COVID-19 disease, as well as complications including death, ICU admission, and the need for assisted ventilation [84].

The investigations of a possible link between the microbial oral flora and COVID-19 also revealed that there is a risk that oral secretions may be aspirated into the lungs and cause infection [85]. Oral bacteria, such as the periodontal pathogens Porphyromonas gingivalis, Fusobacterium nucleatum, and Prevotella intermedia, may accelerate viral infectious diseases such as COVID-19 and aggravate lung damage [50]. Cytokines such as interleukin 1 (IL1) and tumor necrosis factor (TNF), which are present in the saliva as a consequence of their bacterial activity, can easily reach the lungs [84].

Poor oral hygiene, a frequent consequence of low income or psychological troubles, can lead to COVID-19 aggravation due to the aspiration of periodontopathic bacteria, which induces the expression of ACE-2, a known receptor for SARS-CoV-2, and the production of inflammatory cytokines in the lower respiratory tract. Long-term hospitalization of patients with COVID-19 leads to reduced professional oral care. Poor oral hygiene, and limited access to dental care in patients with COVID-19, may increase the inter-bacterial exchanges between the oral cavity and the lungs and thus the risk of a much more severe respiratory infection [86–88].

The degree of periodontal inflammation may help to determine the severity of COVID-19 infection. Routine dental and periodontal treatment may also help decrease the symptoms of COVID-19 [50,85]. The link between poor oral hygiene, bacteria present in the oral cavity, and increased risk of lung damage is presented in Figure 2.

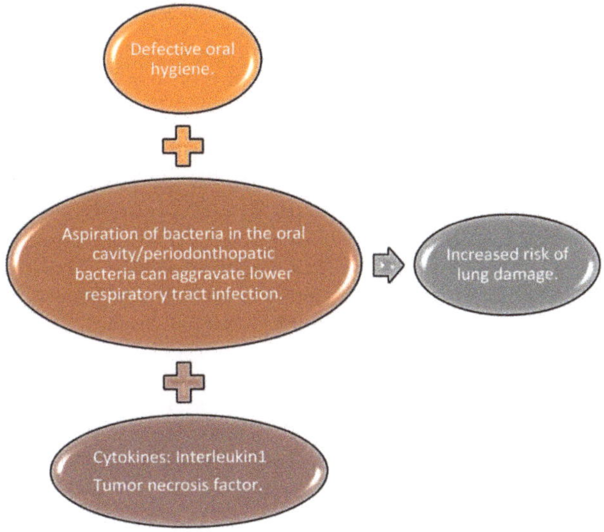

Figure 2. The link between poor oral hygiene, bacteria present in the oral cavity, and increased risk of lung damage.

5. Temporomandibular Disorders Associated with COVID-19 Pandemic

Among the most common symptoms of temporomandibular disorders (TMDs) are soreness in the jaw joint area and jaw muscles and clicking or crunching noises when opening or closing the mouth or when the patient chews, yawns, or even speaks. TMD may be linked with headaches, neck pain, and discomfort in the temple or teeth. TMD reflects the dysfunction of the masticatory system, one of its major causes being stress and psychosocial impairment [89].

Pandemics are stressful, like most public health emergencies. The literature presents aspects of psychological reactions related to epidemics and pandemics, which depend on individual vulnerability, intolerance to uncertainty, perceived vulnerability to disease, and anxiety [90]. The anxiety, depression, and stress people experience during the COVID-19 pandemic may lead to TMD [91].

Uncertainties about the origin and nature of the virus and about governments' abilities to prevent its spread, lack of confidence in the medical system and its ability to cope with new cases, fear of infection, misinformation, and feelings of loneliness and anger in quarantined people due to lack of socialization play important roles in the development and maintenance of TMD [92].

These psychosocial factors, often associated with sympathetic activity and additional release of adrenocortical steroids, may lead to muscle vasoconstriction and increased peripheral vascular resistance. Autonomic insufficiency can increase the sympathetic impulse and the feeling of hyper-excitement that creates and perpetuates sleep disorders, accompanied by sensations such as heat and cold, palpitations, tachycardia, nausea, abdominal pain, diarrhea, and constipation [93].

Reports have noted an increased number of people experiencing teeth grinding and oral pain during the COVID-19 pandemic as a consequence of increased stress due to health worries, the loss of work, and lockdown or separation from family members [94,95]. On the other hand, stress, anxiety, and depression due to COVID-19 lead to increased orofacial pain, TMD, and bruxism symptoms [96,97].

According to another recent study, people with chronic TMD are more susceptible to COVID-19 distress, resulting in deterioration of their psychological status, and increased chronic facial pain severity, supporting the hypothesis that stress acts as an amplifier of central sensitization, anxiety, depression, chronic pain, and pain-related disability in TMD cases [98].

Two concomitant studies aimed to evaluate the effect of lockdown on TMD and bruxism symptoms among 700 subjects from Israel and 1092 from Poland, respectively, by using online questionnaires. The results showed significant altered psychoemotional status, leading to aggravated bruxism and TMD symptoms, accompanied by increased orofacial pain [97].

Even after the lockdown period ended, patients with high risk for severe COVID-19 limited their dental appointments to emergencies only, which was not the case for TMD and bruxism. As they were neglected, these conditions got worse [99].

Medical staff, including dental practitioners, have also been reported to experience moderate to severe levels of anxiety because of possible COVID-19 repercussions [90,94,100].

A study carried out on 641 dental surgeons found TMD in 24.3% of the participants, sleep bruxism in 58%, and awake bruxism in 53.8% [101]. The incidence of TMD reported by a study carried out on 699 dental university students during the COVID-19 pandemic was of 77.5%, accompanied by impaired sleep quality, depression, anxiety, and stress [102]. Another study, based on 113 questionnaires filled out by dental students, also reported that the social isolation and stress due to the COVID-19 pandemic had led to increase symptoms of TMD, anxiety, and depression [103].

6. Dental Medicine during the COVID-19 Pandemic

Health systems around the world were subjected to a great challenge due to the rapid spread of SARS-CoV-2 and the related COVID-19 pneumonia until the vaccine became available. The public health measures during the pandemic forced patients with and without SARS-CoV-2 to remain isolated in order to prevent the spread. The majority of the patients were unable to attend dental services, postponed the appointments, and even neglected their oral hygiene, which can lead to complications [58].

At the beginning of the pandemic, dentistry, as well as oral and maxillofacial surgery and dental radiology, were included among the groups with the highest risk of infection due to inevitable close contact with SARS-CoV-2 asymptomatic and symptomatic patients [104,105].

Dental staff may develop an increased risk of infection due to the proximity of patients, who cannot wear masks during treatment and keep their mouth open [106]. The high risk is also caused by instruments and equipment that generate aerosols that contain oral and respiratory fluids, such as high-speed and ultrasonic scaling devices, both of which use a water-coolant [86,106–108]. Dental radiology, which does not allow the use of a rubber dam, is equally risky, as the patient may cough or gag if the image receptor is placed deep inside the mouth [109].

The high viral load in the nasal cavity in infected patients, even if asymptomatic, puts dentists and maxillofacial surgeons at even higher risk for SARS-CoV-2 infection because of the close contact. Treating patients in these pandemic times has to be undertaken with maximum precautions in order to minimize the infection transmission [110–112].

For a determined period of time at the beginning of the pandemic, dental practices were closed and only dental emergencies that could not be postponed [95] or facial trauma surgery were performed [112,113].

The most common types of facial trauma, generally caused by road or sports accidents, were reduced during this period because of the imposed restrictions, but trauma caused by domestic violence or falls still occurred. Oral and maxillofacial surgeons, head and neck surgeons, and plastic surgeons managed both facial trauma and patient triage by performing COVID-19 buffer tests and helping intubate COVID-19-positive patients with facial trauma [110].

During the peak of the pandemic, when personal contact was avoided as much as possible, telemedicine proved to be a useful tool in dental diagnosis [60,112].

Later on, specific protocols were implemented, combining sanitizing procedures with the wearing of disposable personal protective equipment (PPE). Patient screening by telephone, before scheduling a dental appointment, has been considered necessary to prevent spreading the virus inside the dental office [114,115].

At their arrival, patients must wear a surgical mask and must be unaccompanied (when possible). Patients are requested to leave any personal belongings in certain spaces and sanitize their hands, and they are provided with PPE.

The dental staff have to be equipped with disposable personal protective equipment: gloves, filtering facepiece particle 2 (FFP2) respirator, visor, protective gown, and shoe covers [116,117].

In order to reduce the presence of the virus in the saliva, rinsing with a mouthwash for at least 30 s prior to starting the dental treatment has been advised [118].

During clinical procedures, the use of a rubber dam is strongly recommended to limit the spread of aerosols and potentially infected biological material. The procedures which might cause coughing or gagging must be avoided; for example, the use of an intra-oral scanner instead of a conventional dental impression is preferred [109].

The type of aspirating system used seems to affect the prevalence of SARS-CoV-2 infection across dental offices. Using aspirating systems equipped with HEPA filters, capable of evacuating and dissipating aerosols into specialized areas, is strongly recommended [119].

At the end of the dental appointment, all disposable PPE must be properly discarded [120].

Accurate sanitizing of hands and of all surfaces is equally important, as well as proper ventilation for patients [120–122].

Radiography practices should be kept as simple as possible and minimize staff-to-patient contact. Intraoral radiographs should be avoided as much as possible during the COVID-19 pandemic. Extraoral bitewings represent an alternative for sectional panoramic radiographs and intraoral bitewings. Extraoral bitewings, which involve a radiation dose lower than or comparable to intraoral radiographs while providing a greater field of view, could be further considered, especially in cases of children and adults with difficulties in tolerating intraoral radiographs [123].

7. Conclusions and Future Perspectives

Oral manifestations related to COVID-19, including fungal infections, recurrent HSV, oral ulcerations, drug-related eruptions, dysgeusia, xerostomia or decreased salivary flow, and gingivitis, may be a result of the impaired immune system and/or susceptible oral mucosa [124].

Although, it is difficult to state which of the various oral lesions associated with COVID-19 are the most prevalent, it seems that a higher frequency can be found in older, hospitalized patients with severe infection [125].

A number of factors, such as immune impairment, co-morbidities, poor oral hygiene, adverse drug reactions, stress, secondary hyper-inflammatory responses, and iatrogenic trauma following intubation, may be involved [126].

The hypothesis that the oral manifestations are secondary lesions resulting from the deterioration of systemic health or treatments for COVID-19 is most probably correct. The pharmacological agents against COVID-19 are related to several adverse reactions, including oral lesions [127].

The authors of one study stated that "The oral mucosal examination has been neglected during the pandemic on reasonable grounds" [56]. A routine intraoral examination should always be performed on patients with suspected or confirmed SARS-CoV-2 infection, as it can represent a sign of potentially life-threatening conditions [57,70].

It has also been stated that "Whether the currently emerging new viral variants will have an impact on the oral manifestations is unknown" [125]. It is our belief that extensive knowledge about all possible manifestations in cases of COVID-19, including oral lesions, is of great importance in the present uncertain context. The fourth wave of COVID-19 and the alarming spreading of the Delta strain, which is highly contagious and potentially severe, keep the subject actual; skin manifestations are increasingly frequent. It can be assumed, based on the correlation between skin and oral manifestations, that new outcomes regarding this subject will emerge.

Dentists are not only implicated in providing specialty assistance in times of pandemics but also in fighting against them. A special note that seems worth mentioning is that, during the anti-COVID-19 vaccination campaign in Romania, marathon vaccinations were carried out during weekends in an effort to encourage attendance and limit the spread of the pandemic. Dentists took part as volunteers, together with fellow doctors and students, and 6722 people were vaccinated in the authors' hometown during the first organization of this marathon series.

Author Contributions: Conceptualization, L.-C.R. and L.C.A.; methodology, L.-C.R.; validation, L.-C.R. and L.C.A.; formal analysis, A.M. and C.V.T.; investigation, I.S., E.A.B. and L.C.A.; writing—original draft preparation, I.S., E.A.B. and L.C.A.; writing—review and editing, L.C.A.; visualization, L.-C.R. and L.C.A.; supervision, L.-C.R. and L.C.A.; project administration, L.-C.R. and L.C.A. All authors have read and agreed to the published version of the manuscript.

Funding: This research received no external funding.

Institutional Review Board Statement: Not applicable.

Informed Consent Statement: Not applicable.

Conflicts of Interest: The authors declare no conflict of interest.

References

1. Weiss, S.R.; Leibowitz, J.L. Coronavirus Pathogenesis. *Adv. Appl. Microbiol.* **2011**, *81*, 85–164. [CrossRef]
2. Hui, D.S.; Azhar, E.I.; Memish, Z.A.; Zumla, A. Human Coronavirus Infections—Severe Acute Respiratory Syndrome (SARS), Middle East Respiratory Syndrome (MERS), and SARS-CoV-2. In *Encyclopedia of Respiratory Medicine*; Elsevier BV: Amsterdam, The Netherlands, 2021; pp. 146–161.
3. Ramadan, N.; Shaib, H. Middle East respiratory syndrome coronavirus (MERS-CoV): A review. *Germs* **2019**, *9*, 35–42. [CrossRef] [PubMed]
4. Liu, Y.; Yang, Y.; Zhang, C.; Huang, F.; Wang, F.; Yuan, J.; Wang, Z.; Li, J.; Li, J.; Feng, C.; et al. Clinical and biochemical indexes from 2019-nCoV infected patients linked to viral loads and lung injury. *Sci. China Life Sci.* **2020**, *63*, 364–374. [CrossRef] [PubMed]
5. Zhou, P.; Yang, X.-L.; Wang, X.-G.; Hu, B.; Zhang, L.; Zhang, W.; Si, H.-R.; Zhu, Y.; Li, B.; Huang, C.-L.; et al. A pneumonia outbreak associated with a new coronavirus of probable bat origin. *Nature* **2020**, *579*, 270–273. [CrossRef]
6. Ge, H.; Wang, X.; Yuan, X.; Xiao, G.; Wang, C.; Deng, T.; Yuan, Q.; Xiao, X. The epidemiology and clinical information about COVID-19. *Eur. J. Clin. Microbiol. Infect. Dis.* **2020**, *39*, 1011–1019. [CrossRef] [PubMed]
7. Shi, J.; Wen, Z.; Zhong, G.; Yang, H.; Wang, C.; Huang, B.; Liu, R.; He, X.; Shuai, L.; Sun, Z.; et al. Susceptibility of ferrets, cats, dogs, and other domesticated animals to SARS–coronavirus 2. *Science* **2020**, *368*, 1016–1020. [CrossRef] [PubMed]
8. Zheng, J. SARS-CoV-2: An Emerging Coronavirus that Causes a Global Threat. *Int. J. Biol. Sci.* **2020**, *16*, 1678–1685. [CrossRef]
9. Guarner, J. Three Emerging Coronaviruses in Two Decades. *Am. J. Clin. Pathol.* **2020**, *153*, 420–421. [CrossRef]
10. Hu, B.; Guo, H.; Zhou, P.; Shi, Z.-L. Characteristics of SARS-CoV-2 and COVID-19. *Nat. Rev. Microbiol.* **2021**, *19*, 141–154. [CrossRef]
11. World Health Organization. Novel Coronavirus (2019-nCoV) Situation Report—22—Data as Reported by 11 February 2020. Available online: https://www.who.int/docs/default-source/coronaviruse/situation-reports/20200211-sitrep-22-ncov.pdf?sfvrsn=fb6d49b1_2 (accessed on 15 June 2021).
12. Naqvi, A.A.T.; Fatima, K.; Mohammad, T.; Fatima, U.; Singh, I.K.; Singh, A.; Atif, S.M.; Hariprasad, G.; Hasan, G.M.; Hassan, I. Insights into SARS-CoV-2 genome, structure, evolution, pathogenesis and therapies: Structural genomics approach. *Biochim. Biophys. Acta BBA Mol. Basis Dis.* **2020**, *1866*, 165878. [CrossRef] [PubMed]
13. Harrison, A.G.; Lin, T.; Wang, P. Mechanisms of SARS-CoV-2 Transmission and Pathogenesis. *Trends Immunol.* **2020**, *41*, 1100–1115. [CrossRef] [PubMed]
14. Zou, X.; Chen, K.; Zou, J.; Han, P.; Hao, J.; Han, Z. Single-cell RNA-seq data analysis on the receptor ACE2 expression reveals the potential risk of different human organs vulnerable to 2019-nCoV infection. *Front. Med.* **2020**, *14*, 185–192. [CrossRef] [PubMed]
15. Xu, H.; Zhong, L.; Deng, J.; Peng, J.; Dan, H.; Zeng, X.; Li, T.; Chen, Q. High expression of ACE2 receptor of 2019-nCoV on the epithelial cells of oral mucosa. *Int. J. Oral Sci.* **2020**, *12*, 8. [CrossRef] [PubMed]
16. Chen, Y.; Liu, Q.; Guo, D. Emerging coronaviruses: Genome structure, replication, and pathogenesis. *J. Med. Virol.* **2020**, *92*, 418–423. [CrossRef] [PubMed]
17. Azkur, A.K.; Akdis, M.; Azkur, D.; Sokolowska, M.; Van De Veen, W.; Brüggen, M.-C.; O'Mahony, L.; Gao, Y.; Nadeau, K.; Akdis, C.A. Immune response to SARS-CoV-2 and mechanisms of immunopathological changes in COVID-19. *Allergy* **2020**, *75*, 1564–1581. [CrossRef] [PubMed]
18. Shah, V.K.; Firmal, P.; Alam, A.; Ganguly, D.; Chattopadhyay, S. Overview of Immune Response During SARS-CoV-2 Infection: Lessons From the Past. *Front. Immunol.* **2020**, *11*, 1949. [CrossRef]
19. Wei, C.; Liu, Y.; Liu, Y.; Zhang, K.; Su, D.; Zhong, M.; Meng, X. Clinical characteristics and manifestations in older patients with COVID-19. *BMC Geriatr.* **2020**, *20*, 1–9. [CrossRef] [PubMed]
20. Sciacqua, A.; Pujia, R.; Arturi, F.; Hribal, M.L.; Montalcini, T. COVID-19 and elderly: Beyond the respiratory drama. *Intern. Emerg. Med.* **2020**, *15*, 907–909. [CrossRef]
21. Cui, X.; Zhao, Z.; Zhang, T.; Guo, W.; Guo, W.; Zheng, J.; Zhang, J.; Dong, C.; Na, R.; Zheng, L.; et al. A systematic review and meta-analysis of children with coronavirus disease 2019 (COVID-19). *J. Med. Virol.* **2021**, *93*, 1057–1069. [CrossRef]
22. Panahi, L.; Amiri, M.; Pouy, S. Clinical Characteristics of COVID-19 Infection in Newborns and Pediatrics: A Systematic Review. *Arch. Acad. Emerg. Med.* **2020**, *18*, e50.
23. Zare-Zardini, H.; Soltaninejad, H.; Ferdosian, F.; Hamidieh, A.A.; Memarpoor-Yazdi, M. Coronavirus Disease 2019 (COVID-19) in Children: Prevalence, Diagnosis, Clinical Symptoms, and Treatment. *Int. J. Gen. Med.* **2020**, *13*, 477–482. [CrossRef]
24. De Souza, T.H.; Nadal, J.A.; Nogueira, R.J.N.; Pereira, R.M.; Brandão, M.B. Clinical manifestations of children with COVID-19: A systematic review. *Pediatr. Pulmonol.* **2020**, *55*, 1892–1899. [CrossRef]
25. Lechien, J.R.; Chiesa-Estomba, C.M.; De Siati, D.R.; Horoi, M.; Le Bon, S.D.; Rodriguez, A.; Dequanter, D.; Blecic, S.; El Afia, F.; Distinguin, L.; et al. Olfactory and gustatory dysfunctions as a clinical presentation of mild-to-moderate forms of the coronavirus disease (COVID-19): A multicenter European study. *Eur. Arch. Oto Rhino Laryngol.* **2020**, *277*, 2251–2261. [CrossRef] [PubMed]
26. Ding, Y.; Yan, H.; Guo, W. Clinical Characteristics of Children With COVID-19: A Meta-Analysis. *Front. Pediatr.* **2020**, *8*, 431. [CrossRef]
27. Pal, M.; Berhanu, G.; Desalegn, C.; Kandi, V. Severe Acute Respiratory Syndrome Coronavirus-2 (SARS-CoV-2): An Update. *Cureus* **2020**, *12*, e7423. [CrossRef]
28. Hwang, J.; Ryu, H.-S.; Kim, H.A.; Hyun, M.; Lee, J.Y.; Yi, H.-A. Prognostic Factors of COVID-19 Infection in Elderly Patients: A Multicenter Study. *J. Clin. Med.* **2020**, *9*, 3932. [CrossRef] [PubMed]

29. Liu, K.; Chen, Y.; Lin, R.; Han, K. Clinical features of COVID-19 in elderly patients: A comparison with young and middle-aged patients. *J. Infect.* **2020**, *80*, e14–e18. [CrossRef]
30. Rui, L.; Sirui, L.; Xuebei, D.; Xujun, Y.; Yanggan, W. Clinical observations in very elderly patients with COVID-19 in Wuhan. *Geriatr. Gerontol. Int.* **2020**, *20*, 709–714. [CrossRef] [PubMed]
31. Mahmoudi, S.; Mehdizadeh, M.; Badv, R.S.; Navaeian, A.; Pourakbari, B.; Rostamyan, M.; Ekbatani, M.S.; Eshaghi, H.; Abdolsalehi, M.R.; Alimadadi, H.; et al. The Coronavirus Disease 2019 (COVID-19) in Children: A Study in an Iranian Children's Referral Hospital. *Infect. Drug Resist.* **2020**, *13*, 2649–2655. [CrossRef]
32. Mori, H.; Obinata, H.; Murakami, W.; Tatsuya, K.; Sasaki, H.; Miyake, Y.; Taniguchi, Y.; Ota, S.; Yamaga, M.; Suyama, Y.; et al. Comparison of COVID-19 disease between young and elderly patients: Hidden viral shedding of COVID-19. *J. Infect. Chemother.* **2021**, *27*, 70–75. [CrossRef]
33. Unicef. Available online: https://www.unicef.org/coronavirus/what-you-need-know-about-delta-variant. (accessed on 21 October 2021).
34. Criado, P.; Abdalla, B.M.Z.; De Assis, I.C.; Mello, C.V.B.D.G.; Caputo, G.C.; Vieira, I.C. Are the cutaneous manifestations during or due to SARS-CoV-2 infection/COVID-19 frequent or not? Revision of possible pathophysiologic mechanisms. *Inflamm. Res.* **2020**, *69*, 745–756. [CrossRef]
35. Criado, P.R.; Pagliari, C.; Carneiro, F.R.O.; Quaresma, J.A.S. Lessons from dermatology about inflammatory responses in Covid-19. *Rev. Med. Virol.* **2020**, *30*, e2130. [CrossRef]
36. Torres, T.; Puig, L. Managing Cutaneous Immune-Mediated Diseases During the COVID-19 Pandemic. *Am. J. Clin. Dermatol.* **2020**, *21*, 307–311. [CrossRef] [PubMed]
37. Miodońska, M.; Bogacz, A.; Mróz, M.; Mućka, S.; Bożek, A. The Effect of SARS-CoV-2 Virus Infection on the Course of Atopic Dermatitis in Patients. *Medicina* **2021**, *57*, 521. [CrossRef]
38. Docampo-Simón, A.; Sánchez-Pujol, M.; Juan-Carpena, G.; Palazón-Cabanes, J.; Caso, E.V.; Berbegal, L.; Poveda-Montoyo, I.; Pastor-Tomás, N.; Mataix-Díaz, J.; Terencio-Alemany, C.; et al. Are chilblain-like acral skin lesions really indicative of COVID-19? A prospective study and literature review. *J. Eur. Acad. Dermatol. Venereol.* **2020**, *34*, 445–447. [CrossRef] [PubMed]
39. Daneshgaran, G.; Dubin, D.P.; Gould, D.J. Cutaneous Manifestations of COVID-19: An Evidence-Based Review. *Am. J. Clin. Dermatol.* **2020**, *21*, 1–13. [CrossRef] [PubMed]
40. Recalcati, S. Cutaneous manifestations in COVID-19: A first perspective. *J. Eur. Acad. Dermatol. Venereol.* **2020**, *34*, 212–213. [CrossRef]
41. Freeman, E.E.; McMahon, D.E.; Lipoff, J.B.; Rosenbach, M.; Kovarik, C.; Desai, S.R.; Harp, J.; Takeshita, J.; French, L.E.; Lim, H.W.; et al. The spectrum of COVID-19–associated dermatologic manifestations: An international registry of 716 patients from 31 countries. *J. Am. Acad. Dermatol.* **2020**, *83*, 1118–1129. [CrossRef]
42. Estébanez, A.; Pérez-Santiago, L.; Silva, E.; Guillen-Climent, S.; García-Vázquez, A.; Ramón, M.D. Cutaneous manifestations in COVID-19: A new contribution. *J. Eur. Acad. Dermatol. Venereol.* **2020**, *34*, 250–251. [CrossRef] [PubMed]
43. Galván Casas, C.; Catala, A.; Carretero Hernández, G.; Rodríguez-Jiménez, P.; Fernández-Nieto, D.; Rodríguez-Villa Lario, A.; Navarro Fernández, I.; Ruiz-Villaverde, R.; Falkenhain-López, D.; Llamas Velasco, M. Classification of the Cutaneous Manifestations of COVID-19: A Rapid Prospective Nationwide Consensus Study in Spain with 375 Cases. *Br. J. Dermatol.* **2020**, *183*, 71–77. [CrossRef]
44. Piccolo, V.; Neri, I.; Filippeschi, C.; Oranges, T.; Argenziano, G.; Battarra, V.C.; Berti, S.; Manunza, F.; Fortina, A.B.; Di Lernia, V.; et al. Chilblain-like lesions during COVID-19 epidemic: A preliminary study on 63 patients. *J. Eur. Acad. Dermatol. Venereol.* **2020**, *34*, 291–293. [CrossRef]
45. De Masson, A.; Bouaziz, J.D.; Sulimovic, L.; Cassius, C.; Jachiet, M.; Ionescu, M.A.; Rybojad, M.; Bagot, M.; Duong, T.A.; SNDV (French National Union of Dermatologists-Venereologists). Chilblains is a common cutaneous finding during the COVID-19 pandemic: A retrospective nationwide study from France. *J. Am. Acad. Dermatol.* **2020**, *83*, 667–670. [CrossRef] [PubMed]
46. Andina, D.; Noguera-Morel, L.; Bascuas-Arribas, M.; Gaitero-Tristán, J.; Alonso-Cadenas, J.A.; Escalada-Pellitero, S.; Hernández-Martín, Á.; De La Torre-Espi, M.; Colmenero, I.; Torrelo, A. Chilblains in children in the setting of COVID-19 pandemic. *Pediatr. Dermatol.* **2020**, *37*, 406–411. [CrossRef] [PubMed]
47. Singh, C.; Tay, J.; Shoqirat, N. Skin and Mucosal Damage in Patients Diagnosed with COVID-19: A Case Report. *J. Wound Ostomy Cont. Nurs.* **2020**, *47*, 435–438. [CrossRef]
48. Chaux-Bodard, A.-G.; Deneuve, S.; Desoutter, A. Oral manifestation of Covid-19 as an inaugural symptom? *J. Oral Med. Oral Surg.* **2020**, *26*, 18. [CrossRef]
49. La Rosa, G.R.M.; Libra, M.; De Pasquale, R.; Ferlito, S.; Pedullà, E. Association of Viral Infections with Oral Cavity Lesions: Role of SARS-CoV-2 Infection. *Front. Med.* **2021**, *7*, 571214. [CrossRef]
50. Imai, K.; Tanaka, H. SARS-CoV-2 Infection and Significance of Oral Health Management in the Era of "the New Normal with COVID-19. *Int. J. Mol. Sci.* **2021**, *22*, 6527. [CrossRef] [PubMed]
51. Dos Santos, J.A.; Normando, A.G.; Da Silva, R.L.C.; De Paula, R.M.; Cembranel, A.C.; Santos-Silva, A.R.; Guerra, E.N.S. Oral mucosal lesions in a COVID-19 patient: New signs or secondary manifestations? *Int. J. Infect. Dis.* **2020**, *97*, 326–328. [CrossRef] [PubMed]

52. Picciani, B.L.S.; Santos, L.R.; Teixeira-Souza, T.; Dick, T.N.A.; Carneiro, S.; Pinto, J.M.N.; Avelleira, J.C.R.; Azulay, D.R.; Luiz, R.R.; Gonzaga, H.F.D.S. Geographic tongue severity index: A new and clinical scoring system. *Oral Surg. Oral Med. Oral Pathol. Oral Radiol.* **2020**, *129*, 330–338. [CrossRef]
53. Ansari, R.; Gheitani, M.; Heidari, F.; Heidari, F. Oral cavity lesions as a manifestation of the novel virus (COVID-19). *Oral Dis.* **2021**, *27*, 771–772. [CrossRef]
54. Bezerra, T.M.M.; Feitosa, S.G.; Carneiro, D.T.O.; Costa, F.W.G.; Pires, F.R.; Pereira, K.M.A. Oral lesions in COVID-19 infection: Is long-term follow-up important in the affected patients? *Oral Dis.* **2020**, *1*, 1–2. [CrossRef]
55. Brandão, T.B.; Gueiros, L.A.; Melo, T.S.; Prado-Ribeiro, A.C.; Nesrallah, A.C.F.A.; Prado, G.V.B.; Santos-Silva, A.R.; Migliorati, C.A. Oral lesions in patients with SARS-CoV-2 infection: Could the oral cavity be a target organ? *Oral Surg. Oral Med. Oral Pathol. Oral Radiol.* **2021**, *131*, e45–e51. [CrossRef]
56. Kahraman, F.C.; Çaşkurlu, H. Mucosal involvement in a COVID-19-positive patient: A case report. *Dermatol. Ther.* **2020**, *33*, e13797. [CrossRef]
57. Ciccarese, G.; Drago, F.; Boatti, M.; Porro, A.; Muzic, S.I.; Parodi, A. Oral erosions and petechiae during SARS-CoV-2 infection. *J. Med. Virol.* **2021**, *93*, 129–132. [CrossRef] [PubMed]
58. Corchuelo, J.; Ulloa, F.C. Oral manifestations in a patient with a history of asymptomatic COVID-19: Case report. *Int. J. Infect. Dis.* **2020**, *100*, 154–157. [CrossRef] [PubMed]
59. Tapia, R.O.C.; Labrador, A.J.P.; Guimaraes, D.M.; Valdez, L.H.M. Oral mucosal lesions in patients with SARS-CoV-2 infection. Report of four cases. Are they a true sign of COVID-19 disease? *Spéc. Care Dent.* **2020**, *40*, 555–560. [CrossRef]
60. Rodríguez, M.D.; Romera, A.J.; Villarroel, M. Oral manifestations associated with COVID-19. *Oral Dis.* **2020**, epub ahead of print. [CrossRef]
61. Domínguez-Santás, M.; Haya-Martínez, L.; Fernández-Nieto, D.; Jiménez-Cauhé, J.; Suárez-Valle, A.; Díaz-Guimaraens, B. Acute telogen effluvium associated with SARS-CoV-2 infection. *Aust. J. Gen. Pract.* **2020**, *49*, 1022–1023. [CrossRef]
62. Glavina, A.; Biočina-Lukenda, D.; Mravak-Stipetić, M.; Markeljević, J. Oral symptoms and lesions in SARS-CoV-2-positive patient. *Oral Dis.* **2020**, epub ahead of print. [CrossRef]
63. Jimenez-Cauhe, J.; Ortega-Quijano, D.; Carretero-Barrio, I.; Suarez-Valle, A.; Saceda-Corralo, D.; Del Real, C.M.; Fernandez-Nieto, D. Erythema multiforme-like eruption in patients with COVID-19 infection: Clinical and histological findings. *Clin. Exp. Dermatol.* **2020**, *45*, 892–895. [CrossRef]
64. Kitakawa, D.; Oliveira, F.E.; Neves de Castro, P.; Carvalho, L.F.C.S. Short report—Herpes simplex lesion in the lip semimucosa in a COVID-19 patient. *Eur. Rev. Med. Pharm. Sci.* **2020**, *24*, 9151–9153. [CrossRef]
65. Labé, P.; Ly, A.; Sin, C.; Nasser, M.; Chapelon-Fromont, E.; Ben Saïd, P.; Mahé, E. Erythema multiforme and Kawasaki disease associated with COVID-19 infection in children. *J. Eur. Acad. Dermatol. Venereol.* **2020**, *34*, 539–541. [CrossRef] [PubMed]
66. Shirato, K.; Imada, Y.; Kawase, M.; Nakagaki, K.; Matsuyama, S.; Taguchi, F. Possible involvement of infection with human coronavirus 229E, but not NL63, in Kawasaki disease. *J. Med. Virol.* **2014**, *86*, 2146–2153. [CrossRef]
67. Burns, J.C.; Glodé, M.P. Kawasaki syndrome. *Lancet* **2004**, *364*, 533–544. [CrossRef]
68. Martín Carreras-Presas, C.; Amaro Sánchez, J.; López-Sánchez, A.F.; Jané-Salas, E.; Somacarrera Pérez, M.L. Oral vesiculobullous lesions associated with SARS-CoV-2 infection. *Oral Dis.* **2020**, *27*, 710–712. [CrossRef] [PubMed]
69. Nuno-Gonzalez, A.; Martin-Carrillo, P.; Magaletsky, K.; Rios, M.M.; Mañas, C.H.; Almazan, J.A.; Casasola, G.G.; Castro, E.P.; Arenas, A.G.; Ibarguren, A.M.; et al. Prevalence of mucocutaneous manifestations in 666 patients with COVID-19 in a field hospital in Spain: Oral and palmoplantar findings. *Br. J. Dermatol.* **2021**, *184*, 184–185. [CrossRef]
70. Patel, J.; Woolley, J. Necrotizing periodontal disease: Oral manifestation of COVID-19. *Oral Dis.* **2021**, *27*, 768–769. [CrossRef] [PubMed]
71. Putra, B.E.; Adiarto, S.; Dewayanti, S.R.; Juzar, D.A. Viral exanthem with "Spins and needles sensation" on extremities of a COVID-19 patient: A self-reported case from an Indonesian medical frontliner. *Int. J. Infect. Dis.* **2020**, *96*, 355–358. [CrossRef] [PubMed]
72. Riad, A.; Kassem, I.; Issa, J.; Badrah, M.; Klugar, M. Angular cheilitis of COVID-19 patients: A case-series and literature review. *Oral Dis.* **2020**. [CrossRef] [PubMed]
73. Riad, A.; Kassem, I.; Hockova, B.; Badrah, M.; Klugar, M. Tongue Ulcers Associated with SARS-COV-2 Infection: A case-series. *Oral Dis.* **2020**. [CrossRef] [PubMed]
74. Sakaida, T.; Tanimoto, I.; Matsubara, A.; Nakamura, M.; Morita, A. Unique skin manifestations of COVID-19: Is drug eruption specific to COVID-19? *J. Dermatol. Sci.* **2020**, *99*, 62–64. [CrossRef]
75. Soares, C.; Carvalho, R.; Carvalho, M.; Almeida, O. Letter to Editor: Oral lesions in a patient with Covid-19. *Med. Oral Patol. Oral Y Cir. Bucal* **2020**, *25*, e563–e564. [CrossRef]
76. Pedersen, S.F.; Ho, Y.-C. SARS-CoV-2: A storm is raging. *J. Clin. Investig.* **2020**, *130*, 2202–2205. [CrossRef]
77. Cekici, A.; Kantarci, A.; Hasturk, H.; Van Dyke, T.E. Inflammatory and immune pathways in the pathogenesis of periodontal disease. *Periodontol. 2000* **2014**, *64*, 57–80. [CrossRef]
78. Coke, C.; Davison, B.; Fields, N.; Fletcher, J.; Rollings, J.; Roberson, L.; Challagundla, K.; Sampath, C.; Cade, J.; Farmer-Dixon, C.; et al. SARS-CoV-2 Infection and Oral Health: Therapeutic Opportunities and Challenges. *J. Clin. Med.* **2021**, *10*, 156. [CrossRef] [PubMed]

79. Molayem, S.; Pontes, C.C. The Mouth-COVID Connection: Il-6 Levels in Periodontal Disease-Potential Role in COVID-19-Related Respiratory Complications. *J. Calif. Dent. Assoc.* **2020**, *40*, 68–80.
80. Daniel, R.; Gokulanathan, S.; Shanmugasundaram, N.; Lakshmigandhan, M.; Kavin, T. Diabetes and periodontal disease. *J. Pharm. Bioallied Sci.* **2012**, *4*, S280. [CrossRef] [PubMed]
81. Preshaw, P.M.; Alba, A.L.; Herrera, D.; Jepsen, S.; Konstantinidis, A.; Makrilakis, K.; Taylor, R. Periodontitis and diabetes: A two-way relationship. *Diabetologia* **2011**, *55*, 21–31. [CrossRef] [PubMed]
82. Paul, O.; Arora, P.; Mayer, M.; Chatterjee, S. Inflammation in Periodontal Disease: Possible Link to Vascular Disease. *Front. Physiol.* **2021**, *11*, 609614. [CrossRef]
83. Pitones-Rubio, V.; Chávez-Cortez, E.; Hurtado-Camarena, A.; González-Rascón, A.; Serafín-Higuera, N. Is periodontal disease a risk factor for severe COVID-19 illness? *Med. Hypotheses* **2020**, *144*, 109969. [CrossRef] [PubMed]
84. Marouf, N.; Cai, W.; Said, K.N.; Daas, H.; Diab, H.; Chinta, V.R.; Hssain, A.A.; Nicolau, B.; Sanz, M.; Tamimi, F. Association between periodontitis and severity of COVID-19 infection: A case–control study. *J. Clin. Periodontol.* **2021**, *48*, 483–491. [CrossRef] [PubMed]
85. Takahashi, Y.; Watanabe, N.; Kamio, N.; Kobayashi, R.; Iinuma, T.; Imai, K. Aspiration of periodontopathic bacteria due to poor oral hygiene potentially contributes to the aggravation of COVID-19. *J. Oral Sci.* **2021**, *63*, 1–3. [CrossRef] [PubMed]
86. Brian, Z.; Weintraub, J.A. Oral Health and COVID-19: Increasing the Need for Prevention and Access. *Prev. Chronic Dis.* **2020**, *17*, E82. [CrossRef] [PubMed]
87. Sampson, V.; Kamona, N.; Sampson, A. Could there be a link between oral hygiene and the severity of SARS-CoV-2 infections? *Br. Dent. J.* **2020**, *228*, 971–975. [CrossRef]
88. Botros, N.; Iyer, P.; Ojcius, D.M. Is there an association between oral health and severity of COVID-19 complications? *Biomed. J.* **2020**, *43*, 325–327. [CrossRef]
89. Karayanni, H.; Dror, A.A.; Oren, D.; Sela, E.; Granot, I.; Srouji, S. Exacerbation of chronic myofascial pain during COVID-19. *Adv. Oral Maxillofac. Surg.* **2021**, *1*, 100019. [CrossRef]
90. Consolo, U.; Bellini, P.; Bencivenni, D.; Iani, C.; Checchi, V. Epidemiological Aspects and Psychological Reactions to COVID-19 of Dental Practitioners in the Northern Italy Districts of Modena and Reggio Emilia. *Int. J. Environ. Res. Public Health* **2020**, *17*, 3459. [CrossRef]
91. Saccomanno, S.; Bernabei, M.; Scoppa, F.; Pirino, A.; Mastrapasqua, R.; Visco, M.A. Coronavirus Lockdown as a Major Life Stressor: Does It Affect TMD Symptoms? *Int. J. Environ. Res. Public Health* **2020**, *17*, 8907. [CrossRef]
92. Rokaya, D.; Koontongkaew, S. Can Coronavirus Disease-19 Lead to Temporomandibular Joint Disease? *Open Access Maced. J. Med. Sci.* **2020**, *8*, 142–143. [CrossRef]
93. Almeida-Leite, C.M.; Stuginski-Barbosa, J.; Conti, P.C.R. How psychosocial and economic impacts of COVID-19 pandemic can interfere on bruxism and temporomandibular disorders? *J. Appl. Oral Sci.* **2020**, *28*, e20200263. [CrossRef]
94. Di Giacomo, P.; Serritella, E.; Imondi, F.; Di Paolo, C. Psychological impact of COVID-19 pandemic on TMD subjects. *Eur. Rev. Med. Pharmacol. Sci.* **2021**, *25*, 4616–4626. [CrossRef]
95. Di Blasi, M.; Gullo, S.; Mancinelli, E.; Freda, M.F.; Esposito, G.; Gelo, O.C.G.; Lagetto, G.; Giordano, C.; Mazzeschi, C.; Pazzagli, C.; et al. Psychological distress associated with the COVID-19 lockdown: A two-wave network analysis. *J. Affect. Disord.* **2021**, *284*, 18–26. [CrossRef]
96. Rocha, J.R.; Neves, M.J.; Pinheiro, M.R.R.; Feitosa, M.; Áurea, L.; Casanovas, R.C.; Lima, D.M. Alterações psicológicas durante a pandemia por COVID-19 e sua relação com bruxismo e DTM. *Res. Soc. Dev.* **2021**, *10*, 48710615887. [CrossRef]
97. Emodi-Perlman, A.; Eli, I.; Smardz, J.; Uziel, N.; Wieckiewicz, G.; Gilon, E.; Grychowska, N.; Wieckiewicz, M. Temporomandibular Disorders and Bruxism Outbreak as a Possible Factor of Orofacial Pain Worsening during the COVID-19 Pandemic—Concomitant Research in Two Countries. *J. Clin. Med.* **2020**, *9*, 3250. [CrossRef]
98. Asquini, G.; Bianchi, A.E.; Borromeo, G.; Locatelli, M.; Falla, D. The impact of Covid-19-related distress on general health, oral behaviour, psychosocial features, disability and pain intensity in a cohort of Italian patients with temporomandibular disorders. *PLoS ONE* **2021**, *16*, e0245999. [CrossRef]
99. Alona, E.-P.; Ilana, E. One year into the COVID-19 pandemic—temporomandibular disorders and bruxism: What we have learned and what we can do to improve our manner of treatment. *Dent. Med. Probl.* **2021**, *58*, 215–218. [CrossRef] [PubMed]
100. De Boni, R.B.; Balanzá-Martínez, V.; Mota, J.C.; Cardoso, T.D.A.; Ballester, P.; Atienza-Carbonell, B.; Bastos, I.F.; Kapczinski, F. Depression, Anxiety, and Lifestyle Among Essential Workers: A Web Survey from Brazil and Spain During the COVID-19 Pandemic. *J. Med. Internet Res.* **2020**, *22*, e22835. [CrossRef]
101. Peixoto, K.O.; de Resende, C.M.B.M.; de Almeida, E.O.; Almeida-Leite, C.M.; Conti, P.C.R.; Barbosa, G.A.S.; Barbosa, J.S. Association of sleep quality and psychological aspects with reports of bruxism and TMD in Brazilian dentists during the COVID-19 pandemic. *J. Appl. Oral Sci.* **2021**, *29*, e20201089. [CrossRef] [PubMed]
102. Gaş, S.; Özsoy, H.E.; Aydın, K.C. The association between sleep quality, depression, anxiety and stress levels, and temporomandibular joint disorders among Turkish dental students during the COVID-19 pandemic. *CRANIO* **2021**, *5*, 1–6. [CrossRef] [PubMed]
103. De Medeiros, R.A.; Vieira, D.L.; Da Silva, E.V.F.; Rezende, L.V.M.D.L.; Dos Santos, R.W.; Tabata, L.F. Prevalence of symptoms of temporomandibular disorders, oral behaviors, anxiety, and depression in Dentistry students during the period of social isolation due to COVID-19. *J. Appl. Oral Sci.* **2020**, *28*, e20200445. [CrossRef] [PubMed]

104. Mahdi, S.; Ahmed, Z.; Allana, R.; Peretti, A.; Amenta, F.; Bijle, M.N.; Seow, L.; Daood, U. Pivoting Dental Practice Management during the COVID-19 Pandemic—A Systematic Review. *Medicina* **2020**, *56*, 644. [CrossRef] [PubMed]
105. Ather, A.; Patel, B.; Ruparel, N.B.; Diogenes, A.; Hargreaves, K.M. Coronavirus Disease 19 (COVID-19): Implications for Clinical Dental Care. *J. Endod.* **2020**, *46*, 584–595. [CrossRef] [PubMed]
106. Ahmed, M.; Jouhar, R. Dissemination of Aerosol and Splatter in Clinical Environment during Cavity Preparation: An In Vitro Study. *Int. J. Environ. Res. Public Health* **2021**, *18*, 3773. [CrossRef] [PubMed]
107. Persoon, I.; Stankiewicz, N.; Smith, A.; de Soet, H.; Volgenant, C. A review of respiratory protection measures recommended in Europe for dental procedures during the COVID-19 pandemic. *J. Hosp. Infect.* **2020**, *106*, 330–331. [CrossRef] [PubMed]
108. Soltani, P.; Baghaei, K.; Tafti, K.T.; Spagnuolo, G. Science Mapping Analysis of COVID-19 Articles Published in Dental Journals. *Int. J. Environ. Res. Public Health* **2021**, *18*, 2110. [CrossRef]
109. Peng, X.; Xu, X.; Li, Y.; Cheng, L.; Zhou, X.; Ren, B. Transmission routes of 2019-nCoV and controls in dental practice. *Int. J. Oral Sci.* **2020**, *12*, 9. [CrossRef]
110. Shi, A.H.; Guo, W.; Chng, C.K.; Chan, B.H. Precautions When Providing Dental Care During Coronavirus Disease 2019 (COVID-19) Pandemic. *Ann. Acad. Med. Singap.* **2020**, *49*, 312–319. [CrossRef]
111. Ghai, S. Facial Trauma Management During the COVID-19 Era: A Primer for Surgeons. *Curr. Med. Res. Pract.* **2020**, *10*, 169–173. [CrossRef]
112. Sinjari, B.; Rexhepi, I.; Santilli, M.; D'addazio, G.; Chiacchiaretta, P.; Di Carlo, P.; Caputi, S. The Impact of COVID-19 Related Lockdown on Dental Practice in Central Italy—Outcomes of A Survey. *Int. J. Environ. Res. Public Health* **2020**, *17*, 5780. [CrossRef]
113. Tysiąc-Miśta, M.; Dziedzic, A. The Attitudes and Professional Approaches of Dental Practitioners during the COVID-19 Outbreak in Poland: A Cross-Sectional Survey. *Int. J. Environ. Res. Public Health* **2020**, *17*, 4703. [CrossRef]
114. Al-Omiri, M.K.; Lynch, E.; Patil, S.; Al-Shayyab, M.H.; Al Nazeh, A.A.; Alraheam, A.I.; Malkawi, A.Z.; Alomiri, A.K.; Alzoubi, A.I. COVID-19 and Dentistry: An Updated Overview of Dental Perspectives and a Recommended Protocol for Dental Care and Emergency Dental Treatment. *J. Contemp. Dent. Pract.* **2021**, *22*, 572–586. [CrossRef]
115. Tonkaboni, A.; Amirzade-Iranaq, M.H.; Ziaei, H.; Ather, A. Impact of COVID-19 on Dentistry. *Adv. Exp. Med. Biol.* **2021**, *1318*, 623–636. [CrossRef]
116. Alharbi, A.; Alharbi, S.; Alqaidi, S. Guidelines for dental care provision during the COVID-19 pandemic. *Saudi Dent. J.* **2020**, *32*, 181–186. [CrossRef]
117. Izzetti, R.; Nisi, M.; Gabriele, M.; Graziani, F. COVID-19 Transmission in Dental Practice: Brief Review of Preventive Measures in Italy. *J. Dent. Res.* **2020**, *99*, 1030–1038. [CrossRef] [PubMed]
118. Lo Giudice, R. The Severe Acute Respiratory Syndrome Coronavirus-2 (SARS CoV-2) in Dentistry. Management of Biological Risk in Dental Practice. *Int. J. Environ. Res. Public Health* **2020**, *17*, 3067. [CrossRef] [PubMed]
119. Sarapultseva, M.; Hu, D.; Sarapultsev, A. SARS-CoV-2 Seropositivity among Dental Staff and the Role of Aspirating Systems. *JDR Clin. Transl. Res.* **2021**, *6*, 132–138. [CrossRef] [PubMed]
120. Amato, A.; Caggiano, M.; Amato, M.; Moccia, G.; Capunzo, M.; De Caro, F. Infection Control in Dental Practice During the COVID-19 Pandemic. *Int. J. Environ. Res. Public Health* **2020**, *17*, 4769. [CrossRef]
121. Van Doremalen, N.; Bushmaker, T.; Morris, D.H.; Holbrook, M.G.; Gamble, A.; Williamson, B.N.; Tamin, A.; Harcourt, J.L.; Thornburg, N.J.; Gerber, S.I.; et al. Aerosol and Surface Stability of SARS-CoV-2 as Compared with SARS-CoV-1. *N. Engl. J. Med.* **2020**, *382*, 1564–1567. [CrossRef] [PubMed]
122. Kampf, G.; Todt, D.; Pfaender, S.; Steinmann, E. Persistence of coronaviruses on inanimate surfaces and their inactivation with biocidal agents. *J. Hosp. Infect.* **2020**, *104*, 246–251. [CrossRef]
123. Little, R.; Howell, J.; Nixon, P. COVID-19 and beyond: Implications for dental radiography. *Br. Dent. J.* **2020**, *229*, 105–109. [CrossRef]
124. Dziedzic, A.; Wojtyczka, R. The impact of coronavirus infectious disease 19 (COVID-19) on oral health. *Oral Dis.* **2021**, *27*, 703–706. [CrossRef] [PubMed]
125. Samaranayake, L.; Fakhruddin, K.S.; Bandara, N. Oral Manifestations of Coronavirus Disease 2019 (COVID-19): An Overview. *Dent. Updat.* **2021**, *48*, 418–422. [CrossRef]
126. Sinjari, B.; D'Ardes, D.; Santilli, M.; Rexhepi, I.; D'Addazio, G.; Di Carlo, P.; Chiacchiaretta, P.; Caputi, S.; Cipollone, F. SARS-CoV-2 and Oral Manifestation: An Observational, Human Study. *J. Clin. Med.* **2020**, *9*, 3218. [CrossRef]
127. Godinho, G.V.; Paz, A.L.L.M.; Gomes, E.P.A.D.A.; Garcia, C.L.; Volpato, L.E.R. Extensive hard palate hyperpigmentation associated with chloroquine use. *Br. J. Clin. Pharmacol.* **2020**, *86*, 2325–2327. [CrossRef] [PubMed]

medicina

MDPI

Systematic Review

Awareness, Knowledge, Attitude, and Practice of Teledentistry among Dental Practitioners during COVID-19: A Systematic Review and Meta-Analysis

Galvin Sim Siang Lin [1,*], Sze Hui Koh [2], Karyn Zuhuan Ter [3], Chia Wei Lim [4], Sharmin Sultana [5] and Wen Wu Tan [6]

1. Department of Dental Materials, Faculty of Dentistry, Asian Institute of Medicine, Science and Technology (AIMST) University, Bedong 08100, Kedah, Malaysia
2. Puchong Dental Clinic, Ministry of Health Malaysia, Puchong 47100, Selangor, Malaysia; szehui.koh@gmail.com
3. KK2 Batu Pahat Clinic, Ministry of Health Malaysia, Batu Pahat 83000, Johor, Malaysia; Karyn_ter@icloud.com
4. Taman Intan Clinic, Ministry of Health Malaysia, Sungai Petani 08000, Kedah, Malaysia; lcwei95@yahoo.com
5. Department of Orthodontics, Faculty of Dentistry, Manipal University College Malaysia (MUCM), Bukit Baru 75150, Melaka, Malaysia; sharmin.sultana@manipal.edu.my
6. Department of Dental Public Health, Faculty of Dentistry, Asian Institute of Medicine, Science and Technology (AIMST) University, Bedong 08100, Kedah, Malaysia; tan_wen@aimst.edu.my

* Correspondence: galvin@aimst.edu.my; Tel.: +60-4429-8564

Abstract: *Background and Objectives*: This systemic review aims to appraise and analyse the awareness, knowledge, attitude, and practice of teledentistry among dental practitioners during COVID-19. *Materials and Methods*: This review was registered in the PROSPERO database (CRD42021283404). Cross-sectional articles on dental practitioners' perceptions towards teledentistry published between March 2020 and September 2021 were searched in ten online databases (PubMed, Google Scholar, Web of Science, ScienceDirect, Cochrane, EMBASE, SIGLE, EBSCO, LILACS, and Open Grey). The Joanna Briggs Institute critical appraisal tool was employed to analyse the risk of bias (RoB) of each article, whereas the Oxford Centre for Evidence-Based Medicine recommendation tool was used to evaluate the level of evidence. Data were analysed using the DerSimonian–Laird random effect model based on a single-arm approach. *Results*: Six studies were included and demonstrated Level 3 evidence. A single-arm meta-analysis revealed that dental practitioners had a high level of awareness (70.4%) and attitude (72.5%) towards teledentistry during the COVID-19 pandemic, but their knowledge level (57.9%) was moderate with a poor practice level (35.8%). A substantial heterogeneity was observed with the overall I2 ranging from 90.78% to 98.21%. Furthermore, meta-regression indicated that the sample size of each study had a significant ($p < 0.05$) impact on the degree of data heterogeneity. *Conclusions*: Despite their high degree of awareness and attitude, dental practitioners demonstrated moderate knowledge and relatively poor practice of teledentistry during the COVID-19 pandemic. More well-designed studies are warranted to investigate the alternatives for enhancing dental practitioners' knowledge and practice of teledentistry interventions.

Keywords: coronavirus; dental care; oral health; pandemic; telehealth

Citation: Lin, G.S.S.; Koh, S.H.; Ter, K.Z.; Lim, C.W.; Sultana, S.; Tan, W.W. Awareness, Knowledge, Attitude, and Practice of Teledentistry among Dental Practitioners during COVID-19: A Systematic Review and Meta-Analysis. *Medicina* **2022**, *58*, 130. https://doi.org/10.3390/medicina58010130

Academic Editors: Cesare D'Amico and Pier Paolo Poli

Received: 28 December 2021
Accepted: 14 January 2022
Published: 15 January 2022

1. Introduction

The World Health Organization (WHO) declared the coronavirus disease 2019 (COVID-19) as the first coronavirus pandemic to strike the global healthcare system in March 2020 [1]. Many nations have implemented quarantine and mitigation measures to halt the disease's transmission. Most ordinary non-emergency healthcare was briefly suspended due to the pandemic's lockdown, restricting individuals' contact and access to healthcare concerns, including dental treatment [2,3]. Neglecting oral health issues might result in future dental problems, patient emotional suffering, or even impair their overall quality of life. Dental practitioners are considered high-risk professionals as they are constantly exposed to infections transferred by saliva, blood, or fluid from the nasopharyngeal area due to the nature of dental treatments and close interaction with patients [3,4]. As a result, teledentistry has the potential to give an innovative alternative for continuing dental practice during the pandemic and beyond [2].

Teledentistry, like telemedicine, is the distant or remote delivery of dental care, counselling, education, or treatment using digital technologies rather than physical face-to-face interaction with patients [2]. Telediagnosis, teleconsultation, teletriage, electronic patient records and referrals, and telemonitoring are just a few of the main modalities in modern dentistry practice [2]. Teledentistry has proven to be effective and reliable for distant dental screening, diagnosis, consultation, and treatment planning over the years [1,5]. Moreover, teledentistry is advocated as one of the emergency measures for coping with the COVID-19 pandemic, and a previous study has demonstrated that both dentists and patients feel more secure using teledentistry to minimize non-essential interaction during the pandemic [6]. Since the transition from COVID-19 being a pandemic to an endemic is becoming highly probable, widespread adoption of teledentistry during and after the pandemic is critical, as the primary goal is to avoid face-to-face contact, especially for vulnerable groups, and limit the transmission of this contagious disease [7,8].

Understanding how dentists perceived teledentistry as an alternative tool during the pandemic crisis and how teledentistry may affect future dental professionals' practice are of paramount importance. Although various surveys on dental practitioners' perceptions of the employment of teledentistry during the COVID-19 pandemic have been conducted [3,4,7,8], there has yet to be a systematic evaluation and analysis of dental practitioners' awareness, knowledge, attitude, and practice towards teledentistry. Hence, it is imperative to delve deeper into this context and allow further stakeholders to develop a comprehensive approach for the effective and long-term use of telecommunications for dental care during or even after the pandemic. Thus, the aim of this review is to systematically appraise and analyse the awareness, knowledge, attitude, and practice of teledentistry among dental practitioners during COVID-19.

2. Materials and Methods

2.1. Protocol and Registration

A study protocol based on the Preferred Reporting Items for Systematic Reviews and Meta-Analyses Protocols (PRISMA) was created [9], and the study was registered with a registration number (CRD42021283404) at the Prospective Register of Systematic Reviews (PROSPERO), University of York.

The focus question was developed based on the POT framework, which includes the Population (P), Outcome of interest (O), and Time (T). The POT criteria were: (1). Population: dental practitioners including general dentists, dental specialists, dental educators or lecturers, and postgraduate dental students (2). Outcome: awareness, knowledge, attitude, and practice on teledentistry (3). Time: during the COVID-19 pandemic.

The POT question was 'What is the level of awareness, knowledge, attitude and practice among dental practitioners on teledentistry during the COVID-19 pandemic?' In this context, a dental practitioner is referred to as a dentist who is qualified and certified by the state to provide dental treatments within the extent of their licence and certification. Moreover, the use of information technology and telecommunications for dental treatment, consultation, education, and public awareness is referred to as teledentistry.

2.2. Search Strategy

An electronic search was conducted independently by two investigators (GSSL, SHK) using ten electronic databases to identify relevant articles published between March 2020 and September 2021: PubMed, Google Scholar, Web of Science, ScienceDirect, Cochrane, EMBASE, SIGLE, EBSCO, LILACS, and Open Grey. Two other investigators (KZT, CWL) independently evaluated and appraised the reference lists of relevant papers from the electronic search using computer software (EndNote X9, Thomson Reuters). Keywords such as 'knowledge', 'awareness', 'attitude', 'practice', 'teledentistry', 'e-dentistry', 'COVID-19', and 'pandemic' were applied for each database in conjunction with the use of Boolean operators 'AND' and 'OR'.

2.3. Study Selection

After discarding duplicate articles using EndNote software version x9, two investigators (GSSL, SHK) separately screened the titles and abstracts of all the articles, and the remaining two investigators (KZT, CWL) performed a full-text assessment to identify studies based on the inclusion and exclusion criteria. Articles that fulfilled the following inclusion criteria were considered:

- Awareness, knowledge, attitude, and practice towards teledentistry during the COVID-19 pandemic;
- General dentists, dental specialists, dental educators, or postgraduate dental students;
- Cross-sectional study;
- No limit to any country;
- No limit to any language.
- Articles that fulfilled the following exclusion criteria were omitted:
- Expert opinions, reviews, case reports or case series, letters to the editor, short communications
- Studies performed before March 2020 (as the pandemic was announced by WHO in March 2020)
- Full text unavailable

To evaluate interrater reliability, calibrations between investigators were performed. The average concordance was computed using the Kappa value to compare the investigators' decisions on inclusion and exclusion [10]. Any disagreements that arose throughout the search were addressed and resolved with the fifth investigator (SS).

2.4. Data Extraction

Each article's parameters were extracted and documented by four investigators (GSSL, SHK, KZT, CWL) using customized excel spreadsheet extraction forms: titles of articles, authors, year of publication, country, type of study, sample size, gender, age, assessment method, evaluation criteria, response rate, and overall main results. The fifth investigator (SS) double-checked the accuracy of the filled data and a further discussion with all investigators was conducted if any discrepancies were found.

2.5. Risk of Bias Assessment and Level of Evidence

Three investigators (SHK, KZT, CWL) independently assessed the risk of bias (RoB) of the selected articles using the Joanna Briggs Institute (JBI) critical appraisal checklist for analytical cross-sectional studies [11]. Either 'yes', 'no', 'unclear', or 'not applicable' was assigned for each domain. Subsequently, the studies were categorized as 'include', 'exclude', or 'seek further info'. Any persistent disputes were resolved with the assistance of the fourth investigator (GSSL). The Oxford Centre for Evidence-Based Medicine (OCEBM) guideline was used to establish the level of evidence in each study [12].

2.6. Statistical Analysis

The extracted proportions of the awareness, knowledge, attitude, and practice among dental practitioners towards teledentistry during the COVID-19 pandemic from each study were pooled and estimated using single-arm meta-analysis based on the DerSimonian–Laird random-effects model. The analysis was conducted using the OpenMeta (Analyst) software (CEBM, Oxford, UK) with a significance level of 0.05 and 95% confidence intervals (CI). If the estimated upper limit of the 95% confidence interval was larger than 1.0, the upper limit was defined as 1.0. The Higgins' I^2 statistics were employed to determine the degree of data heterogeneity among the included studies (I^2 less than 30% = acceptable heterogeneity, I^2 between 30 and 60% = moderate heterogeneity, I^2 greater than 60% = substantial heterogeneity) [13]. Subgroup analysis comparing various populations, genders, and age groups with different educational levels was not feasible due to a scarcity of data from the included studies. However, meta-regression was conducted to assess the effect of sample size on the outcomes. Furthermore, Egger's test was performed to identify publication bias.

3. Results

3.1. Study Selection

During the initial search, a total of 1182 articles were retrieved (Figure 1). A total of 438 articles were eliminated after duplication was removed, followed by 724 articles being discarded after screening based on titles and abstracts; the remaining 20 articles were chosen for full-text evaluation. Finally, only six studies were included in the current review encompassing a total of 6904 dental practitioners. The average inter-investigators' Kappa score was 0.82 during the study selection process, which indicates a 'perfect' agreement [14]. Figure 1 depicts the reasons for article exclusion.

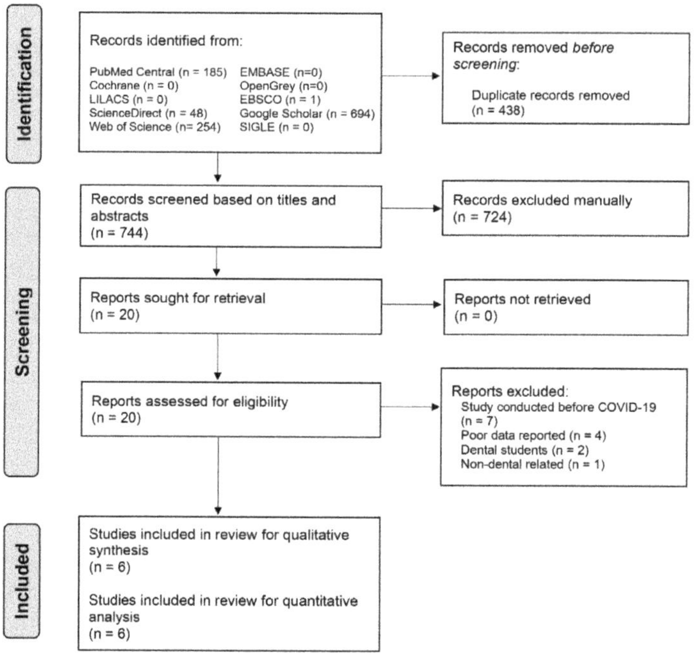

Figure 1. Study selection according to the Preferred Reporting Items for Systematic Reviews and Meta-Analysis (PRISMA) flowchart.

3.2. Study Characteristics

Table 1 summarized the characteristics of each included study. All the included articles were cross-sectional studies. Specific survey questions from each included article were extracted to represent the awareness, knowledge, attitude, and practice towards teledentistry. Five studies focused on the awareness of teledentistry among dental practitioners during the COVID-19 pandemic [3,4,7,8,15], five studies on their knowledge [4,7,8,15,16], four studies on their attitude [3,4,7,8], and three studies on their practice of teledentistry [3,8,15]. Among all the included studies, three articles originated from Pakistan [4,7,15], and one article each from Colombia [3], Saudi Arabia [8], and India [16].

Table 1. Characteristics of the included studies.

Study	Year	Country	Study Design	Sample Size	Gender	Mean Age	Evaluation Tool	Evaluation Criteria	Response Rate	Main Result
Plaza-Ruiz et al. [3]	2021	Colombia	cross-sectional	5370 (2252 GD, 2589 DS)	F: 3878, M: 1492	45	questionnaire	awareness, attitude, practice	16.84%	Knowledge and practice of teledentistry increased since the emerging of COVID-19.
Abbas et al. [7]	2020	Pakistan	cross-sectional	510 (GD, PGDS, DE, DS)	n/a	n/a	questionnaire	knowledge, awareness, attitude	100%	Awareness regarding teledentistry is high among general dentists.
Subhan et al. [4]	2021	Pakistan	cross-sectional	350 (GS, DS)	F: 151, M: 174	n/a	questionnaire	awareness, knowledge, attitude	92.80%	Most of the dental professionals had inadequate knowledge about teledentistry before COVID-19, but their awareness and perception were currently satisfactory.
Zahra et al. [15]	2020	Pakistan	cross-sectional	172 (GD, DS, PGDS)	F: 95, M: 61	n/a	questionnaire	knowledge, awareness, practice	90.62%	In total, 76.6% participants had knowledge of teledentistry, but 80.8% had never used it.
AlAssad et al. [8]	2021	Saudi Arabia	cross-sectional	102 (PGDS, GD)	F: 39, M: 63	n/a	questionnaire	knowledge, awareness, attitudes, and practices	78.50%	Adequate knowledge and awareness of teledentistry during the COVID-19 pandemic.
Save et al. [16]	2020	India	cross-sectional	151 (GD, DS)	F: 99, M: 52	25.72	questionnaire	knowledge	100%	Only 43% of the participants were aware of teledentistry.

DE: Dental educators; DS: Dental specialists; GD: General dentists; PGDS: Postgraduate dental students; F: Female; M: Male; n/a: Not Applicable.

3.3. Risk of Bias Assessment and Level of Evidence

All included studies in the present review were deemed 'include' based on the JBI critical appraisal tool (Table 2). All the included studies were rated 'Yes' for domains 1, 2, 3, 4, 5, 7, and 8, but one study was rated 'No' for domain 6 [4]. All the included studies were ranked as Level 3 based on the evidence of OCEBM. The risk of bias assessment and level of evidence's Cohen's kappa coefficient (κ) were scored 0.78 and 0.80, respectively, indicating a 'substantial' agreement [14].

Table 2. Risk of bias and level of evidence of each included study.

Study	Domains								Overall Appraisal	LOE
	1	2	3	4	5	6	7	8		
Plaza-Ruiz et al. [3]	Y	Y	Y	Y	Y	Y	Y	Y	Include	3
Abbas et al. [7]	Y	Y	Y	Y	Y	Y	Y	Y	Include	3
Subhan et al. [4]	Y	Y	Y	Y	Y	N	Y	Y	Include	3
Zahra et al. [15]	Y	Y	Y	Y	Y	Y	Y	Y	Include	3
AlAssad et al. [8]	Y	Y	Y	Y	Y	Y	Y	Y	Include	3
Save et al. [16]	Y	Y	Y	Y	Y	Y	Y	Y	Include	3

Y: Yes; U: Unclear; N: No; LOE: Level of evidence. Domain 1: Were the criteria for inclusion in the sample clearly defined? Domain 2: Were the study subjects and the setting described in detail? Domain 3: Was the exposure measured in a valid and reliable way? Domain 4: Were objective, standard criteria used for measurement of the condition? Domain 5: Were confounding factors identified? Domain 6: Were strategies to deal with confounding factors stated? Domain 7: Were the outcomes measured in a valid and reliable way? Domain 8: Was appropriate statistical analysis used?

3.4. Statistical Analysis

Table 3 shows the proportions of the level of awareness, knowledge, attitude, and practice towards teledentistry among dental practitioners during the COVID-19 pandemic retrieved from the included studies. Quantitative syntheses were performed when three or more studies were available for each evaluation criteria. For each study, participants such as general dentists, dental specialists, postgraduate dental students and dental educators or lecturers were pooled together. Based on the single-arm meta-analysis (Figure 2), a high level of awareness (70.4%, CI: (64.3, 76.5)) and attitude (72.5%, CI: (60.7, 84.3)) towards teledentistry was noted among dental practitioners during the COVID-19 pandemic. However, the knowledge level (57.9%, CI: (46.0, 69.9)) were deemed moderate, while their practice level of teledentistry (35.8%, CI: (14.8, 56.8)) was found to be poor among dental practitioners. Overall, the I^2 of the weighted mean awareness, knowledge, attitude, and practice level of teledentistry among dental practitioners ranged from 90.78% to 98.21%, indicating a substantial degree of data heterogeneity ($p < 0.001$) among the studies included.

Table 3. Awareness, knowledge, attitude, and practice among dental professionals towards teledentistry during COVID-19.

Study	Year	Participants	Awareness	Knowledge	Attitude	Practice
Plaza-Ruiz et al. [3]	2021	GD, DS	(3368/5370)	n/a	(3198/5370)	(2284/5370)
Abbas et al. [7]	2020	GD, PGDS, DE, DS	(369/510)	(327/510)	(375/510)	n/a
Subhan et al. [4]	2021	GD, DS	(223/325)	(242/325)	(261/325)	n/a
Zahra et al. [15]	2020	GD, DS, PGDS	(120/156)	(66/156)	n/a	(21/156)
AlAssad et al. [8]	2021	PGDS, GD	(75/102)	(66/102)	(79/102)	(53/102)
Save et al. [16]	2020	GD, DS	n/a	(65/151)	n/a	n/a

DE: Dental educators; DS: Dental specialists; GD: General dentists; PGDS: Postgraduate dental students. n/a: Not Applicable.

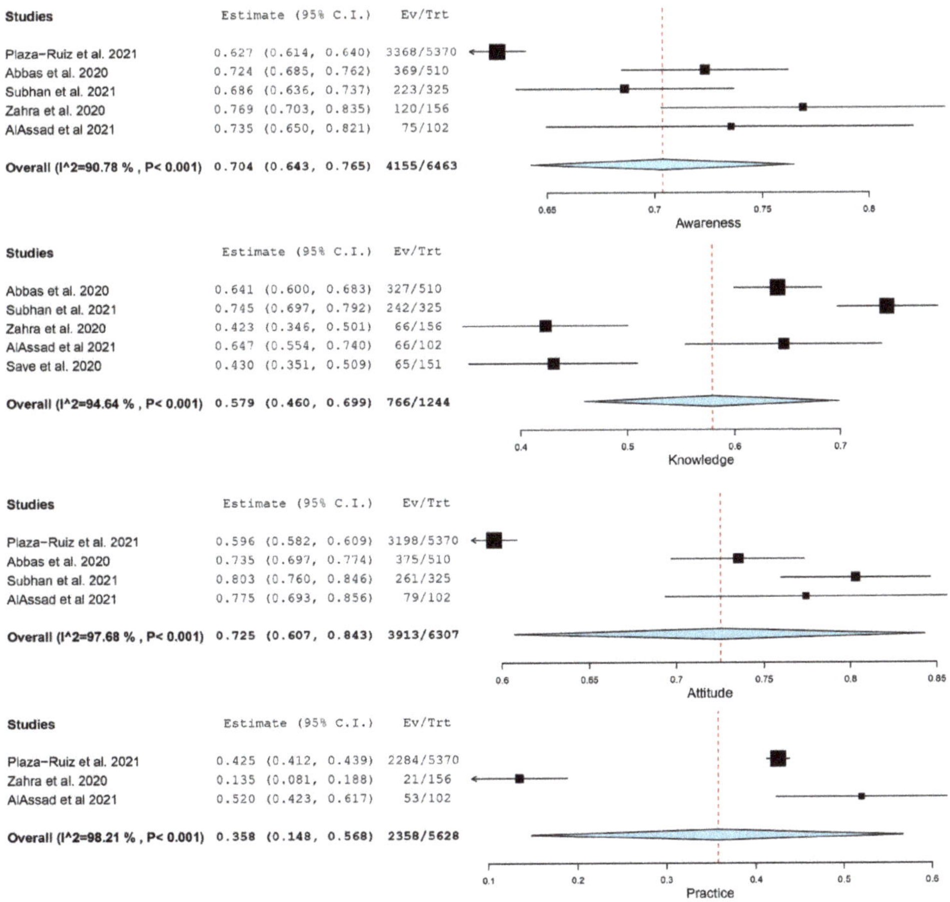

Figure 2. Single-arm meta-analysis showing the awareness, knowledge, attitude, and practice level of teledentistry among dental practitioners.

Sensitivity analyses were carried out by removing each data set one at a time. The highest and lowest weight mean awareness levels were 72.3% (CI: 69.1, 75.5) and 68.8% (CI: 62.7, 74.9), when Plaza-Ruiz et al. [3] and Zahra et al. [15] were omitted, respectively. Furthermore, the highest and lowest weight mean knowledge levels were 61.8% (CI: 50.3, 73.4) and 53.6% (CI: 41.0, 66.3), when Zahra et al. [15] and Subhan et al. [4] were removed, respectively. The highest and lowest weight mean attitude levels were 76.9% (CI: 72.2, 81.7) and 69.8% (CI: 57.9, 81.7), when Plaza-Ruiz et al. [3] and Subhan et al. [4] were eliminated, respectively. Finally, the highest and lowest weight mean practice levels were 46.0% (CI: 37.1, 54.9) and 32.5% (CI: 19.2, 70.2), when Zahra et al. [15] and Plaza-Ruiz et al. [3] were omitted, respectively.

Meta-regression analysis (Appendix A) was also performed to assess the effect of the participants' sample size of each study on the degree of awareness, knowledge, attitude, and practice towards teledentistry. Significant differences were found for all evaluating criteria (p-values: awareness (<0.001), knowledge (<0.001), attitude (<0.001), and practice (0.004)) signifying that the sample size of each study had a direct effect on the degree of data heterogeneity. In addition, Egger's test revealed that there was no indication of significant publication bias in the level of awareness, knowledge, attitude, and practice of teledentistry among dental practitioners during the COVID-19 pandemic (Egger's test: p-value = 0.32, 0.021, 0.05, and 0.11, respectively).

4. Discussion

The current review is the first of its kind to comprehensively evaluate the perceptions of dental practitioners including their awareness, knowledge, attitude, and practice towards teledentistry during the COVID-19 pandemic. Teledentistry enables distance communication and consultation by avoiding face-to-face contact and allowing the exchange of clinical information [2,15]. It also facilitates remote oral care and patient education, which are recommended by healthcare authorities around the globe, particularly during the COVID-19 pandemic, when social distancing should be emphasized to prevent the spread of the coronavirus [2,7]. Despite the current review only covering a small number of relevant primary papers, it uncovered valuable insights regarding teledentistry application among dental practitioners.

In the present single-arm meta-analyses, dental practitioners exhibited a high degree of awareness (70.4%) and attitude (72.5%) towards teledentistry. Such a finding corroborates the findings of a previous systematic review on telehealth in which a high level of awareness and attitude were observed among healthcare professionals [17]. Most dental practitioners agreed that teledentistry is a brilliant invention that may bring certain benefits and requires forward thinking, which has resulted in a more favourable attitude towards teledentistry [7,8]. However, the knowledge level among dental practitioners in the present analysis was somewhat moderate (57.9%), which contradicts other similar studies [18–20]. This could be due to income, legislation, previous undergraduate education, and infrastructural variations that exist between countries [3]. The current finding suggested that dental practitioners are aware of teledentistry and have a favourable attitude toward it, but they are unclear of the knowledge and skills required to utilise it. One probable explanation is that dental practitioners are not well-exposed to teledentistry through workshops, lectures, or seminars [8]. In addition, work experience, postgraduate qualification, and internet access were found to be major predictors of teledentistry knowledge among dental practitioners. It was also reported that junior dental practitioners and those with a postgraduate degree showed a better level of knowledge towards teledentistry [15,21]. This could be due to the fact that teledentistry is a relatively new concept, and senior dental practitioners may not have received sufficient training to cutting-edge technology. Similarly, dental practitioners with postgraduate qualifications may have had more exposure to IT technology throughout their postgraduate studies.

On the other hand, the practice of teledentistry was still found to be uncommon during the COVID-19 pandemic, with only about 35.8% of dental practitioners using it. It is not surprising that teledentistry practice is still limited, despite their adequate knowledge of the subject [18,22]. Dental practitioners' knowledge and comprehension of teledentistry, the skills necessary for its effective application, and a working environment favourable to the adoption of such a new technology are all critical attributes in the widespread acceptance and practice of teledentistry [15,16,23]. Inadequate financial remuneration and disparities in rural regions have also been cited as having a detrimental impact on teledentistry application [3]. However, dental practitioners' knowledge and attitude level towards teledentistry improved during the pandemic period, implying that the increased familiarity and practice of teledentistry would likely continue even when the pandemic entered the endemic phase [3,8].

Another factor that may contribute to a lower level of practice among dental practitioners is that most of the primary studies included in the present systematic review originated from developing countries [4,7,15,16]. While developed countries continue to benefit and expand this technology by encouraging remote health consultation and monitoring with efficient online record-keeping systems, telehealth including telemedicine and teledentistry in developing countries is still in its infancy [23]. Thus, one may postulate that many developing countries still encounter a lack of teledentistry services, and a scarcity of skilled dental practitioners incorporated this technology into their daily practice, making it more challenging to offer remote oral healthcare services during the COVID-19 era, particularly in suburban and remote regions [16]. Despite these issues, the authors believe that the COVID-19 pandemic will provide an excellent opportunity for developing countries to optimise teledentistry by providing greater skills and new technologies that could change the future of dentistry.

Telehealth modalities, such as teledentistry, provide a wealth of advantages, including ease of application, a tendency to enhance outcomes and communication, low cost, the ability to reduce travel time, expand access to treatment, and raise patient self-awareness [24,25]. In light of the present COVID-19 situation and efforts to expand the number of patients treated via teledentistry as a means of limiting virus transmission, dental practitioners may be anticipated to incorporate teledentistry into their work practices on a larger scale. Increased patient acceptance and self-management will likely lead to teledentistry being a more integral element of the care pathway for a variety of oral health issues [2]. Dental practitioners and other dental auxiliaries participating in service design and equipment selection will also assist in boosting teledentistry adoption [26]. Training and continuing professional education can help to enhance teledentistry awareness and knowledge, as well as ensure that dental practitioners are prepared to use it in the treatment pathway [15]. Rather than being viewed as a threat to professional identity and competence, understanding how teledentistry might enable them to accomplish some regular consultation and monitoring activities remotely is essential.

Other factors such as the dental practitioners' age and gender, their work environment, and educational level may have an impact on the overall results [3,8,19]. These characteristics were not evaluated in the current review because the data obtained from the primary studies were pooled together, making it impossible to split the results into numerous age groups or genders for comparison. Notwithstanding this, meta-regression was employed and discovered that different sample sizes had a considerable impact on the findings. It is not odd that this occurred since the included studies contained a large range of sample size, which might increase the likelihood to skew the results in one direction. Furthermore, the inclusion and assessment criteria vary significantly among the studies because different studies define the terms 'knowledge' and 'awareness' differently. In the current review, knowledge refers to a profound comprehension and acquaintance of teledentistry, whereas awareness refers to a superficial understanding.

Most of the included studies were considered to have a low risk of bias in all domains except for one study rated 'No' for domain 6: 'Were strategies to deal with confounding factors stated?' [4]. Subhan R et al. [27] identified cofounding factors including age and gender but did not specify how these factors may affect their findings. Additionally, the recent meta-analyses revealed significant heterogeneity. This might be due to the inclusion of studies with a wide range of sample sizes, as well as the nature of each study's presentation of all evidence using different forms of questionnaires. Unfortunately, due to the small number of studies, subgroup analysis was not possible. When individual participant's data are accessible, the sources of heterogeneity and bias may be fully explored, but most included studies only disclosed aggregate data [28].

The present review provides useful information that paves the way for teledentistry by suggesting the creation of more related programmes and software to fill in the gaps between dental practitioners and patients. Healthcare providers and policymakers are advocated to embrace teledentistry and assist legislation in keeping up with the technology by allowing more funding and infrastructural options for teledentistry. Nonetheless, it is worth noting that the confidentiality of patients' information may be a concern that compromises privacy [4]. Patients' privacy and the establishment of secure information technology networks should be prioritised when contemplating teledentistry adoption [22].

One drawback of the present study is that the included primary studies were still limited in their ability to generalise and extrapolate the findings of the context into a larger population. To ensure accurate inferential outcomes, a substantial amount of primary research should be included in the meta-analysis, but it is understandable that such a criterion is rarely met, particularly in the field of dentistry where the number of selected studies is often very limited [29]. In addition, the absence of subgroup analysis on the impact of dental practitioners' age, gender, working environment, and qualifications due to a scarcity of data may have hampered the current review from developing a greater understanding of teledentistry. Sampling and response bias of each primary study was not addressed in the current review as it was beyond our scope. Thus, more well-designed studies from different countries are warranted to obtain a more general understanding of the level of awareness, knowledge, attitude, and practice of teledentistry among dental practitioners.

5. Conclusions

The present review findings suggested that a high degree of awareness and attitude toward teledentistry was noted among dental practitioners during the COVID-19 pandemic. On the other hand, their knowledge level was moderate, while practice level was relatively poor. Teledentistry offers the promise to provide a new strategy for continuing dental care during and after the pandemic. Hence, it is imperative that future well-designed studies are warranted to investigate alternative approaches to enhance dental practitioners' knowledge and practice of teledentistry. The authors also advocate that future studies should further evaluate participants' characteristics for better comparisons and a deeper understanding of dental practitioners' perceptions towards teledentistry.

Author Contributions: Conceptualization, G.S.S.L. and S.S.; methodology, S.H.K., C.W.L. and K.Z.T.; software, G.S.S.L.; formal analysis, G.S.S.L. and W.W.T.; investigation, S.H.K. and K.Z.T.; writing—original draft preparation, S.H.K., K.Z.T., C.W.L. and W.W.T.; writing—review and editing, G.S.S.L. and S.S. All authors have read and agreed to the published version of the manuscript.

Funding: This research received no external funding.

Institutional Review Board Statement: The study was conducted in accordance with the PRISMA guidelines and approved by the Prospective Register of Systematic Reviews (PROSPERO), University of York (CRD42021283404).

Informed Consent Statement: Not applicable.

Data Availability Statement: Not applicable.

Conflicts of Interest: The authors declare no conflict of interest.

Appendix A

Meta-regression evaluating the effect of sample size of each study on the degree of awareness, knowledge, attitude, and practice toward teledentistry. * Significance at 0.05.

Categories	Coefficient	Confidence Intervals		Standard Error	p-Value
		Upper Bound	Lower Bound		
Awareness	0.729	0.700	0.757	0.015	0.001 *
Knowledge	0.533	0.321	0.745	0.108	0.001 *
Attitude	0.771	0.743	0.798	0.014	0.001 *
Practice	0.319	0.098	0.540	0.113	0.004 *

References

1. Giudice, A.; Barone, S.; Muraca, D.; Averta, F.; Diodati, F.; Antonelli, A.; Fortunato, L. Can Teledentistry Improve the Monitoring of Patients during the Covid-19 Dissemination? A Descriptive Pilot Study. *Int. J. Environ. Res. Public Health* **2020**, *17*, 3399. [CrossRef]
2. Ghai, S. Teledentistry during COVID-19 pandemic. *Diabetes Metab. Syndr.* **2020**, *14*, 933–935. [CrossRef] [PubMed]

3. Plaza-Ruiz, S.P.; Barbosa-Liz, D.M.; Agudelo-Suarez, A.A. Impact of COVID-19 on the Knowledge and Attitudes of Dentists toward Teledentistry. *JDR Clin. Trans. Res.* **2021**, *6*, 268–278. [CrossRef] [PubMed]
4. Subhan, R.; Ismail, W.A.; Musharraf, S.; Khan, M.; Hafeez, R.; Alam, M.K. Teledentistry as a Supportive Tool for Dentists in Pakistan. *Biomed Res. Int.* **2021**, *2021*, 8757859. [CrossRef] [PubMed]
5. AlShaya, M.S.; Assery, M.K.; Pani, S.C. Reliability of mobile phone teledentistry in dental diagnosis and treatment planning in mixed dentition. *J. Telemed Telecare* **2020**, *26*, 45–52. [CrossRef] [PubMed]
6. Menhadji, P.; Patel, R.; Asimakopoulou, K.; Quinn, B.; Khoshkhounejad, G.; Pasha, P.; Garcia Sanchez, R.; Ide, M.; Kalsi, P.; Nibali, L. Patients' and dentists' perceptions of tele-dentistry at the time of COVID-19. A questionnaire-based study. *J. Dent* **2021**, *113*, 103782. [CrossRef] [PubMed]
7. Abbas, B.; Wajahat, M.; Saleem, Z.; Imran, E.; Sajjad, M.; Khurshid, Z. Role of Teledentistry in COVID-19 Pandemic: A Nationwide Comparative Analysis among Dental Professionals. *Eur. J. Dent* **2020**, *14*, S116–S122. [CrossRef]
8. AlAssad, F.; Alqhtani, N.; Alshammery, D. Implementation of Teledentistry in Postgraduate Dental Education During COVID-19 Pandemic in Saudi Arabia. *Ann. Dent. Spec.* **2021**, *9*, 20–26. [CrossRef]
9. Page, M.J.; McKenzie, J.E.; Bossuyt, P.M.; Boutron, I.; Hoffmann, T.C.; Mulrow, C.D.; Shamseer, L.; Tetzlaff, J.M.; Akl, E.A.; Brennan, S.E.; et al. The PRISMA 2020 statement: An updated guideline for reporting systematic reviews. *BMJ* **2021**, *372*, n71. [CrossRef] [PubMed]
10. McHugh, M.L. Interrater reliability: The kappa statistic. *Biochem Med.* **2012**, *22*, 276–282. [CrossRef]
11. The Joanna Briggs Institute Critical Appraisal Tools for Use in JBI Systematic Reviews: Checklist for Analytical Cross Sectional Studies. Available online: https://jbi.global/critical-appraisal-tools (accessed on 21 October 2021).
12. Oxford Centre for Evidence-Based Medicine—The Oxford Levels of Evidence 2. Available online: https://www.cebm.ox.ac.uk/resources/levels-of-evidence/ocebm-levels-of-evidence (accessed on 21 October 2021).
13. Lin, G.S.S.; Hisham, A.R.B.; Ch Er, C.I.Y.; Cheah, K.K.; Ghani, N.; Noorani, T.Y. Success rates of coronal and partial pulpotomies in mature permanent molars: A systematic review and single-arm meta-analysis. *Quintessence Int.* 2021; *in press*. [CrossRef]
14. Landis, J.R.; Koch, G.G. The Measurement of Observer Agreement for Categorical Data. *Biometrics* **1977**, *33*, 159–174. [CrossRef] [PubMed]
15. Zahra, S.; Yousaf, A.; Akram, H.; Sajjad, T.; Bangash, K.; Yousaf, N. Awareness of Dentists Regarding Use of Tele-dentistry During Pandemic of Corona Virus Disease 2019 (COVID-19). *PAFMJ* **2020**, *70*, S489–S493.
16. Save, S.S.; Singh, S.S.; Kalra, D.D.; Jhaveri, S.T.; Avhad, S.K. An overview of teledentistry with a cross-sectional study on relevant knowledge and attitude of dentists in Mumbai. *J. Glob. Oral. Health* **2020**, *3*, 101–109. [CrossRef]
17. Ravi, R.; Gunjawate, D.R.; Yerraguntla, K.; Driscoll, C. Knowledge and Perceptions of Teleaudiology Among Audiologists: A Systematic Review. *J. Audiol. Otol.* **2018**, *22*, 120–127. [CrossRef]
18. Murererehe, J.; Uwambaye, P.; Isyagi, M.; Nyandwi, T.; Njunwa, K. Knowledge, attitude and practices of dental professionals in Rwanda towards the benefits and applications of teledentistry. *Rwanda J.* **2017**, *4*, 39–47. [CrossRef]
19. Pradhan, D.; Verma, P.; Sharma, L.; Khaitan, T. Knowledge, awareness, and attitude regarding teledentistry among postgraduate dental students of Kanpur city, India: A questionnaire study. *J. Educ. Health Promot.* **2019**, *8*, 104. [CrossRef] [PubMed]
20. Martin, A.B.; Nelson, J.D.; Bhavsar, G.P.; McElligott, J.; Garr, D.; Leite, R.S. Feasibility assessment for using telehealth technology to improve access to dental care for rural and underserved populations. *J. Evid Based Dent. Pr.* **2016**, *16*, 228–235. [CrossRef]
21. Ramesh, N.; Pankaj, A.; Archana, J.S.; Kailash, A.; Mridula, T.; Piyush, P.; Nikhil, B. Teledentistry: Knowledge and Attitudes among Dentists in Udaipur, India. *Oral Health Dent. Manag.* **2013**, *12*, 138–144.
22. Zayapragassarazan, Z.; Kumar, S. Awareness, Knowledge, Attitude and Skills of Telemedicine among Health Professional Faculty Working in Teaching Hospitals. *J. Clin. Diagn Res.* **2016**, *10*, JC01–JC04. [CrossRef]
23. Ashfaq, A.; Memon, S.F.; Zehra, A.; Barry, S.; Jawed, H.; Akhtar, M.; Kirmani, W.; Malik, F.; Khawaja, A.W.; Barry, H.; et al. Knowledge and Attitude Regarding Telemedicine Among Doctors in Karachi. *Cureus* **2020**, *12*, e6927. [CrossRef] [PubMed]
24. Kruse, C.S.; Krowski, N.; Rodriguez, B.; Tran, L.; Vela, J.; Brooks, M. Telehealth and patient satisfaction: A systematic review and narrative analysis. *BMJ Open* **2017**, *7*, e016242. [CrossRef] [PubMed]
25. Daniel, S.J.; Wu, L.; Kumar, S. Teledentistry: A systematic review of clinical outcomes, utilization and costs. *J. Dent. Hyg* **2013**, *87*, 345–352. [PubMed]
26. Brewster, L.; Mountain, G.; Wessels, B.; Kelly, C.; Hawley, M. Factors affecting front line staff acceptance of telehealth technologies: A mixed-method systematic review. *J. Adv. Nurs* **2014**, *70*, 21–33. [CrossRef] [PubMed]
27. Innes, N.P.; Evans, D.J.; Stirrups, D.R. The Hall Technique; a randomized controlled clinical trial of a novel method of managing carious primary molars in general dental practice: Acceptability of the technique and outcomes at 23 months. *BMC Oral Health* **2007**, *7*, 18. [CrossRef] [PubMed]
28. Lin, G.S.S.; Cher, C.Y.; Cheah, K.K.; Koh, S.H.; Chia, C.H.L.; Lim, V.R.; Baharin, F.; Wafa, S. Acceptability of atraumatic restorative treatment and Hall Technique among children, parents, and general dental practitioners: A systematic review and meta-analysis. *Quintessence Int.* 2021; *in press*. [CrossRef]
29. Guolo, A.; Varin, C. Random-effects meta-analysis: The number of studies matters. *Stat. Methods Med. Res.* **2017**, *26*, 1500–1518. [CrossRef]

medicina MDPI

Systematic Review

Meta-Analysis of Prevalence of Depression in Dental Students during COVID-19 Pandemic

Javier Santabárbara [1,2,3], Naiara Ozamiz-Etxebarria [4], Nahia Idoiaga [4,*], Beatriz Olaya [2,5] and Juan Bueno-Novitol [6]

1 Department of Microbiology, Pediatrics, Radiology and Public Health, University of Zaragoza, C/Domingo Miral s/n, 50009 Zaragoza, Spain; jsantabarbara@unizar.es
2 Centro de Investigación Biomédica en Red de Salud Mental (CIBERSAM), Ministry of Science and Innovation, 28029 Madrid, Spain; beatriz.olaya@sjd.org
3 Aragonese Institute of Health Sciences (IIS Aragón), 50009 Zaragoza, Spain
4 Department of Developmental and Educational Psychology, University of the Basque Country UPV/EHU, 48940 Leioa, Spain; naiara.ozamiz@ehu.eus
5 Research, Innovation and Teaching Unit, Parc Sanitari Sant Joan de Déu, Universitat de Barcelona, 08830 Barcelona, Spain
6 Psychiatry Service, Hospital Universitario Miguel Servet, 50009 Zaragoza, Spain; elecrijuan@hotmail.com
* Correspondence: nahia.idoiaga@ehu.eus

Citation: Santabárbara, J.; Ozamiz-Etxebarria, N.; Idoiaga, N.; Olaya, B.; Bueno-Novitol, J. Meta-Analysis of Prevalence of Depression in Dental Students during COVID-19 Pandemic. *Medicina* **2021**, 57, 1278. https://doi.org/10.3390/medicina57111278

Academic Editors: Cesare D'Amico and Pier Paolo Poli

Received: 5 October 2021
Accepted: 15 November 2021
Published: 21 November 2021

Abstract: *Background and Objectives*: The COVID-19 pandemic has a negative impact on the mental health of the population in general, and in college students in particular. Dental students have seen their teaching altered and their clinical practice reduced. This study was aimed at conducting a systematic review and meta-analysis of studies reporting levels of depression among dental students during the COVID-19 and estimating the pooled prevalence of depression. *Materials and Methods*: Medline via PubMed and other databases were searched for studies on the prevalence of depression in dental undergraduates, published from 1 December 2019 to 1 September 2021. The pooled proportions of depression were calculated with random effects models. *Results*: We identified 13 studies from 9 countries. The pooled prevalence of depression in dental students was 37% (95% CI: 26–49%) with no variation due to gender, response rate or methodological quality. We only found a significantly higher prevalence of depression in studies from Asia compared to Europe and America. *Conclusions*: Our results suggest that dental students are suffering from higher levels of depression compared with the general population or other college students during the COVID-19 pandemic, with differences across regions. Measures to improve mental health and wellbeing of dental students during the pandemic are needed.

Keywords: depression; dental students; gender; countries; meta-analysis; COVID-19

1. Introduction

Since March 2021, when the World Health Organization (WHO) declared the COVID-19 pandemic [1,2], there have been profound economic, social, psychological and educational changes worldwide [3]. However, the pandemic has not equally impacted different segments of the population [4]. Specifically, several target groups have been studied for the negative psychological impact of the COVID-19 [5]. Among them, university students have concerned the international scientific community [6]. One of the first measures to contain the pandemic, and to stop the spread of the virus, was to close universities, with considerable associated psychological symptoms in this population [7]. University education had to be transformed overnight into a virtual mode [8], and students had to quickly adapt to this change. Students had to deal with delays in academic activities [9], the transition to online education, the administration of homework, projects and other ongoing assessments. Students began to fear that the pandemic could have a serious impact on their careers [10,11] and they were also very concerned about their health, safety and the well-being of their families [12]. Social distancing, lockdowns and other restrictions and norms to stop the spread of the virus are factors related to an increased rates of depression in the general population [13] and particularly in university students [14,15]. This increased level of depression seems to be related to the fear of getting infected and adaptation difficulties to personal, academic and professional restrictions [16,17].

Previous studies have shown that dental students have important levels of depression before the pandemic [18–20]. This previous psychological distress could be caused by the high emotional burden of dental studies due to long study hours, high workload [21], clinical demands, examinations and qualifications [22,23]. Moreover, the levels of depression seem to increase as the years of medical school progress, showing higher symptomatology than medical students [24,25]. In addition, dental students in their clinical practice are especially vulnerable to the risk of COVID-19 transmission [26], as they have to work closely with patients. This proximity may put them at a higher risk of viral exposure and being infected with COVID-19 [27]. In fact, droplets and aerosols produced during most dental procedures are potential methods for COVID-19 transmission [28].

Research has suggested several sociodemographic variables that might be associated with higher rates of depression during the COVID-19 pandemic. In general, higher rates of depression have been observed among females [29–31], although there are studies suggesting that there are no differences between men and women [32,33]. In addition, significant differences have also been found in the prevalence of depression among university students depending on the country [6,34].

Several reports, opinion articles and studies have recently been published about the psychological impact of the COVID-19 pandemic on dental students. However, to the best of the authors' knowledge, there are no studies that synthesize the current scientific evidence on this topic.

Thus, the main objective of this study is to conduct a systematic review and meta-analysis of studies that investigate the prevalence of depression in dental students during the COVID-19 pandemic. Moreover, it will be analyzed whether gender, age or the country were the study was carried out create significant differences in the prevalence of depression among dental students.

2. Materials and Methods

This study follows the methodology of a previous work [35], and was conducted in accordance with the PRISMA guidelines for reporting systematic reviews and meta-analysis [36] (Supplementary Table S1).

2.1. Search Strategy

Two researchers (JS and JBN) searched for all cross-sectional studies reporting the prevalence of depression published from 1 December 2019 to 1 September 2021, using MEDLINE via PubMed, Embase and Scielo databases. The search strategy used in PubMed is detailed in Table 1.

Table 1. Search strategy in Pubmed.

(COVID [tiab] OR COVID-19[tiab] OR coronavirus[tiab] OR SARS-CoV-2[tiab] OR "Coronavirus"[Mesh] OR "severe acute respiratory syndrome coronavirus 2"[Supplementary Concept] OR "COVID-19"[Supplementary Concept] OR "Coronavirus Infections/epidemiology"[Mesh] OR "Coronavirus Infections/prevention and control"[Mesh] OR "Coronavirus Infections/psychology"[Mesh] OR "Coronavirus Infections/statistics and numerical data"[Mesh]) AND ("Depression"[Mesh] OR "Depressive Disorder"[Mesh] OR "depression"[tiab] OR "depressive"[tiab] OR "Depression/statistics and numerical data"[Mesh]) AND ("Students, Dental"[Mesh] OR "dental students"[tiab] OR "dentistry students"[tiab] OR "dental undergraduates"[tiab] OR "dentistry undergraduates"[tiab] OR "university students" [tiab])

No language restriction was made. References from selected articles were inspected to detect additional potential studies. Then, we performed a manual search of the "grey literature" (e.g., medRxiv or Google Scholar) to detect other potentially eligible papers. In addition, the reference lists of selected publications were also screened for potentially eligible studies. Authors of studies were contacted directly when insufficient data were available in articles meeting the inclusion criteria or the full text was not available.

2.2. Selection Criteria

Studies were included if: (1) reported cross-sectional data on the prevalence of depression, or sufficient information to compute this, conducted during the COVID-19 outbreak; (2) focused on dental students; and (3) included a validated instrument to assess or diagnose depression.

We excluded studies focusing only on community-based samples of general population or specific samples that were not dental students (e.g., medical students, medical professionals, patients), as well as review articles.

A pre-designed data extraction form was used to extract the following information: country, sample size, prevalent rates of depression, proportion of women, average age, instruments used to assess depression, response rate and sampling methods.

2.3. Methodological Quality Assessment

Articles selected for retrieval were assessed by one reviewer (JBN) for methodological validity before they were included in the review using the Joanna Briggs Institute (JBI) standardized critical appraisal instrument for prevalence studies [37]. Quality was evaluated according to nine criteria, each yielding a score of zero or one. One score was obtained for each criterion if the study was affirmative in the next questions: 1: Was the sample frame appropriate to address the target population? 2: Were study participants recruited in an appropriate way? 3: Was the sample size adequate? 4: Were the study subjects and setting described in detail? 5: Was data analysis conducted with sufficient coverage of the identified sample? 6: Were valid methods used for the identification of the condition? 7: Was the condition measured in a standard, reliable way for all participants? 8: Was there appropriate statistical analysis? 9: Was the response rate adequate, and if not, was the low response rate managed appropriately?

2.4. Data Extraction and Statistical Analysis

Freeman and Tukey's double arcsine transformation of prevalence to stabilize the variance was applied [38]. A generic inverse variance method with a random effect model was used [39]. The Hedges Q statistic was reported to check heterogeneity across studies, with statistical significance set at $p < 0.10$. The I^2 statistic and 95% confidence interval was also used to quantify heterogeneity [40]. Values between 25 and 50% are considered as low, 50 and 75% as moderate, and 75% or more as high [41]. Heterogeneity of effects between studies occurs when differences in results for the same exposure–disease association cannot be fully explained by sampling variation. Sources of heterogeneity can include differences in study design or in demographic characteristics. We performed meta-regression and subgroup analyses [42] to explore the sources of heterogeneity expected in meta-analyses of observational studies [43]. We conducted a sensitivity analysis to determine the influence of each individual study on the overall result by omitting studies one by one. Publication bias was determined through visual inspection of a funnel plot and also Egger's test [44] (p values < 0.05 indicate publication bias) since funnel plots were found to be an inaccurate method for assessing publication bias in meta-analyses of proportion studies [45].

Statistical analyses were conducted by one researcher (JS) and run with STATA statistical software (version 10.0; College Station, TX, USA) and R [46].

3. Results

Figure 1 shows the flowchart of the literature search strategy and study selection process. In total, 300 records were initially identified from Medline via PubMed, Embase and Scielo, and five extra records were then added after a manual search in a preprints database (MedRxiv) and Google Scholar. A total of 96 duplicate articles were deleted and 166 were excluded after a first screening of the titles and abstracts. After reading the remaining 43 articles in full, we finally included 13 in our meta-analysis [47–59]. Exclusion reasons are detailed in Figure 1.

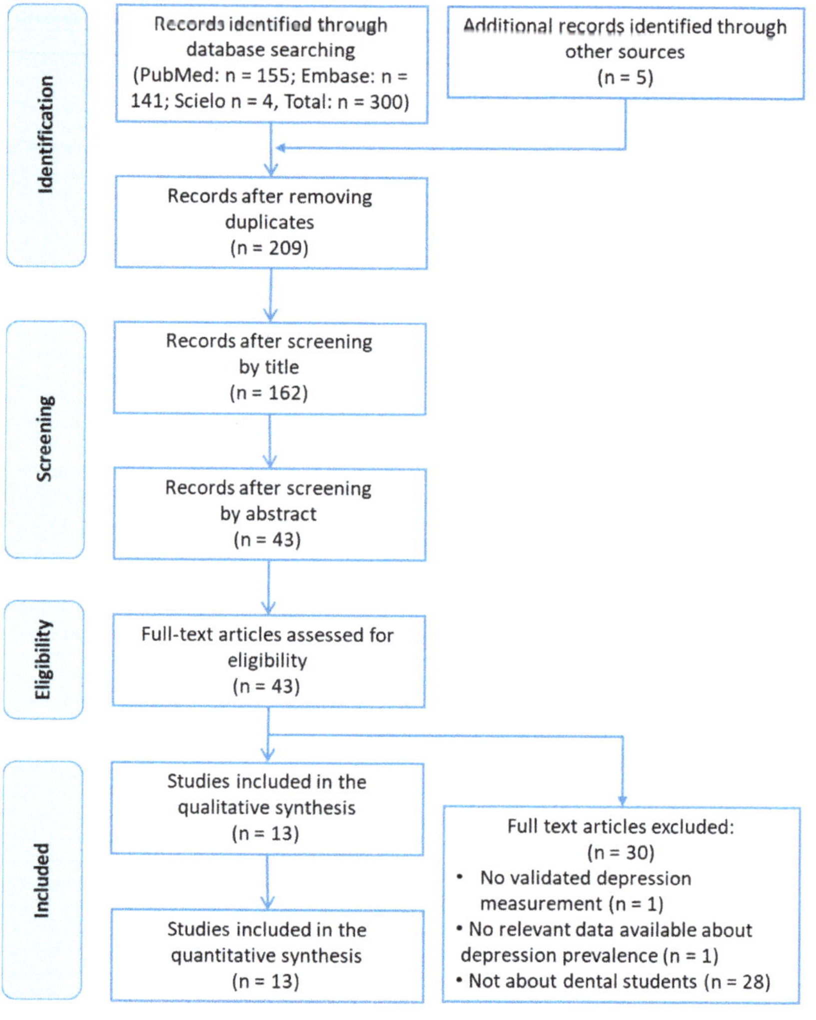

Figure 1. Flowchart of the study selection.

Table 2 shows a description of the studies included. Most of the studies were conducted in Asia (*n* = 10), but we also found studies from Europe (*n* = 1), North (*n* = 1) and South America (*n* = 1), with sample sizes ranging from 97 to 699 participants. Most of the studies involved young students, and gave data referring to the academic year, while only six articles reported the mean age of participants, which ranged from 21.31 to 25.10 years. All studies included both men and women, with a clear predominance of women in all studies. All studies were conducted using online questionnaires and, of those reporting the sampling methodology, all except two used non-random methods. The response rate was reported by eight studies and ranged from 20% to 95.10%. All studies measured depression using standardized scales, most commonly the Depression, Anxiety and Stress

Scale (DASS, n = 10 studies) and the Patient Health (PHQ, n = 2 studies), with one study using the Hospital Anxiety and Depression Scale (HADS).

Table 2. Description of studies included in meta-analysis.

Author (Publication Year)	Country	Mean Age (SD)	% Females (n)	Sample Size (n)	Response Rate (%)	Sampling Method	Depression Assess-ment	Diagnostic Criteria	Prevalence		Quality Assess-ment *
									%	n	
Babadi et al. (2021) [47]	Iran	22.9 (3.3)	53.28% (122)	229	54.5%	Convenience sampling	DASS-21	≥10	28.8%	66	7
Chakraborty et al. (2020) [48]	India	24 (3)	81.55% (137)	168	NR	Convenience sampling	PHQ-9	≥10	53.5%	90	6
Chi el al. (2021) [49]	USA	NR	52.58% (51)	97	35.5%	Convenience sampling	PHQ-9	≥10	14.4%	14	6
Gaş et al. (2021) [50]	Turkey	21.31 (1.9)	64.66% (452)	699	95.1%	Random sampling	DASS-21	≥10	27.2%	190	9
Hakami et al. (2021) [51]	Saudi Arabia	21.76 (1.9)	54.82% (381)	695	NR	Cluster sampling	DASS-21	≥10	60.7%	422	8
Keskin et al. (2021) [52]	Turkey	NR	60.23% (156)	259	NR	Convenience sampling	DASS-42	≥10	75.3%	195	5
Khanagar & Alfadley (2020) [53]	Saudi Arabia	25.1 (NR)	64.55% (71)	110	68.7%	Convenience sampling	DASS-21	≥10	10.9%	12	7
Kwaik et al. (2021) [54]	Palestine	NR	81.19% (354)	436	55.18%	NR	DASS-21	≥10	69.9%	305	8
Medeiros et al. (2020) [55]	Brazil	21.46 (2.37)	76.99% (87)	113	51.36%	NR	HADS	≥8	38.9%	44	6
Mekhemar et al. (2021) [56]	Germany	NR	73.46% (155)	211	NR	Convenience sampling	DASS-21	≥6	26.5%	77	5
Samsudin et al. (2021) [57]	Malaysia	NR	79.43% (139)	175	94.6%	Convenience sampling	DASS-21	≥10	24%	42	6
Shailaja et al. (2021) [58]	India	22.63 (2.88)	82.00% (246)	300	NR	NR	DASS-21	≥10	20%	60	7
Siddiqui & Qian (2021) [59]	Malaysia	22.45 (NR)	79.24% (519)	655	20%	Convenience sampling	DASS-21	≥10	33.6%	220	7

Note. * Quality score based on the Joanna Briggs Institute (JBI) standardized critical appraisal instrument for prevalence studies [Moola et al., 2017]. DASS = Anxiety, Anxiety and Stress scales; HADS = Hospital Anxiety and Depression Scale; NR = not reported; PHQ-9 = Patient Health Questionnaire; USA = United States of America.

Risk of bias scores ranged from 5 to 9 out of a possible total of 9, with a mean score of 6.7 (SD = 1.2) (Supplementary Table S2). The most common limitations were: (a) recruitment of participants not appropriate (11 studies), (b) sample size too small to ensure good precision of the final estimate (9 studies), and (c) response rate not reported, or large number of non-responders (6 studies).

The estimated overall prevalence of depression was 37% in dental students (95% CI: 26–49%), with significant heterogeneity between studies (Q test: $p < 0.001$; $I^2 = 98.3\%$) (Figure 2).

Our meta-regression analysis showed that the prevalence rate of depression was independent of the percentage of women (p = 0.815), mean age at baseline (p = 0.407), response rate (p = 0.727) or methodological quality (p = 0.847). According to subgroup analysis, the only relevant finding was a higher prevalence of depression for studies conducted in Asia (40% (95% CI: 27–53%)) compared to those from Europe or America (29% (95% CI: 16–45%)). We also observed higher prevalence of depression for studies using the PHQ-9 (38% (95% CI: 32–44%)) compared to those using the DASS (−21 or −42) (38% (95% CI: 25–52%)) or HADS (39% (95% CI: 30–49%)); and those using random or cluster sampling methods (44% (95% CI: 41–46%)) compared to those using convenience sampling method (36% (95% CI: 24–50%)).

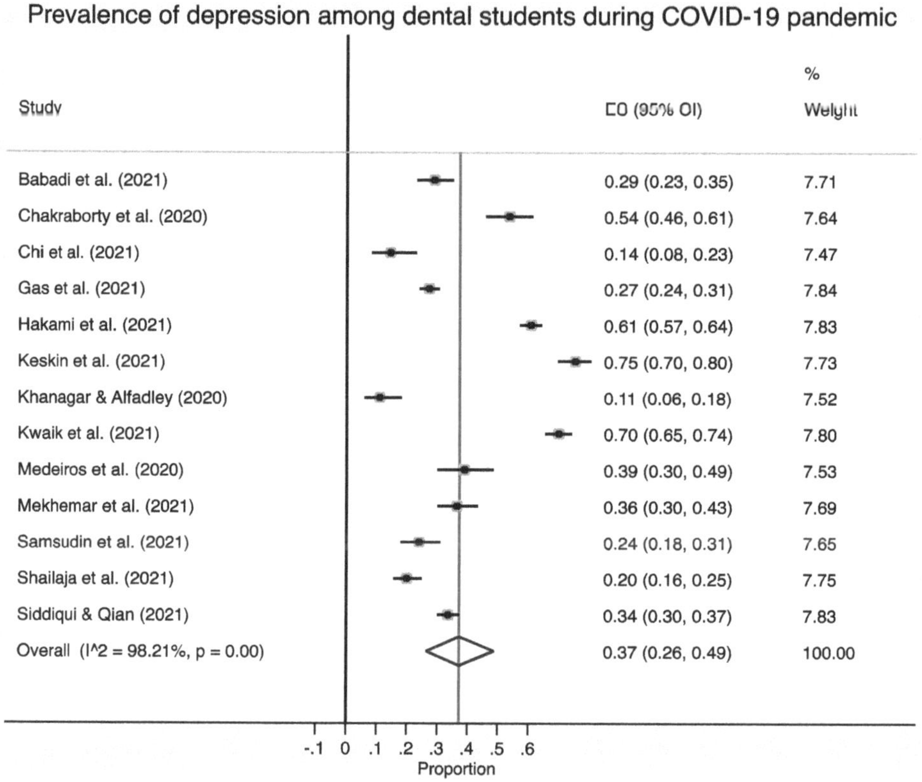

Figure 2. Forest plot for the prevalence of depression in dental students.

Excluding each study one-by-one from the analysis did not substantially change the pooled prevalence of depression, which varied between 35% (95% CI: 24–46%), with Keskin et al. [52] excluded, and 40% (95% CI: 29–52%), with Khanagar & Alfadley [53] excluded. This indicates that no single study had a disproportional impact on the overall prevalence.

Visual inspection of the funnel plot (Figure 3) suggested no publication bias for the estimate of prevalence of depression in dental students, confirmed by a non-significant Egger test ($p = 0.679$).

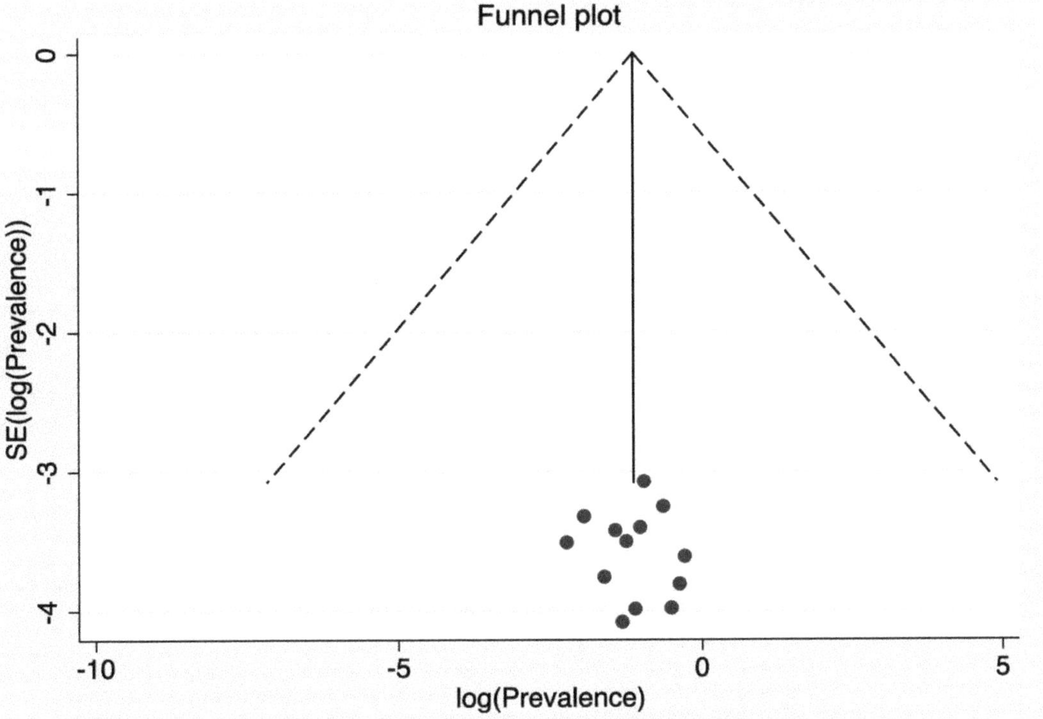

Figure 3. Funnel plot for the prevalence of depression in dental students.

4. Discussion

4.1. Summary of Main Findings

Depression has become one of the most important psychological consequences of the COVID-19 pandemic among university students in general, and dental students in particular. To the best of the authors' knowledge, this is the first meta-analysis reporting pooled depression in dental students during the COVID-19 pandemic. Based on 13 studies, we estimated an overall prevalence of depression of 37%, with higher prevalence of depression found in Asian samples.

Among the studies analyzed, the one that found a lower prevalence of depression among dental students was the one conducted by Khanagar & Alfadley. [53] in 2020 in Saudi Arabia with a prevalence of 20.9%. However, Hakami et al. [51] found a prevalence of 60.7% in the same country in 2021. On the other hand, the highest rate of depression among dental students, 75.3%, was found by Keskin et al. [52] in Turkey in 2021.

Previous meta-analyses on the levels of depression in the general population during the pandemic have reported prevalence rates between 22.8% [60] and 33.7% [61]. As for university students, a great variability has been reported in terms of depressive symptomatology. Previous reviews found that the prevalence rate of depression during the pandemic ranged between 12.2% [62] and 31.2% [6]. However, more recent reviews conducted in 2021 suggest that these rates could be up to 32% [63] and 37% [64].

Our results are consistent with these previous works suggesting that college students, and dental students in particular, are suffering from higher levels of depression than the general population [65]. Moreover, this review also points out that the prevalence of depression among dental students seems to be higher than that observed for university students in general, something that had also been found in studies prior to the pandemic [25,66].

When analyzing differences according to several characteristics, we did not find significant differences by gender or age. These results are not in line with other studies conducted in the general population that found higher rates of depression in women compared to men during the COVID-19 pandemic [29]. This lack of differences may be due to the characteristics of university students, usually young and without family responsibilities. These factors could in turn be risk factors for depression in in women from other types of populations [67,68]. As for the age, one study found that undergraduated students showed higher rates of depression compared with graduated students [69], although they found no significant difference according to the undergraduate year. Our results suggest that in dental students the prevalence of depression does not seem to depend on the age of participants.

According to our findings, the most significant difference of depression was found between geographical regions. In fact, there seems to be a higher prevalence of depression in studies conducted in Asia (42%) compared to those located in Europe or America (27%). This is in line with another meta-analysis conducted in the general population, where the highest prevalence of depression was found in Asia [61] and another that found the highest incidence of depression in the Chinese and Italian general population [70]. In contrast, a previous meta-analysis conducted with the general population and university students found that Asia was the region with the lowest prevalence of depression [6].

The fact that we found a greater proportion of depression among Asian dental students could be explained by differences in the education system across regions. In an international study conducted by Perry et al. in 2017 [71] on simulation and curriculum design in dental studies, it was found that Asian dental colleges were more likely to use alternative methods of learning, such as haptic simulations, the Phantom Laboratory or any simulated teaching aids compared with Europe or America. Since many of these simulated motivating practices had to stop due to the lockdown and social distancing measures during the COVID-19 pandemic, dental studies had to become more traditional for Asian students. This might have increased their work overload and traditional examinations, which are a known major source of depression for dental students [24].

The COVID-19 pandemic seems to be long-lasting, with a significant psychological burden for people. Thus, it is important to stablish preventive and intervention programs to reduce this toll, especially among more vulnerable subgroups, such as dental students. It is also important to continue collecting data about the impact of the COVID-19 on dental students, especially in countries where these data are still not available.

4.2. Strengths and Limitations

The main strength of this study is that it is the first meta-analysis performed about the prevalence of depression in dental students during COVID-19 pandemic. Moreover, this study includes of a large body of literature and it uses of a rigorous approach to identify publication bias (i.e., Egger's test), concluding that there is no bias in the estimation of the pooled prevalence of depression for dental students.

However, this study also has some limitations that should be taken into account. Firstly, the majority of the studies included in the systematic review were based on non-probabilistic samples, but no longitudinal studies were found. Therefore, we do not have scientific evidence to conclude whether the levels of depression have been sustained, reduced or increased over pandemic months [31]. Secondly, the studies included in this study used variety of self-reported standardized questionnaires, being this as a common practice in epidemiological studies [18,72]. However, our results have found that the use of some of these tests was associated with significantly higher prevalence of depression than others. Therefore, ideally, studies should use the same measure of depression and if possible, include a diagnosis based on clinical interviews. Finally, while we were able to include studies from different continents, there were only two studies from the Americas and one from Europe. It would therefore be advisable to carry out more studies in these countries, since there seems to be significant differences depending on the region of study.

5. Conclusions

This meta-analysis concludes that the prevalence of depression among dental students during the COVID-19 pandemic is high, with Asian students showing higher rates than non-Asian students. Taking into account that university students in general and dental students in particular are suffering from higher depressive symptoms, the lack of interventions and policies to improve mental health at universities may bring short and long-term psychological consequences in their personal, academic and professional life [73]. Therefore, universities should also work to adapt their teaching methods to this new situation. For dental studies, for example, it might be convenient to strengthen alternative methods of learning, such as haptic simulations or other simulated teaching, along with blended learning and virtual curriculum [74].

Supplementary Materials: The following are available online at https://www.mdpi.com/article/10.3390/medicina57111278/s1, Table S1: PRISMA Checklist, Table S2: Quality assessment.

Author Contributions: Conceptualization, J.S.; methodology, J.S.; investigation, J.B.-N.; writing—original draft preparation, N.I. and N.O.-E.; writing—review and editing, J.S., J.B.-N., N.I., B.O. and N.O.-E. All authors have read and agreed to the published version of the manuscript.

Funding: Not applicable.

Institutional Review Board Statement: Not applicable.

Informed Consent Statement: Not applicable.

Data Availability Statement: Not applicable.

Conflicts of Interest: The authors declare no conflict of interest.

References

1. Mahase, E. Covid-19: WHO declares pandemic because of "alarming levels" of spread, severity, and inaction. *BMJ* **2020**, *368*, m1036. [CrossRef] [PubMed]
2. WHO. Director-General's Opening Remarks at the Media Briefing on COVID-19—11 March 2020. Available online: https://www.who.int/director-general/speeches/detail/who-director-general-s-opening-remarks-at-the-media-briefing-on-covid-19---11-march-2020 (accessed on 1 September 2021).
3. Nelson, B.W.; Pettitt, A.; Flannery, J.E.; Allen, N.B. Rapid assessment of psychological and epidemiological correlates of COVID-19 concern, financial strain, and health-related behavior change in a large online sample. *PLoS ONE* **2020**, *15*, e0241990. [CrossRef] [PubMed]
4. Khan, K.S.; Mamun, M.A.; Griffiths, M.D.; Ullah, I. The Mental Health Impact of the COVID-19 Pandemic Across Different Cohorts. *Int. J. Ment. Health Addict.* **2020**, 1–7. [CrossRef] [PubMed]
5. Wu, T.; Jia, X.; Shi, H.; Niu, J.; Yin, X.; Xie, J.; Wang, X. Prevalence of mental health problems during the COVID-19 pandemic: A systematic review and meta-analysis. *J. Affect. Disord.* **2021**, *281*, 91–98. [CrossRef] [PubMed]
6. Batra, K.; Sharma, M.; Batra, R.; Singh, T.; Schvaneveldt, N. Assessing the Psychological Impact of COVID-19 among College Students: An Evidence of 15 Countries. *Healthcare* **2021**, *9*, 222. [CrossRef]
7. Viner, R.M.; Russell, S.J.; Croker, H.; Packer, J.; Ward, J.; Stansfield, C.; Mytton, O.; Bonell, C.; Booy, R. School closure and management practices during coronavirus outbreaks including COVID-19: A rapid systematic review. *Lancet* **2020**, *4*, 397–404. [CrossRef]
8. Al Lily, A.E.; Ismail, A.F.; Abunasser, F.M.; Alqahtani, R.H.A. Distance education as a response to pandemics: Coronavirus and Arab culture. *Technol. Soc.* **2020**, *63*, 101317. [CrossRef]
9. Cao, W.; Fang, Z.; Hou, G.; Han, M.; Xu, X.; Dong, J.; Zheng, J. The psychological impact of the COVID-19 epidemic on college students in China. *Psychiatry Res.* **2020**, *287*, 112934. [CrossRef] [PubMed]
10. Idoiaga Mondragon, N.; Berasategi Sancho, N.; Eiguren Munitis, A.; Dosil Santamaria, M. Exploring the social and emotional representations used by students from the University of the Basque Country to face the first outbreak of COVID-19 pandemic. *Health Educ. Res.* **2021**, *36*, 159–169. [CrossRef]
11. Sahu, P. Closure of Universities Due to Coronavirus Disease 2019 (COVID-19): Impact on Education and Mental Health of Students and Academic Staff. *Cureus* **2020**, *12*, e7541. [CrossRef]
12. Zhai, Y.; Du, X. Mental health care for international Chinese students affected by the COVID-19 outbreak. *Lancet Psychiatry* **2020**, *7*, e22. [CrossRef]
13. Arango, C. Lessons Learned From the Coronavirus Health Crisis in Madrid, Spain: How COVID-19 Has Changed Our Lives in the Last 2 Weeks. *Biol. Psychiatry* **2020**, *88*, e33–e34. [CrossRef]

14. Chang, J.; Yuan, Y.; Wang, D. Mental health status and its influencing factors among college students during the epidemic of COVID-19. *Nan Fang Yi Ke Da Xue Xue Bao* **2020**, *40*, 171–176. [PubMed]
15. Kaparounaki, C.K.; Patsali, M.E.; Mousa, D.-P.V.; Papadopoulou, E.V.; Papadopoulou, K.K.; Fountoulakis, K.N. University students' mental health amidst the COVID-19 quarantine in Greece. *Psychiatry Res.* **2020**, *290*, 113111. [CrossRef] [PubMed]
16. Brooks, S.K.; Webster, R.; Smith, L.E.; Woodland, L.; Wessely, S.; Greenberg, N.; Rubin, G.J. The psychological impact of quarantine and how to reduce it: Rapid review of the evidence. *Lancet* **2020**, *395*, 912–920. [CrossRef]
17. Shigemura, J.; Ursano, R.J.; Morganstein, J.C.; Kurosawa, M.; Benedek, D.M. Public responses to the novel 2019 coronavirus (2019-nCoV) in Japan: Mental health consequences and target populations. *Psychiatry Clin. Neurosci.* **2020**, *74*, 281–282. [CrossRef]
18. Galan, F.; Ríos-Santos, J.; Polo, J.; Ríos-Carrasco, B.; Bullon, P. Burnout, depression and suicidal ideation in dental students. *Med. Oral Patol. Oral Cir. Bucal* **2014**, *19*, e206–e211. [CrossRef]
19. Stormon, N.; Ford, P.J.; Kisely, S.; Bartle, E.; Eley, D.S. Depression, anxiety and stress in a cohort of Australian dentistry students. *Eur. J. Dent. Educ.* **2019**, *23*, 507–514. [CrossRef] [PubMed]
20. Bs, A.R.L.; Bs, K.K.Y.; Taylor, G.W.; Saeed, S.G. High depressive symptom prevalence in dental students associated with lifestyle and well-being characteristics. *J. Dent. Educ.* **2020**, *84*, 771–780. [CrossRef]
21. Puthran, R.; Zhang, M.W.B.; Tam, W.; Ho, R. Prevalence of depression amongst medical students: A meta-analysis. *Med. Educ.* **2016**, *50*, 456–468. [CrossRef]
22. Alzahem, A.; Van Der Molen, H.T.; Alaujan, A.H.; Schmidt, H.G.; Zamakhshary, M.H. Stress amongst dental students: A systematic review. *Eur. J. Dent. Educ.* **2011**, *15*, 8–18. [CrossRef]
23. Al-Sowygh, Z.H.; Alfadley, A.; Al-Saif, M.I.; Al-Wadei, S.H. Perceived causes of stress among Saudi dental students. *King Saud Univ. J. Dent. Sci.* **2013**, *4*, 7–15. [CrossRef]
24. Basudan, S.; Binanzan, N.; Alhassan, A. Depression, anxiety and stress in dental students. *Int. J. Med Educ.* **2017**, *8*, 179–186. [CrossRef] [PubMed]
25. Prinz, P.; Hertrich, K.; Hirschfelder, U.; De Zwaan, M. Burnout, depression and depersonalisation—Psychological factors and coping strategies in dental and medical students. *GMS Z. Med. Ausbild.* **2012**, *29*, 1–14. [CrossRef]
26. Posse, J.L.; van Harten, M.; Phadraig, C.M.G.; Freitas, M.D.; Faulks, D.; Dougall, A.; Daly, B.; Dios, P.D. The Impact of the First Wave of the COVID-19 Pandemic on Providing Special Care Dentistry: A Survey for Dentists. *Int. J. Environ. Res. Public Health* **2021**, *18*, 2970. [CrossRef] [PubMed]
27. Kateeb, E.; Danadneh, M.; Pokorná, A.; Klugarová, J.; Abdulqader, H.; Klugar, M.; Riad, A. Predictors of Willingness to Receive COVID-19 Vaccine: Cross-Sectional Study of Palestinian Dental Students. *Vaccines* **2021**, *9*, 954. [CrossRef]
28. García, D.; Akinkugbe, A.; Mosavel, M.; Smith, C.; Brickhouse, T. COVID-19 and Dental and Dental Hygiene Students' Career Plans. *JDR Clin. Transl. Res.* **2021**, *6*, 153–160. [CrossRef]
29. Özdin, S.; Bayrak, Ö.Ş. Levels and predictors of anxiety, depression and health anxiety during COVID-19 pandemic in Turkish society: The importance of gender. *Int. J. Soc. Psychiatry* **2020**, *66*, 504–511. [CrossRef] [PubMed]
30. Vindegaard, N.; Benros, M.E. COVID-19 pandemic and mental health consequences: Systematic review of the current evidence. *Brain Behav. Immun.* **2020**, *89*, 531–542. [CrossRef]
31. Wang, C.; Pan, R.; Wan, X.; Tan, Y.; Xu, L.; McIntyre, R.S.; Choo, F.N.; Tran, B.; Ho, R.; Sharma, V.K.; et al. A longitudinal study on the mental health of general population during the COVID-19 epidemic in China. *Brain Behav. Immun.* **2020**, *87*, 40–48. [CrossRef]
32. Cénat, J.M.; Blais-Rochette, C.; Kokou-Kpolou, C.K.; Noorishad, P.-G.; Mukunzi, J.N.; McIntee, S.-E.; Dalexis, R.D.; Goulet, M.-A.; Labelle, P.R. Prevalence of symptoms of depression, anxiety, insomnia, posttraumatic stress disorder, and psychological distress among populations affected by the COVID-19 pandemic: A systematic review and meta-analysis. *Psychiatry Res.* **2020**, *295*, 113599. [CrossRef]
33. Prati, G.; Mancini, A.D. The psychological impact of COVID-19 pandemic lockdowns: A review and meta-analysis of longitudinal studies and natural experiments. *Psychol. Med.* **2021**, *51*, 201–211. [CrossRef] [PubMed]
34. Ochnik, D.; Rogowska, A.; Kuśnierz, C.; Jakubiak, M.; Schütz, A.; Held, M.; Arzenšek, A.; Benatov, J.; Berger, R.; Korchagina, E.; et al. A Comparison of Depression and Anxiety among University Students in Nine Countries during the COVID-19 Pandemic. *J. Clin. Med.* **2021**, *10*, 2882. [CrossRef]
35. Lasheras, I.; Gracia-García, P.; Lipnicki, D.M.; Bueno-Notivol, J.; López-Antón, R.; De La Cámara, C.; Lobo, A.; Santabárbara, J. Prevalence of Anxiety in Medical Students during the COVID-19 Pandemic: A Rapid Systematic Review with Meta-Analysis. *Int. J. Environ. Res. Public Health* **2020**, *17*, 6603. [CrossRef] [PubMed]
36. Moher, D.; Liberati, A.; Tetzlaff, J.; Altman, D.G.; The PRISMA Group. Preferred Reporting Items for Systematic Reviews and Meta-Analyses: The PRISMA Statement. *PLoS Med.* **2009**, *6*, e1000097. [CrossRef] [PubMed]
37. Moola, S.; Munn, Z.; Tufanaru, C.; Aromataris, E.; Sears, K.; Sfetc, R. Systematic reviews of etiology and risk. In *Joanna Briggs Institute Reviewer's Manual*; Aromataris, E., Munn, Z., Eds.; The Joanna Briggs Institute: Adelaide, Australia, 2017; Chapter 7; pp. 219–226.
38. Freeman, M.F.; Tukey, J.W. Transformations Related to the Angular and the Square Root. *Ann. Math. Stat.* **1950**, *21*, 607–611. [CrossRef]
39. DerSimonian, R.; Laird, N. Meta-analysis in clinical trials. *Control. Clin. Trials* **1986**, *7*, 177–188. [CrossRef]
40. Von Hippel, P.T. The heterogeneity statistic I 2 can be biased in small meta-analyses. *BMC Med Res. Methodol.* **2015**, *15*, 1–8. [CrossRef]

41. Higgins, J.P.T.; Thompson, S.G.; Deeks, J.; Altman, D.G. Measuring inconsistency in meta-analyses. *BMJ* **2003**, *327*, 557–560. [CrossRef]
42. Thompson, S.G.; Higgins, J.P.T. How should meta-regression analyses be undertaken and interpreted? *Stat. Med.* **2002**, *21*, 1559–1573. [CrossRef]
43. Egger, M.; Schneider, M.; Smith, G.D. Meta-analysis Spurious precision? Meta-analysis of observational studies. *BMJ* **1998**, *316*, 140–144. [CrossRef] [PubMed]
44. Egger, M.; Smith, G.D.; Schneider, M.; Minder, C. Bias in meta-analysis detected by a simple, graphical test. *BMJ* **1997**, *315*, 629–634. [CrossRef]
45. Hunter, J.P.; Saratzis, A.; Sutton, A.J.; Boucher, R.H.; Sayers, R.D.; Bown, M. In meta-analyses of proportion studies, funnel plots were found to be an inaccurate method of assessing publication bias. *J. Clin. Epidemiol.* **2014**, *67*, 897–903. [CrossRef] [PubMed]
46. R Core Team. *R: A Language and Environment for Statistical Computing*; R Found Stat Comput: Vienna, Austria, 2019.
47. Babadi, F.; Bazmi, A.; Araban, M. Association between the Fear Induced by the COVID-19 and the Level of Depression, Anxiety, and Stress among Dental Students: A Cross-sectional Study. *Health Educ. Health Promot.* **2021**, *9*, 19–24.
48. Chakraborty, T.; Subbiah, G.K.; Damade, Y. Psychological Distress during COVID-19 Lockdown among Dental Students and Practitioners in India: A Cross-Sectional Survey. *Eur. J. Dent.* **2020**, *14*, S70–S78. [CrossRef]
49. Chi, D.L.; Randall, C.L.; Hill, C.M. Dental trainees' mental health and intention to leave their programs during the COVID-19 pandemic. *J. Am. Dent. Assoc.* **2021**, *152*, 526–534. [CrossRef]
50. Gaş, S.; Özsoy, H.E.; Aydın, K.C. The association between sleep quality, depression, anxiety and stress levels, and temporomandibular joint disorders among Turkish dental students during the COVID-19 pandemic. *CRANIO®* **2021**, 1–6. [CrossRef]
51. Hakami, Z.; Khanagar, S.B.; Vishwanathaiah, S.; Hakami, A.; Bokhari, A.M.; Jabali, A.H.; Alasmari, D.; Aldrees, A.M. Psychological impact of the coronavirus disease 2019 (COVID-19) pandemic on dental students: A nationwide study. *J. Dent. Educ.* **2021**, *85*, 494–503. [CrossRef]
52. Keskin, G. Self-Report Measurement of Depression, Anxiety, and Stress Caused by COVID-19 Pandemic in Senior Undergraduate Dental Students. *Pesqui. Bras. Odontopediatr. Clin. Integr.* **2021**, *21*, 0243. [CrossRef]
53. Khanagar, S.B.; Alfadley, A. Psychological Impact of the COVID-19 Pandemic on Dental Interns in Riyadh, Saudi Arabia: A Cross-sectional Survey. *Int. J. Clin. Pediatr. Dent.* **2021**, *13*, 508–512. [CrossRef]
54. Abu Kwaik, A.; Saleh, R.; Danadneh, M.; Kateeb, E. Stress, Anxiety and Depression Among Dental Students in Times of Covid-19 Lockdown. *Int. J. Dent. Oral Sci.* **2021**, *8*, 1397–1401.
55. Medeiros, R.A.; Vieira, D.L.; Silva, E.V.F.D.; Rezende, L.V.M.L.; Santos, R.W.D.; Tabata, L.F. Prevalence of symptoms of temporomandibular disorders, oral behaviors, anxiety, and depression in Dentistry students during the period of social isolation due to COVID-19. *J. Appl. Oral Sci.* **2020**, *28*, e20200445,0445. [CrossRef] [PubMed]
56. Mekhemar, M.; Attia, S.; Dörfer, C.; Conrad, J. Dental Students in Germany throughout the COVID-19 Pandemic: A Psychological Assessment and Cross-Sectional Survey. *Biology* **2021**, *10*, 611. [CrossRef] [PubMed]
57. Samsudin, A.D.; Jaafar, A.; Idaham, N.I.; Jali@yunos, M.H.M. The Effect of COVID-19 Pandemic on Psychological Wellness among Dental Students of a Malaysian Public University. *Ulum Islamiyyah* **2021**, 87–97. [CrossRef]
58. Shailaja, B.; Shetty, V.; Chaudhury, S.; Thyloth, M. Exploring cyberchondria and its associations in dental students amid COVID-19 infodemic. *Ind. Psychiatry J.* **2020**, *29*, 257–267. [CrossRef] [PubMed]
59. Siddiqui, F.; Qian, G. Psychological impact of self-quarantine on malaysian dental students during COVID-19 pandemic. *Med. J. Dr. D.Y. Patil Vidyapeeth* **2021**. [CrossRef]
60. Pappa, S.; Ntella, V.; Giannakas, T.; Giannakoulis, V.G.; Papoutsi, E.; Katsaounou, P. Prevalence of depression, anxiety, and insomnia among healthcare workers during the COVID-19 pandemic: A systematic review and meta-analysis. *Brain Behav. Immun.* **2020**, *88*, 901–907. Available online: https://www.sciencedirect.com/science/article/pii/S088915912030845X (accessed on 8 July 2021). [CrossRef]
61. Salari, N.; Hosseinian-Far, A.; Jalali, R.; Vaisi-Raygani, A.; Rasoulpoor, S.; Mohammadi, M.; Rasoulpoor, S.; Khaledi-Paveh, B. Prevalence of stress, anxiety, depression among the general population during the COVID-19 pandemic: A systematic review and meta-analysis. *Glob. Health* **2020**, *16*, 57. [CrossRef]
62. Wang, Z.-H.; Yang, H.-L.; Yang, Y.-Q.; Liu, D.; Li, Z.-H.; Zhang, X.-R.; Zhang, Y.-J.; Shen, D.; Chen, P.-L.; Song, W.-Q.; et al. Prevalence of anxiety and depression symptom, and the demands for psychological knowledge and interventions in college students during COVID-19 epidemic: A large cross-sectional study. *J. Affect. Disord.* **2020**, *275*, 188–193. [CrossRef]
63. Deng, J.; Zhou, F.; Hou, W.; Silver, Z.; Wong, C.Y.; Chang, O.; Drakos, A.; Zuo, Q.K.; Huang, E. The prevalence of depressive symptoms, anxiety symptoms and sleep disturbance in higher education students during the COVID-19 pandemic: A systematic review and meta-analysis. *Psychiatry Res.* **2021**, *301*, 113863. [CrossRef] [PubMed]
64. Wang, C.; Wen, W.; Zhang, H.; Ni, J.; Jiang, J.; Cheng, Y.; Zhou, M.; Ye, L.; Feng, Z.; Ge, Z.; et al. Anxiety, depression, and stress prevalence among college students during the COVID-19 pandemic: A systematic review and meta-analysis. *J. Am. Coll. Health* **2021**, 1–8. [CrossRef]
65. Shah, S.M.A.; Mohammad, D.; Qureshi, M.F.H.; Abbas, M.Z.; Aleem, S. Prevalence, Psychological Responses and Associated Correlates of Depression, Anxiety and Stress in a Global Population, During the Coronavirus Disease (COVID-19) Pandemic. *Community Ment. Health J.* **2020**, *57*, 101–110. [CrossRef] [PubMed]

66. Uraz, A.; Tocak, Y.S.; Yozgatlıgil, C.; Cetiner, S.; Bal, B. Psychological well–being, health, and stress sources in turkish dental students. *J. Dent. Educ.* **2013**, *77*, 1345–1355. [CrossRef] [PubMed]
67. Ardoino, G.I.; Queirolo, E.I.; Barg, G.; Ciccariello, D.A.; Kordas, K. The Relationship Among Depression, Parenting Stress, and Partner Support in Low-Income Women From Montevideo, Uruguay. *Health Care Women Int.* **2013**, *36*, 392–408. [CrossRef]
68. Seto, M.; Morimoto, K.; Maruyama, S. Effects of work-related factors and work-family conflict on depression among Japanese working women living with young children. *Environ. Health Prev. Med.* **2004**, *9*, 220–227. [CrossRef]
69. Chirikov, I.; Soria, K.M.; Horgos, B.; Jones-White, D. Undergraduate and graduate students' mental health during the COVID-19 pandemic. *eScholarship* **2020**.
70. Luo, M.; Guo, L.; Yu, M.; Jiang, W.; Wang, H. The psychological and mental impact of coronavirus disease 2019 (COVID-19) on medical staff and general public—A systematic review and meta-analysis. *Psychiatry Res.* **2020**, *291*, 113190. [CrossRef] [PubMed]
71. Perry, S.; Burrow, M.F.; Leung, W.K.; Bridges, S.M. Simulation and curriculum design: A global survey in dental education. *Aust. Dent. J.* **2017**, *62*, 453–463. [CrossRef]
72. Faisal, G.G.; Radeef, A.S. Stressors and Their Association with Symptoms of Depression, Anxiety and Stress in Dental Students. *Makara J. Health Res.* **2018**, *22*, 58–62. [CrossRef]
73. Adolescent Mental Health. 2021. Available online: https://www.who.int/news-room/fact-sheets/detail/adolescent-mental-health (accessed on 2 September 2021).
74. Haroon, Z.; Azad, A.A.; Sharif, M.; Aslam, A.; Arshad, K.; Rafiq, S. COVID-19 Era: Challenges and Solutions in Dental Education. *J. Coll. Physicians Surg. Pak.* **2020**, *30*, 129–131. [CrossRef]

MDPI
St. Alban-Anlage 66
4052 Basel
Switzerland
www.mdpi.com

Medicina Editorial Office
E-mail: medicina@mdpi.com
www.mdpi.com/journal/medicina

www.ingramcontent.com/pod-product-compliance
Lightning Source LLC
Chambersburg PA
CBHW062039220926
51850CB00010B/2606
* 9 7 8 3 0 3 6 5 9 6 1 4 3 *